A TIME TO LEARN

The Dial Press
New York
1973

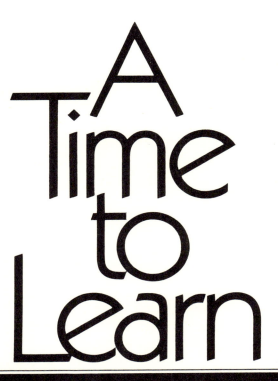

A Time to Learn

A Guide for Parents to the New Theories in Early Childhood Education

Ruth Langdon Inglis

Library of Congress Cataloging in Publication Data

Inglis, Ruth Langdon, 1927–
  A time to learn.

  Bibliography: p.
  1. Education, Preschool. I. Title. II. Title:
A guide for parents to the new theories in early
childhood education.
LB1140.2.I48   372.21   73–10026

*To my children, Diana
and Neil, who have
provided me with some
of the raw material for
this book, and to my
sister, Louise van Agt,
who was its tireless,
generous researcher*

Contents

1 The Importance of Books,
Films and Comics in
Childhood
3

2 The Urgent Need for
Language Learning in the
Earliest Years
22

3 The Way Children Learn
to Speak and Think
44

vii

4 *The Nursery School:
Learning in the Preschool
Years*
67

5 *Language Deprivation:
Effect on Speech and
Behavior*
91

6 *IQ Tests*
115

7 *Television: The Child's
Third Parent*
127

8 *What Does Television
Teach?*
158

9 *TV and the Child's
Emotional Development*
180

10 *Children's Literature
Today: Changing Patterns*
205

11 *Some Modern Solutions
for Teaching the
Under-Tens*
235

References
271

A TIME TO LEARN

1

The Importance of Books, Films and Comics in Childhood

When a child begins to read alone at about six or seven, his mind has a special receptive quality that makes the first book that moves him as significant as his first love later on. If only we could occasionally re-create the total absorption and receptivity of those first reading years.

For my own part, I remember Frances Hodgson Burnett's *A Little Princess* as if it had scarred my brain. Reaching back into my memory with difficulty, I have tried to analyze the book's power over me then. I had a strange, happy childhood, often lonely but never miserable. My father was an American diplomat posted as the U.S. consul general to Mukden, Manchuria, an uneasy role in that decade of the thirties when I grew up there, because America refused to recognize Japan's rule in Manchuria. My father was thus left in a nebulous, rather dangerous position, for the Japanese were certainly there in full illegal military occupation and had been since they routed Chiang Kai-shek's troops from the country in 1933 and installed the unfortunate young Manchu emperior P'u-yi as a puppet and symbol. America's refusal to lend official recognition to the regime was a slap on the wrist that caused the Japanese little remorse or discomfiture. The United States refused to export certain commodities to the Japanese rulers as a further sting. To my two older sisters and myself, living in a luxurious but rather isolated house and compound in the center of Mukden, the greatest hardship was the export ban on American films. Our movie-going, in that amazing period of Hollywood fecundity, was a limited affair as a result of the ban.

Inexplicably one American film, *The Ghoul,* starring Boris Karloff, had slipped through the nonrecognition net. With sad regularity, the three of us, aged fourteen, thirteen, and eight, trooped into Mukden's shopping center to see Boris Karloff raise his death-stained and shroud-ridden form, stepping from a creaking coffin to go about his awful business. *The Ghoul* arrived at the cinema two or three times a year, as inexorably as do Fred Astaire and Ginger Rogers on the television screens today, but with considerably less wholesomeness.

I suppose that, given this dearth of outside stimuli, books were bound to explode into my brain like depth charges. When my mother took my sisters off to Peking to enroll them at an American high school there, my lack of company was almost complete. Up to that time, she had taught them by correspondence with the Calvert Course, a plan of instruction conceived in Baltimore,

Maryland, seventy-four years ago, and still a lifesaver for stranded mothers in remote foreign parts who are determined to keep their children with them. The sprinkling of English and American children of my own age in Mukden whose fathers worked for the British American Tobacco Company had been sent home to escape the lack of schooling and the uneasy political situation. My busy father, left in charge of me, sweetly and rather abstractedly handed me the current assignments from the Calvert Course (one, which I remember above all others, was listening endlessly to Bizet's *Carmen* in order to write essays on it). At night he read me Hugo's *Les Miserables* and Dickens's *Tale of Two Cities.*

In retrospect, I realize that I could have done a great deal worse. For diversion, I played Monopoly with Wher-chiao ("Little Flower"), the cook's daughter, who had a lightning intelligence and who could, in spite of the fact that she knew no English, reel off the names of the game's London properties, Pall Mall, Trafalgar Square, Elephant and Castle, as if they were the main streets of Mukden. But like all Chinese daughters in northern China, she was her mother's major helper and had little time to relax with me, away from the demands of tending her smaller, more cherished brothers.

So Sara Crewe in her lonely attic garret in Miss Burnett's story became a closer friend than even Wher-chiao. The memory of the book that lingers with me now is largely a sensuous one. I can almost feel the black velvet dress Sara wore when she first entered her young ladies' boarding school in London as the cossetted daughter of a diamond mine owner. This was the black dress that was to become her badge of pauperism when the cruel headmistress, Miss Minchin, disposed of Sara's rich wardrobe after her parents had died abroad, leaving her orphaned.

Mukden's winter cold was intense, a dry, crackling, numbing kind of cold that turned horses' droppings into frost-covered balls moments after they hit the streets. I knew about frostbite. I could feel the cold beneath Sara's feet as she padded through the London streets with holes in her shoes, see the tapering, aristocratic hands go red in her freezing attic room. An empathy for all stray, abandoned animals that gripped me in those days and had me picking up any sick, starved bird or mangy, stray dog that came my way (and in the Orient, they are abundant) made Sara's lonely friendship with sparrows and mice seem unbearably poignant. Miss Minchin's petty cruelties were recognizable. My closest friend, a half-English, half-American girl, who had just departed from Mukden, had had an extraordinarily harsh mother who kept her incarcerated in a mansion across town like some victimized fairy princess. At one point, my friend and I could communicate only by carrier pigeon. My own family's enormously good-natured coolie, Lao-ma (which translates cruelly as "Old Horse"), would take a pigeon over to her; she would write me a note, attach it to the pigeon's leg, and back the bird would come.

It was sad to pick up *A Little Princess* again some years ago to read aloud to my daughter. This story that had given me evocations of chill and loneliness, of seemingly unmotivated adult cruelties, of bravery in the face of persecution, a smell and feel of a smoky, class-ridden London of the nineteenth century, now came across like a slap of wet drapery in the face, full of clumsy, flagrant snobbishness. How was it that I had missed Miss Burnett's repellent suggestion that an aristocratic child will always be a lady no matter what her circumstances, or her mewling admiration for Sara's bounty to the poor Cockney maid, Becky?

The attempt to approximate Becky's crippled Cockney accent made the gorge rise on rereading (" 'Oh, miss! Oh, miss!' she stuttered. 'I arst yer pardon, miss!' "). And how could Sara's patronizing ways have seemed winsome?

> She put her hand on Becky's cheek. "Why," she said, "we are just the same—I am only a little girl like you. It's just an accident that I am not you, and you are not me!"

I remember choking with emotion at her magnanimity. My own daughter, raised, blessedly, in more democratic times, said: "Conceited little cow."

The sheer handsomeness of the 1933 Scribner volume undoubtedly increased the story's power over me; glossy, beautifully produced illustrations by Ethel Franklin Betts made the finery of the children's clothes at Miss Minchin's, their tea sets and dolls, their glowing fireplaces, reek of wealth's aroma. Poverty is exotic to someone who has never known it, and Sara's cell, with its peeling walls, bad light, cracked floors, and patched quilts, in contrast to the earlier illustrations of parlored luxury, was redolent of that state. To a fortunate diplomat's daughter with two ponies, a bicycle, and the attention of a staff of fourteen servants, Sara's story was romance indeed.

In response to a mildly complaining letter of mine at the time, Aunt Dee Dee, my crusty old spinster aunt in Washington, D.C., wrote:

> It's good for you to have little else to do but read, dear. Boredom can be a disguised virtue. If you had lots of friends, you might just be a social butterfly. Being alone turns you in on yourself—makes you more reflective, forces you to rely on your own brain for amuse-

ment. Now, you see, if you ever get taken prisoner and are put in a cell, you wouldn't crack.

As there seemed to be no prospect of imminent imprisonment or relegation to solitary confinement (though, on occasion, the Japanese-U.S. tensions did rumble round us menacingly; a Japanese officer had kicked my sister on a crowded train when she refused to give him her seat), I could not see any relevance in my Aunt Dee Dee's remarks. I had no one to play with—this was my small personal tragedy—and I did not see why childhood should be a grooming for an eventual life of personality adjustment in a cell.

My isolation had some pleasant and some unpleasant effects. It did force me to read voraciously but it also made me garrulous and cocky with my father's friends at night, anxious to air my opinions at the dinner parties he misguidedly asked me to join. The wife of an old China hand recalls one dinner in particular. My father's vice-consul at the time, John Paton Davies, who rode an Arabian stallion, spoke and wrote Chinese fluently, and had the forehead and high cheekbones of a Leslie Howard (when he once absentmindedly put an arm around the shoulders of my chubby sister, Louise, she passed out) was present at the dinner. He was just about to travel to Hankow to see Generalissimo Chiang—in those days still something of a hero, even to liberal Americans like Davies, who also, at about that time, had visited Mao Tse-tung in Yenan and became impressed with Mao's young, rival regime (in the 1950s John Paton Davies was pilloried by Senator Joseph McCarthy for these sentiments and was forced to leave the State Department, a wrong that the department only recently, and belatedly, righted). While everyone wanted to talk to Davies, I monopolized him painfully, the

woman recalls with a little laughing shudder, composing aloud
my own letter to Chiang, which Davies had charmingly prom-
ised to deliver by hand. She says that at nine years old, I headed
the table like a mature hostess, and was very vocal about wanting Davies to make sure that Chiang came back to Manchuria
to reclaim his rightful land from the Japanese. I feel for those
long-suffering guests.

The enforced idleness and long hours alone produced a kind
of fringe delinquency, too. When the eyes began to liquefy and
blur from too much reading, there was always the game of
stunning the servants—doing circus tricks on my bicycle in the
courtyard, standing on the bars with hands outstretched; bringing my thick-haired Mongolian pony up the kitchen steps to
frighten the amah at her lunch hour; picking at the servants'
saucepans of delicious bean curd and noodle brunches at noon
when their backs were turned (the Manchurians ate only twice
a day, and so this first meal of the day was crucial). When all else
failed and my gyrations left them unmoved and uninterested, I
would take to stagily guzzling ice water straight from the bottle
out of the refrigerator, draining it to the bottom without stopping. This really got them. Accustomed to their own Siberian-
like winters, inadequately heated huts, and high incidence of
pneumonia and viral stomach disorders, they looked upon cold
water at any season, even though it had been boiled, as a kind
of instant diarrhea, perhaps even a shortcut to the grave—to
gulp down such a quantity of it iced was suicide. In my case, I
wonder why they cared.

When my stomach began to distend uncomfortably from ice
water and all other diversionary tactics began to pall, I was once
again at the mercy of my media, Bizet, Sara Crewe (beautiful,
circumspect, nothing like me), and some battered Oz books cast

aside by my sisters. I identified totally with the pragmatic heroine of Frank Baum's Oz books—tough talking, no-nonsense Dorothy from Kansas. While Sara Crewe had romance and star quality, remoteness, endless forbearance, Dorothy was a more recognizable creature. She was impatient, forthright, somewhat plain, an earthy farm girl, literally sucked from her own background by events she could not control—in her case, a cyclone; I felt for this lone, human, flesh-and-blood American girl in a landscape peopled by capricious gnomes, talking hens, and temperamental robots. She soldiered through it all, remaining cheerful without being saccharine. Like her cool predecessor, Alice, whom I liked a great deal less, she never lost the ballast of her own common sense, while, unlike Alice, she stopped short of imperiousness and condescension.

Faced with some very alien happenings in my own life, I tried to emulate Dorothy's sangfroid. I remember particularly one summer's day when Wher-chiao and I had sat on the compound wall and watched an opium addict expire on the footpath beneath us. A Japanese policeman directed traffic at the busy intersection, shouting at the bicycle-rickshaw men who were not pumping by him fast enough. He paid no attention to the cadaverous-looking man who had crumpled to the ground, a bag of bones in a light coolie vest and ragged trousers. We had seen him lay himself down on the gravel with dignity and serenity. He looked as if he were slipping under a coverlet to sleep, except that no normal sleep produced such a yellow-to-ash hue on the countenance. Wher-chiao and I agreed that he was dying. It all seemed very unremarkable. Passersby stepped round him, scarcely looking down. If it make us feel queasy, we said nothing about it, and soon slipped off the wall to buy some popsicles— long, thin, fuchsia-colored ones that my mother forbade me to eat, saying that they were just sticks of frozen cholera.

At times like these, when even horror had a commonplace quality because of the lack of public reaction to it, it was comforting to return to the land of Oz and to Dorothy's hard head. I could sympathize with her homesickness for her homespun Uncle Henry and Aunt Em back in Kansas when the going got really rough in Oz. As Dorothy's thoughts turned to Aunt Em, mine focused, in times of stress, on my Aunt Dee Dee's apartment in Washington, the one permanent base in our family's peripatetic existence, the unshakable still center.

The measure of the power of a book over a child's mind is presumably just this: the ease of identification, the ability to extract relief as well as amusement from it, the capacity of the story to facilitate spiritual removal, at least, from one's surroundings. The staying power of a children's classic—and classics in the making appear every year, thankfully, in spite of the technological society—is that it follows you through life, remaining in the index file of your memory until the end of your days. Recently Katharine Whitehorn, a sometime colleague of mine on the London *Observer*, commented on a devious editor we both knew: "Oh, he's the wicked witch of the West." She didn't have to explain. We were both Oz raised and bred.

Everyone is shaped by early tastes and by memories of the first intense pleasure the printed page can give. And how can one in fairness be pompous about what this might be? I cannot be critical of my son when he pores over his favorite weekly comic (he shuts himself up in his room so that he can read it in solitude, relishing the interlude it takes to read it). I recall too well my own exquisite enjoyment at the bimonthly set of "funny papers" Aunt Dee Dee sent to Mukden from two Sundays' worth of the *Washington Post*. Nothing since has ever seemed as tantalizing as those fat brown paper cylinders did then. I would peel off the tightly bound wrapper the way a

gourmet might uncap a jar of Beluga caviar, slowly and voluptu-
ously. Then—there they were!—the Katzenjammer Kids (whatever happened to them?), Little Orphan Annie with her shoe-
button eyes and her libidinous Daddy Warbucks, Mutt and Jeff,
the beanpole and the midget. The pleasure was orgiastic; deprivation had been a fine preparation for simple ecstasy.

Perhaps I am being farfetched, but I believe that my special
life circumstance in Mukden, one that isolated me from my
contemporaries, gave children's media a special power over my
childhood, placing me in the same position of detachment that
a great many city children experience today. The child who
lives in a high-rise apartment and has no play space and few
playmates, the child for whom school has not yet begun, whose
father (if he is lucky enough to have one around) is practically
a stranger except on the weekends and whose mother tends to
register little more than a distracted impatience with his constant presence, is as desperately dependent on his daily ration
of television as I was on books and bimonthly comics.

Children's entertainment media carry a voltage for the
cramped urban child that was lacking for the nineteenth-or
early-twentieth-century child. The latter could play in the
streets from the moment he began to walk and so devised those
complicated street games, endless varieties of hopscotch and
jump rope, which were accompanied by versifying and rhyming
—rich, sociable fun. Today's urban child might get run over
playing in the street, the playground is far away and put together with cement and lack of imagination (those careful rows
of swings, the single slide, a few seesaws), and so he stays at
home with mother. For the young in compressed, urban quarters, the media is not so much the message these days as their

very lifeline. With parents in modern nuclear families as isolated as they are today, children begin to resemble that type of
flour called "self-rising."

A fine fictional example of the modern self-raised child, dependent for nourishment on media, rather than on human contact, is the sad, hustling cowboy from James Leo Herlihy's novel
Midnight Cowboy, which John Schlesinger adapted so faithfully
and so skillfully for the screen. Joe Buck, raised by a man-crazed
grandmother hardly conscious of his existence, sucks all experience from the cathode tube. A school dropout at fourteen, he
moons about at home, never switching off the set. Gradually,
subliminally, he garners his life-style from the box; he becomes
a fantasy cowboy turned quasi real. He acquires the boots, the
Stetson, the rolling walk, the sleepy smile. The sight of a real
prairie or the whinny of an actual horse would be as alien to him
as a Hong Kong sampan village, but as far as he is concerned,
he is Gary Cooper, Henry Fonda, and Will Rogers all wrapped
up in one. Television has molded his tastes and concepts, made
him what he is, illiterate, inarticulate, a fiasco human.

Joe Buck is a monster for our age, an extreme result of lonely
media mania, never very bright to begin with and ripe for total
tube-rearing. However, cowboy Buck apart, it is good to recall
the television-viewing figures for North American children
given in 1961 by the Stanford University sociologists Wilbur
Schramm, Jack Lyle, and Edwin B. Parker in *Television in the
Lives of Our Children*. They write that throughout the years of
school, an American child spends within 5 per cent as much time
on television as on school, devoting about one-sixth of his waking hours to the medium, spending more time on television than
on any other activity except sleep.

In England the viewing time is lessened by the fact that children's weekday leisure television does not begin until about 4:30 in the afternoon, with Saturday afternoon television devoted to sports events and Sunday afternoons to educational television and religious programs. So the slightly diminished viewing in Great Britain is caused by circumstances rather than by children's individual choice. As Dr. Hilde Himmelweit, the British sociologist, writes in her book *Television and the Child*, television is so cherished by the young viewer that it has in early viewing years a kind of "halo quality," literally shimmering with mesmerizing interest. If there were hours of cartoons to be seen on weekend mornings, the British child would almost certainly be there watching, encouraged by Mother.

No one can honestly blame the restricted, apartment-dwelling mother for using television as a kind of baby-sitter for all seasons. Mothers living in high-rise, high-density apartment houses are fearful of sending their under-fives out to play on their own. Fear of molestation, traffic accidents, elevator breakdowns, broken bones on the concrete playground—all these very real anxieties contribute to the urban mother's wish to keep her children indoors.

Play space and playgroups for the under-fives in urban settings are universally inadequate. The editor of the journal of the U.S. Parent Cooperative Preschools International wrote me in 1971 that there were 232 member schools in the United States and 65 in Canada that year—hardly a vast number for two North American countries. However, it should be emphasized that the PCPI is not the sole organization for the provison of preschool learning. A statistic quoted in a May 1972 issue of *Newsweek* stated that 40 per cent of all three- to five-year-olds in the United States are enrolled in some sort of pre–primary school program. While this is not a disheartening statistic, it cannot occasion any complacency, either, especially when one considers that 60 per cent of the nation's children is a great number of children and they are probably just those disadvantaged preschoolers most in need of nursery school stimulation.

In a 1970 report written by the British National Society for the Prevention of Cruelty to Children, *Children in Flats: A Family Study,* it was found that less than 10 per cent of the parents of young children interviewed relied on any form of playgroup. In fact, most of the mothers surveyed did not know of the existence of any such group anywhere in the area. This was realistic of them; in the majority of cases, none existed.

Still, help is certainly on the way for the British mother. In the new White Paper published on December 7, 1972, called *Education: A Framework for Expansion,* Margaret Thatcher, the secretary of state for education, outlined a ten-year plan in which all three- and four-year-olds will be able to enjoy part-time nursery education on demand by 1982. In what she calls a "general strategy," the first great mushrooming of nursery schools, to be attached to the existing primary schools, will be completed by 1974–1975. To this end, this forthright Tory lady is spending £15 million—or $36 million—in the next two years, and admits that her eye is mainly on the poor, inner city areas, at least initially.

When enlightened educators such as Mrs. Thatcher think of the deprived urban child, they are very likely to be concentrating on children in city tower blocks. It is one of the greatest ironies of this post-World War II period that the growth of high-rise buildings, the cement realizations of Gropius and Le Corbusier, and the growing belief that they are crippling to the human spirit, especially that of a young child, should coincide with the development of a new theory about how young children learn first postulated by the Chicago psychologist Benjamin Bloom. Bloom believes that a child's most important intellectual development, more than half of what he will attain during his whole lifetime, occurs in the earliest years, before he is four years old. Bloom has thus harnessed us with a rather dreadful realization: a child needs the stimulation of creative media, play, and socialization most crucially before the age of five—but the majority of city-bred children, and particularly those housed in high-rise blocks, are the least likely to get those stimuli. Cramped, two-room apartments, restricted quarters, the constant "shushing" by parents, lack of anywhere to play—these are the virtually mind-extinguishing conditions surrounding a frighteningly large number of children today. The only intellectual nourishment he is likely to get flows from the not too bounteous teat of the television set in the corner, gushing out the second-rate—sadomasochistic cartoons, old movies, tasteless family situation "comedies," turgid Westerns. There is some hope—"Sesame Street" in America, the British Broadcasting Company's magazine and story-reading programs for children in Britain. But good children's programs are still scarce. Children's minds are being neglected on a worldwide scale.

No one interested in child development can remain unmoved by the exciting discoveries concerning children that have been reported or given new emphasis in the past fifteen years. Some stunning, revolutionary concepts and theories have been offered up for parental consumption: Bloom's hypothesis concerning early development, the growing credence given Maria Montessori's idea of a child's early "period of sensitivity," Piaget's experiments as to how children learn to conceptualize, the growing belief that a stimulating environment can raise a child's intelligence, the final laying away of the old idea that a child has

a *fixed* intelligence at birth, and the new belief in a correlation
between the acquisition of richer language patterns in early
years and developing intelligence. These concepts are not only
revolutionary, but deeply disturbing, too, since now that we
know so much more about a young child's receptivity and need
for stimuli in his earliest years, we are faced with society's
apparently equally deep inability to cope with that young
child's needs. It is as if we had been offered a big, rough diamond
and knew nothing about cutting that gem, nor where to find a
setting for it.

We can thank the psychologists and sociologists for handing
the educators and planners this big, ticking stick of dynamite—
the young child's urgent need for stimulation—but our grati-
tude would be more fulsome if we knew exactly how to go about
giving it to him. I sometimes think that society might have been
more prepared to handle this new dynamite if the theories and
postulations concerning the mind of the under-fives had been
more comprehensible, less dispersed, more cohesive, more lu-
cidly delivered. We might greatly admire Jean Piaget's discovery of how a child deals with the concept of volume, for example, but I seriously doubt if any nonprofessional parent can sit
down and read through Piaget's elucidation of his findings with
any ease.

While I do not believe the world's child experts are deliberately trying to mystify parents, I do think they often hamper
widespread comprehension of their important theories and discoveries with the use of rather incestuous, intramural jargon
which only they can understand.

This struck me particularly when I was sent by the London
Observer to cover the Sixth International Congress of Child Psychiatry at Edinburgh in 1966. The only journalist there from a

national newspaper, I was given a front-row seat in a huge, stately hall, part of the University of Edinburgh, among twelve hundred psychiatrists from thirty-three countries. It occurred to me then that my situation was quite extraordinary and reflected a kind of breakdown of communications between professional child experts and the press—and of course, those people who would be likely to read the press coverage of the conference, the parents. Robert Shields, the *Observer*'s psychology correspondent, a psychoanalyst, had sent me to the congress when he was unable to go himself. He was not surprised when I told him of my lonely status, explaining that the *Observer* was unique among national newspapers in Britain in its interest in and coverage of psychiatry.

The congress centered on the subject of adolescence, this at a time when the so-called generation gap was first gaining its frightening momentum and when most fathers and mothers were just beginning to feel stunned and betrayed by their children's naked hostility. For five days, the disturbed adolescent was analyzed on a vast international scale. Why did he go about unwashed? Behave in a surly way? Drop out of school? Break windows? Overeat? Have casual sex? Get deeply depressed? Commit suicide? Bouncing off the domed ceilings of the austere auditorium were words that would have made John Knox blanch, or at least recoil: *hypersexual, penis growth, penis envy*. And certainly words were aired there that would have been inexplicable to a great many parents who had sired these same adolescents—*internalization, compulsive neurotic, transference, fantasy guidance, psychic equilibrium, tensional outlets, ego-syntonic fixity, peer cultures, ego-identity*.

The next four years were to see the full outbreak of the adolescent rebellion against parental and establishmentarian values, the growth of the hippie cult on an international scale, the drug phenomenon, student violence. One wonders what would have happened if those clever professionals at the congress, who seemed to be so conversant with adolescent disturbance, had been less close with their knowledge. Would parents the world over have been more prepared for the outbreak of rebellious behavior and would they have handled it with less heartbreak and confusion when it finally hit them?

The congress was dominated by the high priestess of children's psychoanalysis, Anna Freud, daughter of Sigmund Freud, then in her early seventies. Gray-haired and clad in a simple, calf-length black dress, she appeared vaguely nunlike and very shy. But when she stood on the auditorium stage, her shyness dropped away dramatically and she gave a stirring, hard-hitting speech to the transfixed audience. She deplored the fact that the adolescent's environment was at its most demanding when he had "the greatest stress inside." Added to his physiological growth explosion, she noted, was the grotesque fact that he also had to meet the most arduous academic challenges at the same time. Her plea for understanding of the adolescent was convincing and moving—but who was going to know about it except the readers of one newspaper?

It seems ironic that these specialists in children's behavior who work so earnestly to bring about the liberation of the spirit of their young patients should be so tight about airing their findings. It is a great pity that they tend to keep their discoveries within their profession, although this may be in no way deliberate but may spring from an inability to translate them into lay language.

For example, when I first began to do some research for this book and was concentrating particularly on the link between the growth of intelligence in children and verbal fluency, I came upon a reference to the "case of Anna" in a book entitled *Social Learning and Its Measurement* by the British child expert Kellmer Pringle. I remembered trying to contact Dr. Pringle previously. She had been one of the experts who, because of the pressure of work, had been unable to help with an *Observer* magazine series, "The Mind of the Child," that I helped produce in 1966. The series had been a rather oversimplified description of the various stages of mental and physical development of the child, aged one to ten, its simplification an unavoidable outcome of the limitations of the color supplement magazine format. But simple or no, it had turned out to be a winner with parents and was the newspaper's first intimation of a widespread desire for knowledge about child development that was not being satisfied.

In her textbook, a professional work *for* professionals, Dr. Pringle spoke of a baby's task of "learning to become a human being" and the importance of early dependency relationships, first on the mother and father and then on other people; she viewed the key role of "socializing" with others as being a prime factor in normal development. She mentioned the "distortion" of development in those children who have been "socially isolated" from birth and then referred to the "case of Anna" as an illuminating example of this kind of "distortion." She assumed that her reader knew to which Anna she referred. I did not know. How many other interested laymen would? Dr. Pringle did little to enlighten me in her reference, though she did make a note about her source in the bibliography at the end of the chapter.

That was the beginning of my week-long search for Anna, who turned out to be a tragic little Pennsylvania girl of five whose mother had not wanted her and had hidden her in an upstairs room, giving her little attention since her birth except regular bottles of milk. The social welfare authorities discovered her in 1938 and removed her into care. The case had been written up by Kingsley Davis in the *American Journal of Sociology* in the 1940s. London libraries did not stock the journal; the Tavistock Clinic did but its volumes began only after 1950. The British Museum Library finally revealed Anna (about whom more later) to me but only after a red-tape-ridden two days spent obtaining a permanent pass to the library, and dredging back into the lists of periodicals. I wished Dr. Pringle had not assumed so much from me originally.

But then she, like so many of her colleagues both in England and America, is concerned with the detailing of data, the cataloguing of caseloads, the piling up of convincing and sufficiently abundant statistics to back up certain hypotheses and theories—to convince others in the same profession of the correctness of these stands and postulations. Admirable work, but where does the public figure?

In this book, I have tried to outline and clarify some of the newer findings of those who work with or study very young children, to write a sort of layman's guide to these revolutionary new theories the professionals, perhaps unconsciously, have tended to keep to themselves. Most of all, I have tried to show how their theories about a child's mental development relate to the media that fill the modern child's life; to find out if the media are helping young minds to develop, or failing to do so.

2

The Urgent Need for Language Learning in the Earliest Years

The phrase "neglected child" once conjured up visions of a runny nose, ragged shirt, and split shoes. Today the concept of neglect has become less linked with appearances only, and the truly impoverished child may be the one whose verbal skills are as sparse and threadbare as his clothes.

A startling new concept about language ability and its relationship to a child's mind has been growing in England, Russia, and the United States over the past decade, with experts in child development and sociologists saying much the same thing but in different languages and usually independently of each other. What they say is that a child not only enlarges his experience

22

through speaking but that speech gives him fresh ways of adjusting his mental activities. In other words, speech is no longer considered to be just a method of communicating—which is important enough, we know—but a way in which a child may have those internal monologues that facilitate abstract thinking. The link between linguistic ability and intelligence is irrefutable, a complex process of cross-fertilization between tongue and mind. When this crucial interaction is absent, we have a truly deprived child.

If a child lives in a silent world from the time of his birth until he is three or four years old, the chances are that he will never learn to speak adequately and will have acquired an irreversible incapacity to learn any language. He will have been deprived of one of the most important developmental tools a child has been given. Professor Eric Hawkins of the York University language center in England explains the process poetically as teaching human songbirds to sing; those who fail educationally are too often, in his words, "the human songbirds who never learned to sing."

There have been many instances of socially isolated children whose progress after discovery has been painstakingly documented, and they have been found to have been just this— "silent songbirds"—throughout their adult lives. What the believers in environmental influence have done is to examine these child casualties and then ask: Why *are* they casualties? Why are they irredeemably backward? What factor common to all has produced such an amazing similarity in developmental behavior?

Every now and then a child is born who touches off something psychotic in a mother or in both parents. Usually the child is illegitimate, a cause for shame, or simply a mistake, the last in a stream of unwanted progeny. A kind of madness overtakes the parent upon the arrival of this unwelcome child, and instead of dealing it active physical blows (like that growing number of parents who *do* batter an unwanted baby), the parent hides it, locks it up, and deals it an impassive form of cruelty, that of cutting it off from all outside stimuli. Whether the child has been abandoned in an Indian jungle, chained in a hole in Germany, or tied to a chair in a Pennsylvania farmhouse, one characteristic has been common to all such children who have been recovered and cared for later—adequate speech eludes them for the rest of their adult lives.

Cases involving such children have been reported in the newspapers almost since printing presses were invented. As long ago as 1799, a provincial journal in Aveyron, France, reported that a wild boy of about eleven had been captured in the woods of the area. The reporter went on to describe the child in some detail. He was almost naked, scarred all over from apparent skirmishes with forest animals, and could only grunt like a beast. Apart from a loping, ambling trot or gallop in which he placed the palms of his hands on the ground as he moved, his only other predominant movement was a slow rocking back and forth on his heels, rhythmic and despairing, like that of a caged animal. The newspaper report described a scar from a deep incision on his neck and suggested that the child might have been wounded deliberately before being abandoned in the woods. Certainly whoever had abandoned him hoped he would not live, and it was assumed that the culprit was his mother, hiding her shame, an illegitimate birth.

In some extraordinary way, the boy had managed to survive in this wild state, through freezing winters, on a diet of acorns, roots, and spring water. When first sighted by hunters, he scrambled up a tree with the agility of a monkey. They caught him, however, and took him to a village in the canton of St. Sernin, where he stayed for a few months until his story was described in the Aveyron journal.

The story of the wild boy's discovery hit the Paris medical community like a bombshell. At that time, the French intelligentsia was still reeling under the impact of Jean-Jacques Rousseau's concept of a "noble savage," pure and free of society's corrupt influences. And here was one in the living flesh! Or so they supposed until he was brought to Paris and put on view like a circus freak. What they saw was a filthy boy-animal, given to biting and clawing out, to making frightening, spasmodic, rocking movements, and uttering only subhuman, guttural sounds. Few of his senses had been developed. Perfume and pig swill held the same apparent aroma for him; he did not jump or react even to the sound of a pistol shot near him; he had no sense of hot or cold. At one point, he picked a potato out of boiling water and did not respond to the shock of heat on his hand. Dr. Pinel, the famous director of the National Institute of the Deaf and Dumb in Paris, pronounced the boy's "wildness" a fake (the popular description for this "wildness" then was "feral") and said he was a congenital idiot, pointing out that severely retarded children also lacked the essential faculties of hearing, smelling, or feeling temperature differences.

But a keen, idealistic, twenty-five-year-old doctor at the deaf-mute institute, Jean-Marc-Gaspard Itard, refused to accept Pinel's diagnosis and decided to take over the boy's education on his own. Itard's first step was to remove the boy from the institute where he had been so wretched, clawing out at the other boys and registering a kind of impassive contentment only when he was let loose in the garden. Itard placed him in the care of a comfortable matron, Mme. Guerin, who lived on what was then the outskirts of Paris near the Luxembourg Gardens and gave him frequent outings there (to the end of his life, he was happiest out of doors).

Itard and Mme. Guerin devoted their full energies to the boy. Mme. Guerin provided maternal warmth and excellent physical care while Itard brought his considerable professional talents to the task of educating him. A methodical man with a passion for recording his studies, Itard wrote a careful history of the wild boy's progress.* The first step in the business of humanizing the boy was to give him a name. As he seemed to make the sound *oh, oh* more than any other, Itard decided to give him a name with an *o* in it to which he might respond more readily. He selected the name Victor.

By this time, the child was beginning to respond to people with a few rudimentary signs of feeling, especially to Mme. Guerin. Now when he was separated from her, he would weep pathetically, still mute. He would smile radiantly when she returned to him. These signs of humanity encouraged Itard to set up an ambitious program of aims for the boy:

> 1st Aim. To interest him in social life by rendering it more pleasant to him than the one he was then leading, and above all more like the life which he had just left.
>
> 2nd Aim. To awaken his nervous sensibility by the most energetic stimulation, and occasionally by intense emotion.

---

*With the help of Itard's meticulous diary, the French film director François Truffaut, taking the part of Itard himself, made a touching and reasonably faithful film of the wild boy's education. I say "reasonably faithful" because he neglected to mention that the wild boy never learned to speak. The film, called *L'Enfant Sauvage* (*The Wild Child* in the United States), was released for world distribution in 1970.

3rd Aim. To extend the range of his ideas by giving him new needs and by increasing his social contacts.

4th Aim. To lead him to the use of speech by inducing the exercise of imitation through the imperious law of necessity.

5th Aim. To make him exercise the simplest mental operations upon the objects of his physical needs over a period of time afterwards inducing the applications of these mental processes to the objects of instruction.

Considering these ambitious aims, Itard actually accomplished very little with Victor, especially in the realm of speech. Lesser men might have despaired long before he did. At the end of two years of conscientious training, Victor could utter only two different expressions or words: one was *lait,* the word for milk, his favorite drink, the other *Oh, Dieu,* the frequent "oh, God" which burst from Mme. Guerin's lips and which he imitated. Even these two expressions were uttered more as exclamations of pleasure than as ways of getting something he wanted. It was only after he received the crock of milk that he uttered the appreciative word *lait,* never beforehand. Though virtually mute, Victor revealed a keen intelligence. He devised his own "language of action," as Itard called it. If he wanted a second helping of milk or water, he would go find a jug and point at it meaningfully, or bang at the jug with his fork at the table.

Boyishly, he loved being given a ride in a wheelbarrow and would run out into the garden and push the empty wheelbarrow around wistfully until someone got the point. More encouraging even than these signs of increasing intelligence was the fact that Victor began to pick up an extensive reading vocabulary; for example, seeing the word *key* written on the blackboard, he would dutifully run off to fetch it off its latch. It became obvious that he could hear. This discovery caused Itard to write such disconsolate entries, underlined, as: "If he is not deaf why does he not speak?"

Itard was touched by the child's sense of occasion. While Victor never reached out for physical contact during their obviously rather grim lessons, he would allow himself to soften at bedtime. Itard writes:

> When I go to the house in the evening just after he has gone to bed, his first movement is to sit up for me to embrace him, then to draw me to him by seizing my arm and making me sit upon his bed, after which he usually takes my hand, carries it to his eyes, his forehead, the back of his head, and holds it with his upon these parts for a very long time. At other times he gets up with bursts of laughter and comes beside me to caress my knees in his own way which consists of feeling them, rubbing them firmly in all directions for some minutes, and then sometimes laying his lips to them two or three minutes.

There is no question that, in spite of being moved by Victor's shows of affection, Itard was a tough taskmaster, almost obsessive in his sworn aim of civilizing the savage. Disappointed in the boy's speech development, or total lack of it, he dug into the poor child's psyche. Did Victor have a moral sense, a concept of justice or injustice? To find out, Itard pretended rage and tried to push him into a closet, his occasional punishment when Victor misbehaved. The boy fought back and ended up by biting his hand. Itard writes:

> It would have been sweet to me at that moment could I have made my pupil understand and have told him how the pain of his bite filled my heart with satisfaction and made amends for all my labor.

. . . It was an incontestable proof that the feeling of justice and injustice . . . was no longer foreign to the heart of my pupil.

Pleased as Itard was at this growth of moral consciousness, his enthusiasm for his project began to flag after five years of hard work; he felt he had failed. This sensation of defeat cut deeply into his beliefs. Itard had a faith in the power of good environment and dedicated teaching that amounted to a religion. At the outset he believed that Victor's isolated beginnings had blanked out his senses and mind and that, with proper training, these could be recovered. In this, Itard foreshadowed the theories of the progressive educators of today who say that no child is ineducable. It is not merely coincidental that Itard's work should have indirectly influenced Maria Montessori over a hundred years later. Itard taught Séguin, whose writings inspired Montessori's belief that subnormal children could be taught, a conviction she later proved by teaching retarded children to read and write at an institute in Rome in the 1920s.

Itard's disappointment over the fact that he never drew Victor into speech, that "phenomena," in his own words, "which is without question, the most marvelous act of imitation, is also its . . . principal promotor of education," is most understandable. He had succeeded in so many other ways. He had taught Victor to comport himself like a young man, to walk upright, to understand certain written words, to respond to affection and verbal commands, to enjoy the sights and sounds of nature in an active way. The doctor seemed to feel, however, that Victor had let his theories down, an unforgivable lapse where a dedicated theoretican like Itard was concerned. He had provided an environment for Victor that should have effected staggering changes in the boy's development, and had given five years of his busy time trying to make the experiment work. What Itard missed was that Victor had indeed been shaped by his environment and his environment *had* shaped him—irrevocably. Itard did not realize that the right environment could come too late. Today we know that if a child does not hear or imitate the sounds of an attentive adult before he is three years old, he may never acquire the ability to speak.

I was interested to hear a friend who had been working with autistic children in a small day school in Southwest London say that she had noticed many similarities in their behavior and Victor's, especially in his single-mindedness over the wheelbarrow, for example, and in his occasional outbursts of petulance and rage. However, if, as I understand it, autistic children are suffering from an acute inability to respond to any outside stimuli, ostensibly retreating from all contact through some inchoate wish for total emotional withdrawal, they would not resemble Victor. No one could have been more demonstrative or tactile than Victor, as Itard so movingly described.

It is remarkable that Itard did not further damage the child with his stern, Gallic, unrelenting tutelage. When you consider that Victor was discovered in his prepubertal phase and was somehow ferried through the trauma of adolescence while being subjected to a barrage of strange intellectual exercises and incessant demands for a rigid discipline of mind, it is only remarkable that he did not become violently disturbed. Itard was lucky that a bite was all he got! As it was, Victor grew peacefully into adulthood, becoming reasonably self-sufficient, it appears, but never speaking. He died at the age of forty leaving Itard to survive him by another ten years.

Most of the accounts of abandoned or isolated children convey the quality of a Gothic horror tale, but the case of Caspar

Hauser, a German adolescent discovered in Nuremberg in 1828, seems to be more Grimm's tale than anything even the brothers themselves could have invented. Every society probably gets the sensational news story it deserves and Germany at the time, overly romantic, quixotic, melodramatic, might have been waiting explicitly for a grotesque such as Caspar Hauser.

According to the records of the Nuremberg police at that time, the miserable boy, aged about seventeen, dressed in tattered peasant clothes, was found staggering and weeping in the streets, apparently drunk. Taken to a Horse Guards barracks and examined there, he was found to be completely sober but in a state of nervous collapse (a nervous excitability that only increased with time, unfortunately). He was nearly dumb, and spoke only one phrase he kept repeating incomprehensibly: "I will be a rider as my father was." His feet and legs were pitifully misshapen. The sight of these along with his snufflings and whimperings soon melted the reserve of the tough, suspicious guards and they took him in and fed him.

He carried a letter with him addressed to the captain of the guards. The letter said that he had been abandoned by his mother and begged the captain to give him "a good Christian education." Explaining why he himself had abandoned Caspar, the letter-writer said that he was a poor peasant with ten children of his own. As the days passed, the guards were able to piece Caspar's history together bit by bit. As far as they could tell, Caspar had been kept in a hole where he had always been forced to sit upon the ground. Doctors examining him found that he had a curious formation at the back of his knees (which lay flat on the ground, without the normal hollows there). This suggested that he had never lain flat but had sat up with his back supported against his cell wall and his legs stretched out. Vaccination marks on his arms led his discoverers to believe that he had had upper-class parents, as only the rich in Germany at that time could afford to be inoculated. This initial supposition blossomed later into wild conjecturing about his background; many believed that he was the son of Stephanie de Beauharnais and the Grand Duke Charles Louis and thus was the hereditary prince of Baden, cruelly suppressed by another Baden princess who wanted her own firstborn on the throne. There has never been any proof of this theory, but it fit the mood of the times to envision him as a blueblood in chains.

Caspar's behavior and speech patterns interest me more than his parents' pedigree, however. Like his sad counterpart Victor, he responded sweetly to adult concern and sympathy (in fact, his biographers imply that he eventually became addicted to it). Anger did not seem to be part of his docile, naive makeup, and he spoke of his former captor without rancor as "the man I was always with." Scientists and doctors were fascinated by him; his every reaction and saying was recorded. They noted his tastes in food and drink; he detested meat and wine, and for a long time would touch only bread and water, presumably because this was the fare to which he was accustomed. He could not bear bright lights or the sight of panoramic landscapes. He was revolted by all smells, whether they were of cheese or of roses. He adored horses. He had a passion for order and liked playing with wooden toys, usually models of horses, and seemed to enjoy ranging them together in neat columns. He later managed to explain that two wooden horses were all he had had in his cage or hole.

So much doubt has been cast upon the Caspar Hauser story because of the somewhat hysterical conjecture about his being a royal prince that much of the real fascination of his story has been obscured. The possession of only two toys to play with in his isolation is a point in fact. It is quite possible that these two bits of external stimuli kept the boy from degenerating into total idiocy. His fingers were as nimble when he was discovered as his feet were clumsy, and only the constant touching of the smooth toys, making them run and prance by his side, could have given him this coordination and kept him from a life of total passivity and stupefaction. His docility toward his observers led them to believe that the man who had been his captor had not been brutal. Caspar said that he had never seen the man's face. He did not refer to him or to anyone disparagingly. In fact, he appeared to like his fellow men. On one occasion, he registered terror at the sight of a chimney sweep, apparently because of his black face. He never learned to dissociate inanimate from animate objects, which made him appear touchingly childlike. The sight of a crucifix moved him to tears, not for its sad religious connotations but because he could not bear to see the little man hung up in this painful fashion. His guardians had to restrain him from trying to detach this hanging man from every crucifix he saw.

When Caspar was moved to the home of a kindly educator, Professor Georg Daumer, he bloomed. He learned to play chess with the professor, made intricate pasteboard cutout figures, and showed great love for the professor's old mother, whom he too called Mother. However, his language, except for the long phrases he could parrot, remained truncated and incomplete. Anselm von Fuerbach, the famous jurist who tried to track down his long-term captor to have him criminally prosecuted, described Caspar's speech at some length:

> His enunciation of words which he knew was plain and determinate, without hesitation or stammering. But coherent speech was

not yet to be expected from him, and his language was as indigent as his stock of ideas. It was therefore also extremely difficult to become intelligible to him. Scarcely had you uttered a few sentences which he appeared to understand, when you found that something was mingled with them which was foreign to him, and if he wished to understand it, his spasms immediately returned. In all that he said, the conjunctions, participles and adverbs were still almost entirely wanting; his conjugation embraced little more than the infinitive; and he was most of all deficient in respect to his syntax, which was in a state of miserable confusion. "Caspar very well," ... he generally spoke of himself in the third person, calling himself Caspar.

As Fuerbach points out, Caspar's sentences lacked all the richness of proper speech; he left out all conjunctions, participles, adverbs. In this, he resembles children of the lower socioeconomic groups, whose language has been studied in great detail both in Britain and the United States. Caspar had great difficulty in placing himself in his speech, a fact which suggested that his sense of identity had been severely damaged by his deprived background. It should be stressed here that while language helps a child to order his mind, it also contributes to his ego growth, the ability to attach words to emotions, and enhancement of a feeling of self that is crucial to healthy emotional growth. Children from disadvantaged homes whose language development has been inadequate also tend to refer to themselves in the third person far beyond the age where this is normal. Robert Coles and Maria Piers, two child-study experts who worked with Boston slum children in the mid-1960s, reported that these deprived preschoolers constantly referred to themselves in the third person, as if, the authors write, they were "unaware of their own separateness or uniqueness or worth."

The early lack of any affectionate adult with whom he could identify or engage in a loving flow of conversation robbed Caspar of the capacity for adequate speech and a strong sense of self for the remainder of his sad, dramatic life. Even when a savage attempt was made to kill him when he was eighteen, presumably by his former captor who was afraid of being prosecuted, he could hardly explain that the failed act had been committed against *him*. Lying bleeding with a sharp wound deep in his forehead, he shouted: "Man! Man! Man beat—black man, like sweep—tell professor! Tell Mother. [Daumer's mother] . . . hide in the cellar."

It took him some time to come around to the word *me*, although the attack had certainly been upon him. His life grew no happier after he escaped this first attack. He was shuttled between caretakers, who seem to have grown a little tired of his oddness. When he was twenty-three, he was discovered to have a deep stab wound. He died three days after he was wounded, and as there was no proof of an outside evildoer in the case, it was assumed that the wound had been self-inflicted as a pathological attention-getter. If Caspar's beginnings had been Gothic, his ending was even more so.

If the tale of a socially isolated child is dramatic enough, as in Caspar's case, it is usually greeted with a healthy amount of public skepticism. The tendency to dismiss these children's histories as poppycock and fabrication is never more evident than with cases of so-called wolf children, infants abandoned by their parents and "brought up" by wolves. Since the time of the myth of Romulus and Remus and the founding of the Roman Empire, these tales have cropped up to form local, spellbinding lore both in Asia and in Europe.

In 1920, in a village called Godmuri near the town of Midnapore in West Bengal, two girls, Kamala, aged about eight, and Amala, apparently her sister, aged two, were discovered living in a wolves' den. An Indian missionary, the Reverend J. A. L. Singh, had sought them out after hearing stories from the villagers about a "man-ghost" that would appear at the edge of the jungle, emerging from a large mound made by white ants. Ant mounds tall enough for tunneling through are found all over India, and in this case the wolves had made their den in the heart of one of these curious structures, not a usual practice for wolves, it seems. This uncharacteristic behavior, coupled with the emergence of the "man-ghost," made the situation even more terrifying for the villagers. Undaunted, the Indian clergyman stood watch near the mound for several nights and saw that the so-called ghost, following out of the narrow tunnel after several wolf cubs, was actually two children with great balls of matted hair, crawling on all fours with a scuttling, hopping movement, "like squirrels," as he later recalled.

Mounting quite an elaborate operation, Singh paid some diggers to open up the mound and a gunman to shoot the mother wolf (a step he regretted taking but felt was necessary). The wolf cubs and two hideous-appearing children huddled together as the men entered the tunnel and Singh directed his men to separate the children from the cubs by throwing sheets over them and bundling them away.

Singh started writing a diary after making this astounding discovery. In it, he ponders about the wolf-human connection —but only briefly. Certainly, he reasoned, the children and the wolves had been together, but how, or why, or how the children were fed he chose to leave for others to puzzle over.

Well, and how *did* they live? Did they scratch an existence
from roots and berries like the wild boy of Aveyron? Or did they
pick up raw meat scraps left on the den floor by the mother
wolf? Was their proximity to the mother wolf and her cubs an
accident, or was it significant? We will never know.

Singh, a humane, educated man, decided to concentrate on
the children's development *after* their discovery. As his diary
shows, he was particularly fascinated by the older child,
Kamala; possibly she was more appealing and responsive than
Amala. In any case, he took them back to his orphanage in
Midnapore, keeping their sensational discovery to himself and
jotting down diary notes (meticulous ones like Itard's) on their
progress. Eventually, the news of their existence leaked out and
he was besieged by visitors. The publicity was a shock for Singh,
who had simpler plans for the girls. At that time, he wrote: "We
[himself and his wife] . . . simply wanted to rear them as human
children found in the jungle with the wolves. . . . One thing
occurred to my mind that I should keep a diary of the daily
improvement in everything as they stayed with us and grew."

Singh and his wife cut the children's hair and scrubbed their
filthy bodies, applying carbolic soap, carbolic lotion, tincture of
iodine, zinc, and boric acid to their dirt sores. In three weeks'
time, the girls' sores had disappeared and they looked quite
human. Their behavior was still very wild, however. They
would eat nothing but raw meat and milk. They could not stand
erect but ran very fast in that hopping, squirrel-like way that
Singh first noticed. He observed that their hands were longer
than those of most humans, presumably because of the unusual
use to which they had been put, clamped to the ground like
animals' paws. At first, they were drawn to a year-old orphan,
Benjamin, choosing his company exclusively, Singh guessed,
because the baby boy was also on all fours. However, this brief

association came to a dramatic halt when the wolf-children one day bit and scratched Benjamin. After this, they shunned all the other children, babies included, and crouched together in a corner for hours "as if meditating on some great problem," Singh wrote.

Except for a strange howling at night, the children appeared to be mute. The sound, Singh said, was rather beautiful, rich and reverberating, neither animal nor human, and soon everyone took this occasional nocturnal howling for granted. After eighteen months at the Singh orphanage, Kamala and Amala began to utter a sound like *bhoo, bhoo* when they were hungry or thirsty. Like Victor, they soon acquired the "language of action" (which also suggested a normal intelligence), and Kamala, in particular, would go to the pitcher of milk or water kettle when she was thirsty. Kamala also learned to shake her head for no and nod for yes, and at the same time began to register certain human emotions; she showed Mrs. Singh that she wished to wear a dress instead of a loincloth. Kamala also adored the color red (in this, she resembled Victor) and fell in love with a pair of bright red pajamas. In other words, except for her speech, she was starting to behave like any other little girl, with feelings of vanity as well as of modesty. She was also beginning to respond to affection, and made it plain that she wanted Mrs. Singh by her bed continuously when she was ill, which unfortunately was frequently, since she was rather delicate in spite of her harsh background—or perhaps because of it.

Convalescing from a severe illness, Kamala began to imitate the speech of the other children at the orphanage. Singh wondered if the illness had loosened her tongue. She showed herself much more articulate than either Victor or Caspar. However, her delivery revealed an unexpected impediment. While she could articulate the first syllables of words (she said *bha* for *bhat*, which means "rice" in Bengali, for example), she never managed to speak the second or third syllable: "her defective tongue failed to bring out the clear phonetic sound," Singh wrote. Sometimes she would pronounce the end of words rather than the beginnings, but she never formed them as a whole.

The reverend made a careful analysis of her vocabulary and pronunciation. For years after her discovery in 1924, she had a vocabulary of only forty-five words. Listed here are ten of them, with her renditions of the Bengali and English translations. Her vocabulary is seen to consist entirely of nouns, all of which had practical significance for her. In this, Kamala, like Caspar, reflected the characteristic of linguistically deprived children in both modern urban and rural surroundings, where the preponderance of nouns and sprinkling of verbs suffices for communication at its most limited, though immediate level.

Kamala's Words	*Bengali Equivalents*	*English Equivalents*
ud	ashud	medicine
doo	dudh	milk
foo	phul	flower
khel	khalena	toy
go	goru	cow
puz	pyjamah	pajama
go-ga	goru gari	bullock cart
bag	baghan	garden
joot	juta	shoe
zo	jal	water

That Kamala captivated both Mr. and Mrs. Singh is quite clear. In one triumphant moment, Kamala even joined the other children in a thank-offering service, kneeling to pray with them.

The missionary Singhs were understandably gratified. She stayed at the orphanage for a total of nine years, dying at seventeen, of what Mr. Singh does not say. She had apparently grown into a delightful person, but she always spoke in the broken way Singh described. Singh hardly ever mentioned the younger girl Amala, presumably because her progress and ability to respond were less impressive.

In the history of the language development of socially isolated children, Kamala made more impressive verbal strides than many others. Her impediment remained but her fluency was considerable and her vocabulary grew slowly but steadily. It has been suggested that Kamala's superiority in this realm might have been due to her listening to the cries of the wolves at night and at least hearing some vocalization. I would think it much more likely that the children were abandoned when Kamala was five or six and her sister only a baby and that Kamala had already learned some language, which she forgot entirely when she became wild but which had lingered in her subconscious mind nonetheless.

As we have seen, most of the men and women who have cared for these once abandoned children have been relative amateurs at the business of diagnosing their psychiatric states (with the exception of Itard, although his eighteenth-century knowledge of child psychiatry was limited). This was not the case, however, in the story of Anna, the case history mentioned earlier which, though as familiar as the name of Freud to many child experts, takes, as I discovered, some little digging to uncover if the facts of the case are unknown to you. Anna's case is one of the best known in the psychiatric profession because she was examined shortly after her discovery by a psychiatric social worker, Kingsley Davis, who studied her subsequent progress and recorded it in sympathetic, descriptive, and yet highly professional detail in the *American Journal of Sociology* a few years after she was found.

Anna was discovered in 1938, and the shocking circumstances of her imprisonment written up in the *New York Times* a day afterward. The *Times* reported that the child, just over five years old, was found "tied to an old chair in a storage room on the second floor of a farm house" in rural Pennsylvania. Her mother, a large, mentally retarded woman of twenty-seven, lived with her own parents, and as she had already enraged her father by giving birth to one illegitimate child, she was forced to keep Anna, the second one, out of sight. The mother regularly gave the child milk to drink but had not bathed her, trained her, fondled her, or spoken to her since infancy. At first, Anna had to be tied to a bedroom chair, but eventually her leg and arm muscles atrophied so that she could not move of her own free will, in any case. The older child, a son, slept on the bed at night but did not enter the room otherwise, so that Anna was cut off from this negligible social contact.

Kingsley Davis visited Anna three days after she was removed to a children's institution, and found her lying in a "limp, supine position, immobile, expressionless, indifferent to everything . . . believed to be deaf and possibly blind." After massage and a vitamin diet, she could sit up, and her small, pretty features began to register slightly more expression. According to Davis, at that time she neither smiled, cried, nor reacted to toys. The only sound she made was "a slight sucking intake of breath with the lips." On the fifth day at the children's home, Anna literally "found her tongue," writes Davis, and delighted in sticking it out. She began to show signs of affection toward other humans, rubbing heads with a favorite nurse. At the end of two months' stay, she laughed aloud, and proved that she was not blind by nodding in recognition to certain nurses. By 1939, more than a year after her discovery, she had learned to go down stairs by sitting on each step successively as she descended. She could drink from a cup, feed herself, and responded to spoken commands. In the words of the by then adoring nurses at the home, "she was learning a new trick every day."

But the one trick that she did not learn was how to speak. Her speech ability ranked below that of a one year old—she could only say *da*. Though presumably of normal intelligence (her learning ability in other directions tended to prove this), she never learned to speak properly, causing Davis to comment that the most important characteristic of the socially isolated child is his "universal failure to learn to talk with any facility." Davis concluded that these children were not innately or congenitally retarded but that their isolation in infancy had made them so.

Until recently, there has been a commonly held and rather romantic view that affection and love could warm these once cruelly isolated children back to normality. The sad fact is that while they learn certain motor activities—how to walk, eat, dress themselves, and other acts of social competence—impressive enough accomplishments for such damaged children, admittedly, the damage to the tongue is irreversible. There is strong reason to believe that if a child does not learn to speak before he is five, he will never do so.

So to return to the question first asked: What factor common to all has produced such an amazing similarity in developmental behavior? The answer is similar environments. Environment has been aptly described by the Chicago psychologist Benjamin Bloom as "the conditions, forces and external stimuli which impinge upon the individual." In the cases of these children, there was a total absence of external stimuli, a lack of any valid contact with a loving adult, someone with whom to identify, to imitate, and with whom to speak. Their environments are described by the sociologists and psychologists as "extreme." Other "extreme" environments that produce similar characteristics (inability to verbalize and a correspondingly low intelligence quotient) are orphanages and other children's homes, where again there is a minimum of contact with interested adults.

3

The Way Children Learn to Speak and Think

I have tried to show how the four unfortunate children, Victor, Caspar, Kamala, and Anna, failed to acquire the one skill most crucial to any human being—that of language. Of course, these are hardly typical children. They were sensational victims of cruelty, neglect, and their own bizarre environments. And yet they shared the one destructive experience, that of having no meaningful interaction with an adult during their formative young years. And what they lost—the ability to verbalize—they could never regain. In their different ways, these four dramatically deprived children tend to give credence to Benjamin Bloom's theory that the "loss of development in one period

44

cannot be fully recovered in another period" and that "extreme environments can have far greater effects in early years of development."

It is a curious fact that a child can develop a number of crucial skills without help from an adult. Give a normal, healthy child room in which to move and nothing in this world will prevent him from eventually rising to his feet somewhere around his first year or shortly after it, clasping a piece of furniture for support, and moving along in the stumbling beginnings of a walk. But speech is not a skill one can acquire on one's own; it is a complex, mysterious ability dependent on contact and interaction with an attentive adult. To quote the glib phrase "Man is a social animal" is to be more profound than one realizes. A child raised with the minimum of social—or, more specifically, *linguistic*—contact from a parent or some other interested, affectionate adult can, as we have seen, be intellectually stunted for life.

As anyone who has listened to an infant knows, a normal baby of two to three months will start making cooing and gurgling noises; sometimes these are contented sounds, and at other times the cries are sharp and angry, cries of discomfort. However, at some point, it becomes clear to any observant parent that the baby himself is aware of the sounds. He stops delightedly after a certain babble or coo and listens to it and then tries it again (in more scientific language, this is called *autism*, or "self-stimulation"). Naturally, this tentative self-appreciation and listening process occurs when the baby is full and contented. As Dr. M. M. Lewis, the British speech expert, points out, the pleasure a baby experiences in hearing his own babbling advances a step further when he not only plays with sounds but begins to experience a second kind of pleasure, "that of enjoyment in the *patterns* of his repeated sounds." Lewis believes that the key to language development lies in a child's babbling; he calls it the "beginning of delight in language for itself, for its own sake, the rudimentary beginning of the enjoyment of the art of language."

At the same time that the infant is becoming aware of his own babbling sounds, he is also beginning to be conscious of the sounds outside himself, noises that he is not making himself but that are obviously beamed at him. The smallest baby, barely a month old, can be soothed from his stressful crying by the comforting words his mother murmurs over his crib. In a few months' time, when he is about three months old, he will smile back at her soothing noises, and perhaps coo in response. This complex orchestration of sounds—the baby's own babblings and sound patterns, the effect of his mother's or father's voice on him, his vocal response to these sounds directed at him—all tend to build up into a powerful interrelationship, child to parent, parent to child. This interpersonal interaction forms the maximum beneficial environment for the flowering of speech in a child.

When the parent comforts a child with soothing sounds, the baby's response is, of course, emotional. Language learning is so complex—and often a sad and imperfect process—because it appears based largely on feeling and on reciprocity of affection and verbal interaction. Dr. Gertrud Wyatt, a speech therapist who has worked extensively with children with speech defects in the Boston area and elsewhere, believes that a child learns language through imitating a mother's sounds and through a reciprocal feedback process between himself and his mother. The child needs a high degree of this feedback, she believes, particularly of a corrective nature, at the time that he first begins to attach names to objects. The child experiments with sounds and imitates words he hears, and the mother, in an affectionate manner, monitors and corrects him as he says them. Later on, when the child is speaking more fluently, at the age of three or four, the mother becomes an *interpreter* as well as a corrector, interpreting strange symbols for him ("No, that does look like a bus, dear, but it's only a truck," and so on).

Usually a mother will fall naturally into this process. I did not know that I was involving myself in "corrective feedback" when my daughter was three and experimenting with language but I recall tirelessly correcting certain words: "No, not 'muk,' *milk*," and "Not 'yagg,' *egg*." The process became automatic, like a litany after a while (she tended to cling tenaciously to her own pronunciations). If a child is of normal mentality and has a normal speech apparatus, this feedback can seem an entrancing game, a way to get an affectionate reaction, a testing process, a means of making all-important contact. The mother is the child's first and most crucial language teacher—she *is* the medium.

When I met Dr. Benjamin Spock in New York City in 1970, he commented that he wished fathers and mothers could make serious efforts to stay with their children for the first years of their lives. "The quality of care the first three years is especially crucial. Both parents have equal responsibility. I used to assume that mothers had the greater obligation to stay at home. Now I say that if a mother wants an uninterrupted career, a father has an equal obligation in housework and child care."

Spock went on to say that "after the age of three a child will not be deprived if he attends a good nursery school half or two-thirds of a day. It is preferable that he not be away from parents all day till the age of seven." If neither parent is willing to give up time to care for a child, he added, "I'd advise them not to have one."

The more I have studied the subject of language learning in children, the more I have tended to agree with Spock that the relationship with the parents in the first three years is crucial. Where else but with a mother or father would a child manage to find this same feedback process? It would have to be a pretty special parent substitute or day-care center with an unusually dedicated staff that could rival the painstaking feedback cycle, edged with affection and concern, that a parent can muster for his or her child. Of course, some parents, particularly those mothers who are alone and struggling to survive economically, are either unable or unconscious of the need to provide this reciprocal feedback. In such cases the home is not necessarily preferable to a day nursery or well-run kindergarten.

But given the existence of an emotional, interpersonal relationship between parent and child, language tends to burgeon. Dorothea McCarthy, who studied speech development in the young child at the University of Minnesota in the late 1920s, was one of the first psychologists to investigate this subject. In the now seminal monograph summarizing her findings, she concluded that "the child's involvement with the environment usually has to be *emotionally charged* before his efforts to communicate spill over into verbal responses which may subsequently become words." Speech is acquired in an interpersonal setting. Test this process for yourself if there is a reasonably contented baby within speaking distance. Look into the baby carriage or crib of this happy baby and smile and say his name. With any luck, you can see him go stiff with excitement, start to smile himself, and swivel his arms and legs about in a crisis of pleasure. Then he may coo, literally *spill* into sound. Language, or early sounds in an infant, are often a result of this spillover of emotional excitement, response of a very high key. A child's response to a mother's smile can be even more highly charged than the one he accords a friendly stranger. If his mother accompanies the smile with a word, the overspill into responsive language is uncontrolled delight, vocally expressed.

As Lewis says, nothing is less *neutral* for the child than this verbal contact: "The word comes to him charged with emotion, as much a part of his experience of his mother at this moment as her physical presence." Lewis goes on to say that a child is most likely to respond vocally when he is actively encouraged. He reports an experiment made with a ten-week-old boy who made only four sounds in three minutes when his father was silent but increased his vocalization to *eighteen* sounds in the same amount of time when his father said hello to him every ten seconds.

This highly revealing experiment moved Lewis to entreat parents to involve themselves more in dialogue with their children ("Play the dialogue game," he begs them). This game encourages the child to try to imitate more closely what he hears, writes Lewis. If a parent ignores his child's constructive, meaningful babble, he warns, and fails to respond to it vocally, the child's development of his power of imitation may be severely retarded. However sensible and ideal Lewis's suggestion of increasing mother-child dialogue may be, it is impossible not to reflect on how untenable a game it must be for some mothers to play. One has only to think of a frantic, single mother, oppressed by poverty, bringing up a large family alone in a small, city apartment project on welfare benefits to smile wryly at the picture of her stopping in her weary tracks to play the "dialogue game" with baby. It just does not happen, and the sad effects have been well charted, as I hope to show.

Still, if a mother can carry on a relaxed, happy dialogue with her baby, she is helping him immeasurably. A baby is a helpless explorer in the unknown, more bewildered by stimuli and objects that he does not understand than any moon traveler. A mother attaches "signs" to the objects, gives them names, and helps the infant to relate to his bewildering universe. Robert Thomson, psychology professor at Leicester University in northern England, writes that with the use of language

> the environment, quite early in life, becomes meaningful at every glance. Although we do not use words, when we perceive the world, it is in virtue of having learned to name, describe, and relate what is commonly perceived that we come to know a structured, consistent, and ordered world. Language assists us to build up a detailed and understood map of the world we inhabit.

So by giving a child these signs, words for objects he sees, one is handing him a kind of symbolic compass. From naming objects, the child can then proceed to a more *cognitive* awareness of them; this is to say that he soon gets a kind of Platonic idea, a concept, *behind* the words, when he is three or four years old. To put it in its simplest terms, when a child of two or three sees a dog, he will name it "doggie," or whatever, to his mother, who will say, "Yes, a dog," nodding and agreeing. He has named it correctly and his mother approves this infant sign-posting. However, when he sees a horse and again says "dog," she shakes her head and corrects him. In doing so, she is forcing his *cognitive* development, his idea of all dogs, the abstract image.

When one stops to think of how varied the canine species is —big or squat, hairy or hairless, resembling anything from bears to rats to sausages, depending on their breed—one can only marvel at the child's ability to identify any dog as one of

a species at the age of three or four. This process is called
conceptualization, and it is essential to a child's intellectual development. Children who have not been corrected, helped with
their signs and labels, are left with faulty compasses and are
partial strangers in their own environments. Knowing the right
sign for the right object helps a child to *accommodate* to his
surroundings, in Jean Piaget's now famous definition.

Language helps a child feel better in his skin in a variety of
ways. First of all, it gives a sense of self; he can put the "I" of
himself into his surroundings, get a better idea of where he
stands in them. A child who has been deprived of adequate
language learning and subsequent cognitive development has
difficulty in personalizing himself; almost eerily, he may speak
of himself in the third person ("this kid's lousy clay model," a
deprived four-or five-year-old preschool child will say, referring
to his own handiwork). He has been robbed of a sense of identity
by his oppressive circumstances and language starvation. A
child who can think aloud, or speak, and who can also think
inside his head, internalize his speech, tends to be less frustrated,
not as prone to hit and kick out, less tempted to roll himself into
a little ball of inarticulate rage. A black nursery school teacher
in the Boston area summed it up briskly for me this way: "Once
a kid can begin to explain what it is he wants, he stops smashing
up the joint."

When a child can think in his head, internalize his speech, he
is far more capable of solving small but frustrating practical
problems. In his London lectures in the early 1960s on the role
speech plays in human behavior, the Russian psychologist, A. R.
Luria spoke of a colleague's experiment with a group of preschool children. He would ask children to perform simple tasks
such as drawing and tracing and then make the job more diffi-

cult by giving them blunt pencils or no thumbtacks to fasten down the tracing paper. The three- to four-year-olds asked for help. "The children of five, given no help," Luria writes,

> tried to get round difficulties, but their behavior showed a marked change . . . evoking outbursts of *active speech* addressed to anyone. At age 6 or 7 this unattached, unfocused speech begins to disappear . . . becomes fragmentary . . . and it thus gradually passes over into *abbreviated internal speech* which is an invariable part of the thought process.

We see that the child who can "speak in his head" approaches problems with more cool than the younger child who is still thinking out loud. A really linguistically deprived child who could not think or speak adequately inside *or* outside his head would undoubtedly collapse in the face of such an experiment, and we can assume that he would throw paper, pencil, and tacks to the ground. The inference that Luria makes from his colleague's experiment is that adequate active speech and its sequel, *internal speech,* can modify behavior. The ability to solve a problem by thinking it through calms a child's actions, Luria appears to be saying.

One of the most valuable messages that Jean Piaget has given the world is one that may appear obvious (and, as with so many "obvious" ideas, had not been thought of before he began his work in the late 1920s); that is, that children think differently from adults. This different view of the world accounts for some of their loveliest flights of fantasy, the poetry in their written verse, their fresh and accurate images. Adults delight in their quixotic statements; they are refreshed by children's unpredictability, their different perspective. This special way of thinking is something few parents would wish to change.

Two Australian teachers were struck by the freshness of speech of forty kindergarten children, aged three and one-half to five, and taped their spoken thoughts; the random stories and ideas seemed to exhibit admirably the quality of verbal spontaneity a preschooler possesses. The two women, Ruth Bodman and her assistant, Margaret McNichol, teachers at Ewing Memorial Kindergarten in East Malvern, recorded "cooperative" stories of children—where one child starts a story and others add bits to it. These were published in 1966 in the *Melbourne Herald*. They were as the newspaper put it, a "glimpse of a Melbourne child's world as pictured in children's own words." For example:

Linda:	Brides get married at church.
Ian:	Yes and you throw perfetti at them.
Julie:	Spaghetti you mean.
John W.:	Then they go on a holiday called a honeymoon, don't they?
John R.:	After they're married they can have plenty of children.
Mark R.:	But first they have to go to the hospital to get babies because children are babies first you know.
John R.:	Yes, unless they don't want to have any children, but then they have to do all the work themselves, 'cos children can help mummies can't they?
Michael:	A snake is a very long thing with a very long tail and it bites.
Richard:	A worm.
Jayne:	It looks like a worm but it's not, you know.

Alastair: They haven't got legs—they move the curly
            part.

John W.:   "Branded" means a cowboy film on
            television.

John R.:   It means you have milk on bran.

Jocelyn: It means your jumper is bran new.

Ian: Matthew's bird died because of old age didn't
            it. Old things die, don't they? But oranges
            don't die up to heaven, do they? They just
            get old with all that fluffy stuff on them.

Matthew: When you look in the water you think you're
            upside down.

The healthy child whose parents have helped him to verbalize places himself at the center of his own universe and his speech is egocentric. Up to the age of seven, he is almost incapable, according to Piaget, of keeping his thoughts to himself: "Egocentrism must not be confused with secrecy," writes Piaget.

Reflexion in the child does not admit of privacy. Apart from thinking by images or autistic symbols which cannot be directly communicated, the child up to an age, as yet undetermined but probably somewhere about seven, is incapable of keeping to himself the thoughts which enter his mind. He says everything. He has no verbal continence . . . the child really speaks . . . first and foremost to himself, and that speech, before it can be used to socialize thought, serves to accompany and reinforce individual activity. . . . Almost everything he does is to the tune of remarks such as "I'm drawing a hat," "I'm doing it better than you."

Piaget then goes on to show how a child's egocentric language moves from the "I, I, I" soliloquy state to the more sociable stage where some sort of colloquy with his mates comes into play.

Piaget's experiments and findings at the Maison des Petits in Geneva as outlined in his book *Language and Thought of the Child* are compelling and enlightening in many ways but should be read, I believe, with the type of child he is studying in mind. It is clear that Piaget's young subjects are drawn from the more fortunate Swiss middle classes, children who have been given a rich linguistic background. Some of the examples Piaget gives us as representative of egocentric speech, while no doubt of impeccable scholarly accuracy (for example, "Well, I'm the strongest all the same," says Pie, aged six and one-half), could not have been said by a slum child from Liverpool or Chicago. A superlative such as *strongest* would simply not be in his vocabulary. It is perfectly valid that Piaget should have studied those children who came into his scientific reach, but they should not be compared with children from other classes and backgrounds. Many of his hypotheses and conclusions would not be applicable to British or American slum children. As so many of these children arrive at school almost mute except for a smattering of nouns and verbs, it would be impossible to categorize their speech as egocentric.

But bearing in mind these class and economic differences, what Piaget has shown us is invaluable. He reveals how it is that children grow gradually into certain ideas, ideas of volume, distance and number, morality (what is a black or a white lie?). Every adult concept concerning such ideas and abstractions requires years of development before becoming crystallized in a child's mind. In other words, a child grows very slowly from the idea of the *concrete* object to the larger Platonic idea of the concept or abstraction behind it. Studies of linguistically deprived children in urban and rural areas of America show that without an adequate grasp of language (and this does not necessarily mean a small or large vocabulary), a child takes a much longer time than even Piaget's more fortunate Swiss children to move from the concrete to the abstract.

An excellent example of this inability of deprived children to grasp the larger abstraction behind the concrete and visible is given by Robert Coles and Maria Piers, in their description of shopping with a group of "rock-bottom-poor" preschool children in a two-year experimental program in Boston called the North Point Project, which ended in 1967. At the age of three and four, these children could cross dangerous intersections in order to buy household items, such as cigarettes or coffee for their mothers. Teachers found that if they took the children (four year olds, in this case) to a supermarket with which they were familiar, they were capable of picking out certain items that they had been accustomed to finding for their mothers. However, if they were moved to another supermarket, in another area, no matter how similar in appearance, they became completely disoriented,

> running about heedlessly and sidling up to strangers. The children could not name any of the objects in the store nor point to those the teacher named. . . . In every area of the children's functioning in nursery school, one is struck by their poor capacity to translate what was learned in one situation to another. It was as though they reacted without inner commitment and inner comprehension. . . . He [the child] needs to understand the abstract principle underlying grocery stores.

So these children could not make the transition from the idea of *one* supermarket to the idea of *all* supermarkets; in other words, they had not begun to *conceptualize*. According to Piaget, this process does not begin, in any case, until the age of seven. In his assiduous researches on children, he shows us how they arrive slowly at an abstraction, a longer and more tortuous trip than one realized before Piaget made his marvelous studies. One of his most interesting tests on children under the age of seven explored their concepts of distance. He would draw two lines from one spot to another, pretending this was a walk; on one of the lines from one point to another, he would ask the child to pretend he had to perform a duty, like mailing a letter. Invariably, the child was convinced, if he had been involved in some errand on the way, the walk had been longer.

Piaget's writing can sometimes be highly abstruse—or perhaps just badly translated—but in any case occasionally the impact of what he is saying is lost. It is far more telling, I have found, to stop after reading one of his conclusions about a child's way of thinking and to test it out unobtrusively on one's own child or on a friend's. At the time I was reading Piaget's studies on the child's concept of distance, my daughter, then seven, provided me with some living proof of the accuracy of his observations on a child's inability to judge what is longer or shorter. She had a mile-long walk from her school at the top of London's Baker Street and sometimes was rather vocal about being tired afterward, especially if there was a television program she wanted to see ("Rests me," she would say, sprawling out in front of the set). One day I asked her if she was tired, as this time she genuinely looked it, and she said no, not at all, because they had had swimming that day and she had had less distance to walk home. Now the public swimming pool that the children used when they had swimming lessons at the end of the school day was exactly halfway back from school. In other words, she had only broken her usual homeward journey in half. No amount of patient explanation would convince her that she had walked exactly the same distance that day and had merely broken her journey in two. She would stamp her foot in exasperation. "No, Mummy, I only had to walk half the way today because I had swimming this afternoon!"

Perhaps the most famous of all Piaget's tests on children has been his water measurement or "conservation" test. Using two beakers of water, one squat and wide brimmed, the other thin and tall, he poured the same volume of water from the short, fat beaker to the tall one before the children's eyes and asked them which contained the largest amount of water. Without fail, children under the age of six pointed to the tall beaker, saying that it held more water because the water came up higher; only after the age of seven did the children answer that there was the same in both. The young child accepts his *perceptual* image, as Piaget puts it, the evidence of his eyes. Piaget concludes that the young child has no clear idea of invariant qualities or of equivalence. He discovered that when he puts the same number of beads into each of two jars, the children again judged the number by the shape of the jar containing them, even though the beads had been counted out in front of them before being placed in the containers. "We are well aware," he writes, "that perception of the quantifiable qualities such as length, weight, etc., leads to systematic distortions, and that the child finds it extremely difficult to perceive the constancy of these qualities."

Piaget has emphasized that even when a child is at his most egocentric, with his language centered entirely on himself, he is encouraged to embroider and verbalize even more by the presence of his mother. This is not necessarily the case when a child is playing with other children. He has to break off his monologues occasionally when surrounded by his own schoolmates in order to protect his property or stand up for himself in some way. With his nonabrasive mother, his soliloquies can flow on uninterruptedly ("I must finish this steeple," "I'm drawing on this sheet," "Now, I'm making an animal," to give some of Piaget's examples).

When a child gives his activities his own running commentaries, it is like a flexing of verbal muscles, and is absolutely necessary to his language growth. In spite of their apparently egocentric nature, these childish monologues are highly social in nature, Piaget believes.

> The child loves to know that he is near his mother. He feels that he is close to her in each of his acts and thoughts. What he says does not seem to him to be addressed to himself but is enveloped with the feeling of a presence, so that to speak of himself or to speak to his mother appear to him to be one and the same thing. His activity is thus bathed in an atmosphere of communion or syntonization.

What a lovely image! There is the patient, educated Swiss mother assuming her chosen role of adoring listener and occasional monitor, and next to her the highly verbal child describing his own activities in a richly descriptive monologue. Undoubtedly, this kind of communion does exist in homogeneous societies of high economic prosperity such as Switzerland, and such a background would afford the maximum potential for a child to develop his speech and thought. A sadly different mother-child picture is afforded by those sociologists who have studied the speech patterns of the poor in America and Britain. Basil Bernstein with his children from London's East End and Martin Deutsch, with his New York City slum children, for example, have discovered that a poor (other more high-flown terms for it are "socially disadvantaged," or "culturally deprived" but they reduce to being poor) mother does not share in this luminous communion that Piaget describes. A poor mother tends to speak entirely in *imperatives*—"do this," "do that," "shut up"—limiting her conversation to controlling her children's behavior. If a slum child of three talks to himself, no one is likely to be listening, certainly not his harassed and frantic mother. Language learning does not appear to be a very egalitarian process; in fact, it is distressingly class-oriented.

Other conditions that depress a child's language-learning capacities are deafness and institutionalization. Slum children, children from orphanages, and some deaf children have many characteristics in common, the most telling of which is a crippling inarticulateness and a lowered intelligence. As language sharpens thought processes (in a system of "complex reciprocity," as Bernstein puts it), it can be assumed that this lowered intelligence springs from language deprivation, the lack of an interpersonal setting which encourages verbal flowering, rather than from any fixed, genetic predisposition at birth.

As I have described earlier, the infant begins to flex his linguistic muscles at the very earliest moments by babbling in his crib and by stopping to enjoy his own happy noises and then trying to imitate the sounds made to him by his parents. A deaf child is not necessarily born with less intelligence, nor any particularly different vocal apparatus. However, the fact that he cannot hear his own babblings will naturally discourage any attempts on his part to play with his own sounds. As we have seen, an infant also learns by a system of *reinforcement*, by the fact that his own sounds are obviously appreciated by his parents and may be underscored by them with a smile, along with additional, encouraging words such as *hello*. But, as Morris

Lewis writes, in a deaf child's development, "the auditory defect may impair both the development of expressive sounds and the development of babbling . . . and the potential ability to solve problems (in later stages of the deaf child's development) that is, 'innate intelligence'—can, like any other inborn capacity, be made more or less effective by the influences that are brought to bear upon the growing child." Because deaf children live in a silent world during their crucial early language-learning years, their handicap does depress their intelligence, and deaf children are frequently found to have IQs two years behind those of normal children.

The deaf child is at a disadvantage in a variety of ways; the most far-reaching of these is that circumstances prevent him from receiving any significant auditory help from the adult world; he misses the crucial feedback cycle, for example. He also misses learning by trial and error. According to scholar-linguist, Noam Chomsky, a normal child of average intelligence increases and extends his command of language by making bold sorties into unfamiliar syntactic territory. The child says that he can make things "more better" than his mates at school or that he "goed" for a walk. These linguistic bloopers are fun for him to concoct and usually delight a parent who can enjoy the language-bending before correcting it. A deaf child necessarily has to restrict his own outlandishness with language. He would naturally try to get the word right from the offset and stick to it. Just as he has not been able to play with sounds in infancy, he is not able to play fast and loose with grammar and syntax in his preschool years. In vocabulary tests with deaf children, Lewis has found that they have trouble with prefix elements such as *un* (*unlike, unkind*), with words denoting family relationships (such as *aunt* or *sister*), and with words describing emotional states (*unhappy*). It is quite possible that a deaf child's enforced isolation has weakened his sense of self and that he has difficulty placing himself in proper perspective; hence his inability to label certain relatives correctly, to recognize their connection with him, and also his struggle to describe himself as "angry," "sad," or "happy," states that the ego-centered child with normal hearing is only too fascinated to attach to himself.

Children in institutions also have difficulty in placing themselves squarely in the middle of their own universe. Institutions form the archetypal passive background for a young child. Here children's questions are rarely answered (especially if the staff is inadequate in number and overworked); shapes and colors and sizes go unexplained; and physical contact is at a minimum. By the age of eight years, the institutionalized child is likely to have an IQ thirty points lower than the average—and irreversibly lower at that. Children appear to grow and bloom most happily in situations of maximum stimulation and expectation. The sterile background of an orphanage or a large children's home simply does not provide the requisite stimulation. The most crucial deprivation among institutionalized children is in the realm of language. Speaking has met with no echoing adult response; as a result, institutionalized children use words largely to communicate feelings of discomfort or unhappiness, and these in monosyllables or in short, truncated sentences.

While a deaf child probably has loving parents he cannot hear and thus cannot imitate, a child in an institution is deprived of any meaningful relationship with an adult because of the very nature of these large, impersonal homes. In this respect, a deaf child is far more fortunate than his peer in an institution (and the results show clearly in IQ scores: a deaf child's may be twenty points lower than a normal child's, but an institutional-

ized child's is thirty points lower). The late Dr. D. W. Winnicott, a famous British child analyst, once said that a child in an
institution has small hope of developing into robust emotional
health because he cannot work off his intense rages or feelings
of love or guilt or aggression on any *single* person, since he is
tended by a wide variety of differing adults. It is no good for an
orphan to hit out at a nurse or attendant in the early morning,
for example, feel intermittently guilty about it during the rest
of the day, and then see a different nurse at night when he had
hoped to see the original one he had abused. He is stopped from
making his childish attempts at reparation or apology. The
effect of this is to make him wish to stifle his feelings altogether.
Hate is repressed as a result of this kind of frustration, writes
Winnicott: ". . . the capacity to love people is lost. . . . In the
larger care centers . . . there is a merging of identity with the
other children in the group. This involves both loss of personal
identity and loss of identification with the total home setting."

It should be stressed that institutions come in all shapes and
sizes, and the smaller ones can come close to providing almost
the same degree of stimulation and affection as, say, some of the
most passive and uninspiring home backgrounds. However, the
large number of persons required to administer a huge institution make it difficult for the child to depend on any specific adult
or to identify with any single older person. Thus the infant in
his own home, no matter how mediocre, has the edge over the
institutionalized child. This is made evident when children
from such homes are transferred to foster homes. An institutionalized child with a low IQ (say, of about 85; 80 is where
normal intelligence begins, 120 is university standard) can raise
his intelligence level by as much as twenty points upon entering
the more personalized atmosphere of a foster home. We need

only cast our minds back to some of the more highly publicized biographical accounts of life in a foster home (Marilyn Monroe's, for instance) to know that they are not ideal. However, even if they are imperfect, the one-to-one relationship a child can often build up with a foster parent gives him just that much more richness—both emotional and intellectual—than he can find in a large institutional setting. The result is a quicker and less mute, deadened, and hopeless child.

It has been extremely difficult for sociologists and psychiatrists to follow the lives of institutional children from their childhood entry into a home through their adolescence and then into adulthood. However, three British psychiatrists, Drs. F. Bodman, M. McKinley, and M. Sykes, were assiduous enough to keep track of the lives of fifty-one institutionalized children and follow them into maturity. They selected nineteen girls and thirty-two boys who had spent three years in an institution, comparing their lives with opposite numbers ("controls" in sociological terminology) who had similar deprived backgrounds but who had entered foster homes. Of the institutional children, most of whom had been deserted by their mentally ill parents, 30 per cent had no contacts with their parents, 56 per cent had siblings in the institution, and 30 per cent had occasional family visits. They were characterized by low IQs (mostly under 85 but some near 70) and an air of hopelessness. The little socializing in which they engaged was confined to the institution; they made no attempt to make friends on the outside, although they were encouraged to explore the neighborhood and given free access in and out of the home. They registered little or no interest in their own futures, but if pinned down about what they proposed to do when they left the home, they chose unglamorous jobs: factory or farm posts. One child burst

into tears when he was asked what he wanted to do when he
grew up.

Their peers who were lucky enough to escape into foster
homes registered far more vitality and hope and became altogether less dull after their transfer. Whereas only 40 per cent
of the institutionalized children were successful in obtaining the
jobs of their choice in maturity, 60 per cent of the controls
moved into jobs of their own choosing. The institutionalized
children rarely married in later life, seemingly unable to abandon their lonely pattern of living even after leaving the home.
If they did marry, the marriages usually ended in separation and
divorce. Most of the controls married and raised families of their
own. One concludes from the Bodman, Sykes, and McKinley
study that the habit of isolation (or not *connecting*) is self-perpetuating. Such an alienated life appears to depress the intelligence and the spirit. The very definite inference is that even an
inadequate parent or home is preferable to the impersonality of
an institution. Contact with an interested adult in early life on
a sustained basis seems as necessary to the growth of the human
psyche as is oxygen to the body.

Other factors that can depress language development, intelligence, and ego growth in a young child are being born into a
large family or being a twin. These may seem like strangely
disparate situations but on examination one finds that they are
not. A child in a large family is liable to get very little adult
attention; a twin, because he has a built-in alter ego to play and
talk with, does not seek adult attention. The results are uncan-
nily similar. Just as a child in a large family is apt to get lost in
the hurly-burly and shuffle, an only child will become the center
of his parents' universe. The result of this undiluted attention
may be unfortunate for an only child's personality development

(we have all seen examples of the self-centered only child, or the owlish one, the child of older parents), but the fact is that an only child usually has a far higher IQ than the child from a large family.

The many studies of institution children, twins, children from large families, and only children have convinced a large body of experts in child development that the environment is a powerful molder and enhancer of human intelligence. In other words, human intelligence is like a rare instrument: pay attention to it and nurture it and its tone deepens and becomes enriched; leave it untended, untouched, or barely so, and it loses whatever capacity for melody-making it had. And the strings on the instrument? The ability to verbalize, to handle language— a child's most crucial skill.

4

The Nursery School: Learning in the Preschool Years

I recall vividly my feeling of revulsion several years ago when I read the title of a book by two child-development experts—*Give Your Child a Superior Mind*. Why should one wish to add twenty points to a child's IQ, as these child psychologists, Siegfried and Therese Engelmann, invited all parents of preschoolers to do? It smacked to me of loathsome parental competitiveness, the stretching of tiny minds on an unnecessary rack.

I was feeling particularly sensitive about pushing children at that time. My son, then just four and at a London nursery school, had been described by his teacher as "exceptional." She suggested that he be moved up one class, to be with children six months older than himself. Instead of pleasure at her assessment and advice, I experienced an irrational dread at her words (wasn't being bright another kind of problem?). I asked her to please leave him where he was, as he had just made his first close friend, an exotic half-Maori New Zealander who wrote him loving Valentines at all times of the year and who bossily planned their premature wedding. Her attentions were boosting my son's ego, helping to dissipate his then almost crippling shyness. I thought the teacher ought to find their close association as important an event as I did, more significant and useful to him than his almost embarrassing ability to read like a ten-year-old. I resented the woman for the grudging way in which she agreed to do so. Maybe she had been reading too many books from Chicago, I thought. How could you gauge the intellect of a child of four and attempt to stretch him accordingly?

My reaction, I now realize, was misguided, but understandable. The concept of a nursery school as a developer of intellect was new and a little repellent. I cannot have been alone in this kind of thinking. Parents have traditionally tended to view the nursery school as a safe retreat from adult pulls and tensions, a snug harbor where a child floats for a few years before pushing into the rougher seas of a formal primary education. The parental views vary of course with the type of father or mother. A tender, hovering parent might view the nursery school as a place where the child can learn a measure of independence, play contentedly in a happy cocoon, and learn how to put out social tendrils. A less benign, more irascible parent might look at the nursery school or play group as a dumping ground for a vigorous child, as a two- or three-hour respite from the ransackings of an apparent demon who would rather hurl lampshades to the floor than placidly count beads. But whether the parents have been loving or selfish, they have rarely, up to now, regarded the nursery school as crucial to the child's growing intelligence, a place where he can flex his mental muscles, and, even more essentially, fix his future performance as an adult.

But more and more, this is what a nursery school—or like forms of early education—are thought to be. It was Dr. Benjamin Bloom, of whom I have already spoken a great deal (it would be impossible not to—he emerges as a kind of educational Cassandra of this mid-century), who first crystallized this kind of thinking, causing a gentle revolution in early childhood education in the 1960s. In 1964 he wrote that between birth and the age of four, half of all growth in human intelligence takes place; another 30 per cent occurs between the ages of four and eight. So, Dr. Bloom pointed out startlingly, two-thirds of a person's intellectual development has come to fruition before he begins what we now regard as his formal education (Dr. Bloom's findings, assessed from the results of a thousand different studies of child development, are outlined in his highly technical and scholarly work, *Stability and Change in Human Characteristics*, a book that is, sadly, more comprehensible to his colleagues than to parents who perhaps need it more).

The very young child has always been thought of as having a magical quality—the way he can pick up words like a lawn-mower does grass, the painless manner in which he can become bilingual or even trilingual. Even the most W. C. Fieldsian child-hater cannot always resist the charm of a child's pungent imagery. In his book *From Two to Five*, the Russian scholar Kornei Chukovsky lists some examples that poets would not be ashamed of: "Don't put out the light, I can't see how to sleep!" "I'll get up so early that it will still be late." "A turkey is a duck with a bow around its neck."

The Italian educator Dr. Maria Montessori was one of the first to marvel at what she called the preschool child's "absorbent mind" ("they are endowed with this ability to absorb cultures," she wrote wonderingly). She contented herself with pulling young minds ahead, most remarkably a group of slum children in Rome in 1906–1907 who under her tutelage learned to read fluently at four and five. She worked with intuition and imagination, and her writings on her work are poetical, but she attempted little in the way of the scientific approach, the data-assessing, and the IQ-taking of our day. But the remarkable coincidence in the work of this educational pathfinder and the Englemanns is that both came to similar conclusions about the crucial absorbent quality of the young child's mind by studying "disadvantaged" children (a term few can pretend to like but one which seems, like so much else now firmly established in the glossaries of sociology, here to stay). By discovering how deprived a child could be by living in a culturally impoverished environment, it seemed also possible to gauge how much he *could* have learned had a rich cultural environment been available.

Maria Montessori spoke of her slum children, delinquent little vandals before she took them over, as "souls concealed in a hermetic cell." Their behavior beneath her guidance amazed her. They soon learned to read and write, showed unexpected powers of concentration, and seemed to enjoy creating their own order, putting things away without being asked (she never speaks of her own charisma—could just anyone have produced this group miracle?). At the San Lorenzo Children's House, a schoolroom she created out of one of the unused rooms in the tenement apartment house where the children had roamed, neglected by their factory-worker parents, she designed some of the teaching materials that are still used in nursery schools today. She believed that children learn by touching as well as by hearing. Her children learned the alphabet by feeling sandpaper letters. In order to give them some idea of shape and form, she devised a graded wooden cylinder with corresponding wooden pegs where the child could slip the pegs in and out of the holes in the wooden block.

One day at the Children's House, she was astounded to see a three-year-old taking out the cylinders and putting them back in the block with an almost trancelike concentration. On impulse, Montessori lifted the child, still holding her cylinders, up into the air in her small chair. The child did not seem to notice; she kept right on with her exercise until she had done it forty-two times. When the child was put back on the ground, she repeated the activity again, still stopping at forty-two, apparently responding to some numerical law of her own. Montessori came to believe that a child's ability to push through with a task until he himself has decided that it has come to its conclusion was most likely to appear in a "period of sensitivity of development."

Most observant parents will recognize the sense of what Montessori says. It would be a sad father or mother who has not noticed one of these sensitive periods in his own offspring, a sudden breakthrough when a child seems stripped of dullness and apathy and acts like someone driven, when he literally breaks into speech, or reading, or writing, or delves into a hobby like someone possessed. I remember when my own daughter, at about six, was playing with an encyclopedic series on famous artists, using the magazines like bricks. One day she stopped making piles of them and began to study the pictures, gazing with particular fascination at the more gory scenes of Christ's crucifixion as rendered by the early Italians. I felt a smug sense of pride on discovering, when I took her to museums, that she could identify the early Italians, Duccio, Giotto, Caravaggio. A baby genius, I thought (since, she has leveled off into decent normal intelligence). But she had hit upon the magazines in a sensitive period. A Montessori disciple once likened a child's period of sensitivity to that adult reaction of total, blinding, quick response when averting an accident on the road, with all his senses flashing and flickering at top capacity.

Montessori was convinced that these sensitive periods could be encouraged to occur. She thought that if you gave a child an unrepressive environment, the right materials, and his self-respect, this sensitivity would explode into being, especially in the younger child, beginning at about three and a half. She suspected that if these periods were neglected, the child would sink into apathy, that the sensitivity would dull, and that it would be increasingly difficult as the child grew older for him to have these magical explosions of receptivity.

In the past ten years, specialists in child development have come more and more to concur with her views. Head Start workers in the United States, in the course of their efforts to teach some fundamentals about numbers, the alphabet, shapes, and sizes, to ghetto and other poor children under six years of age, make the distressing discovery that many of the children were already, at four and five, irretrievably far behind their more fortunate peers and would never catch up in later life.

The argument about *how much* to teach the under-fives rages on. In England, children start the first grade at five instead of six as in America, so that British children are beginning to learn to read and write a year before their American counterparts. However, even in England where the clock is put back a year for the very young, there is an extreme reluctance to teach a bright child to read at nursery school, especially at the state or public schools. This reluctance is based on the "readiness" argument, which is a boiling issue on both sides of the Atlantic. Once when I was writing an article on preschool education in Britain, I went around asking the mothers of children in expensive private kindergartens (or nursery schools, as they are more often called in England) why they had elected to spend a great deal of money—from $100 to $135 a term—to send their preschoolers there rather than to the state-run nursery schools. This was a fair question. In England, the private nursery schools are often down-at-heel affairs run in church halls or in seedy private houses, and the equipment is often equivalently shabby. The state kindergartens, on the other hand, though crowded, are better staffed, better equipped—in all ways, more attractive, modern affairs. Most mothers answered that they did not feel that their children ever *learned* anything in the state nursery schools, which are guided largely by the "playing is learning" theory. I was amazed to discover that snobbery had little to do with the choice of these mothers.

"I don't really care if Lucy talks like a pint-sized Cockney because she goes to a local free kindergarten," one mother told me. "I just want to see her with a paper and pencil in her hand. The poor child is dying to learn to read. She wants to do more than play with beads and plasticine. I really can't afford to send her to a private nursery school but I just had to ignore my own finances and go ahead. Why should I frustrate her?"

The readiness argument appears to be fed by complacency and lack of a spirit of adventure. First-grade teachers in England and America have a vested interest in having their children reach them with an equal amount—or lack—of knowledge. It is obviously easier to begin classes where the children are on an equal footing, without one or two who are already ace readers. Few state educators are as revolutionary as California's Wilson Riles, the superintendent of public instruction, who would like to start all of his state's 4,408,000 children a year before the present kindergarten age of five. He wants preschoolers to begin first grade work in kindergarten instead of cutting out paper dolls and building sand castles. Riles feels that the state laws regarding early schooling are outmoded, clinging to antediluvian feelings about when a child is *ready* to tackle the printed page. "Our youngsters are more ready than the schools are," he says.

But Riles is meeting with a great deal of recalcitrance and skepticism from his fellow educators. Don't shock the little minds with too much learning too soon, is the feeling. To a large extent, the great shadow of Jean Piaget is responsible for this widespread reluctance to move children forward. As Freud dominates psychoanalysis, so Piaget casts his formidable presence over Western thought regarding learning for the young. Perhaps Piaget never intended to shape thinking this way, but the very fact that he insists that certain concepts of volume and number can only be understood at particular stages has made everyone in education very age conscious. Why teach them at young ages when they cannot absorb what they are being taught? This is the complacent question posed by proponents of the status quo.

But there is a powerful movement among certain educators to lower the school entrance age. They believe that the critical learning age for man is much earlier than we have thought. When I asked Harvard educator and early education advocate Professor Jerome Bruner if he thought the primary school age should be lowered to three years, he flashed the reply "Three is already too late."

Bruner believes that the concept of educating infants is so revolutionary that people cannot or will not meet the idea head on. "One of the main reasons that the idea frightens people," he told me, "is that no one knows exactly how to go about setting it up. Up to now, education has been guided by the idea that there is only one way of going about teaching the young. I think we just have to forget that monolithic approach and try diversity. The structure is not so important now. Let's try three or four methods all at the same time and study as we go."

It is important to note that Bruner speaks of trying "three or four methods" of teaching the very young. Too often when the advocates of early teaching speak of educating the toddler, an image of the unfortunate tot rooted to his desk and being almost forcibly fed reading and writing techniques springs to an appalled parent's mind. But this is not what Bruner and his colleagues mean to convey, and this is why the educator's reference to "three or four methods" is so significant. Reading and writing and arithmetic—these agelong skills which were as necessary to acquire a hundred years ago as they are today—are now taught in any number of creative ways. Sometimes a child learns to recognize words almost by osmosis, just by putting a word together with a picture that he himself has conceived.

When revolutionary educators such as Bruner speak of "early learning," they are not suggesting force-feeding methods, the rote memory learning of C-A-T spells *cat* and monotonous incantations of the ABCs. They tend to support open-ended, informal teaching methods; in the field of reading and writing, that technique which is often called "language-experience" learning. In this relatively new method, a child invents a sentence from everyday experience, writes it down with the help of a teacher and an illustrative drawing of his own, and more often than not, has it placed upon a wall for all to see. He may also write about a trip with school friends to a museum or a supermarket (if he is very young, a word or two culled from this experience would be enough); thus reading is part of the process of enjoyment, of making friends at school, sharing events and pleasures with them, and, most important of all to his young, developing ego, of putting his own special stamp on an event. Reading thus becomes a part of his life, rather than something superimposed upon it.

Bruner's idea that people are frightened of the idea of teaching children younger and sooner is echoed by British educator Willem van der Eyken, of suburban London's Brunel University. He also agrees that the thought of building different plants to house the younger child is a deterrent.

"What is really impeding progress in nursery education," says Van der Eyken, "is the idea of buildings. But we must try to get a broader view of the nursery school situation and not try to separate it from the whole educational system. We've got to think in terms of a *program* and not a pile of expensive new bricks. I'm trying to get provisions to open up the existing primary schools. We should lower the school starting age to three and use our existing facilities. Young children shouldn't be separated off from the rest. The idea that you have a group of children who are different in kind and are called 'pre-school' children is purely the result of administrative history. There are in fact no such children. I use the term myself because it's a bit of short-hand that everyone understands. But I don't like it. What I'm trying to do is just to get it recognized that these are younger versions of what we have in primary schools."

Van der Eyken is emphatic that children under five must not be relegated to some shadowy, neglected niche, their minds lying fallow, being virtually ignored by stimulating, interested adults, and losing the best intellectual years of their lives. After the critical age of five, he warns, "aid or reinforcement is meaningless." He cites the experiment made on some red squirrels who were not given nuts to crack at an early age and in later years never acquired the skill of cracking them. The squirrel-human analogy could be dismissed contemptuously if there were not so much data, as with the Head Start findings, to back it up. Dr. Bloom said it some years earlier, and circumstances and research seem to be bearing him out. He wrote: "What we have hypothesized is . . . that deprivation in the first four years of life can have far greater consequences than deprivation in the ten years from 8 through 17. . . ."

Whether we agree with such thinkers as Bloom, Van der Eyken, and Bruner about the necessity of teaching a child while he is still toddling or not, it would be difficult to deny that learning must start much sooner than it does at the moment. There are few educators in either England or America who would now opt for a passive, hit-or-miss, let-him-just-grow-until-primary-school kind of early learning background. On the matter of parental responsibility for early learning, the pendulum swings back and forth. A few years ago, parents were told that they were becoming too "Spock self-conscious," too quick to feel guilty about a child's bad behavior. Bruno Bettelheim, the new child-guidance guru, positively encourages parents to be tougher on their bairns. "Be guilt-free!" he says solacingly. But it is not as easy as this. As early learning is so crucial, and parents, especially mothers, are almost wholly responsible for teaching their children basic language patterns, it just might be that parents will have to feel responsible, even a little guilty again, Bruno Bettelheim notwithstanding. Giving a child sufficient stimulation during his early years, or trying to see that he gets it at a nursery school, appears to be as necessary to intellectual growth and future success as iron for the blood. Giving a child a passive background is a kind of insurance for later school failure—a frightening parental responsibility if what the experts of this new thinking about children are telling us is true.

Up to recent years, a child's intelligence was thought to have been genetically fixed at birth. Recent studies of "passive" and "active" backgrounds and their effects on the very young child, such as the studies in children's institutions by the three British sociologists already cited, have shown that intelligence is *not* fixed at birth, but is elastic, and that an IQ can be retarded by as much as twenty points by dehumanized, deadening surroundings, and expanded by twenty points by a stimulating one. This gap of twenty points is a fairly profound one; it can separate the normal from the retarded, the college graduate from the semi-skilled laborer. This elasticity of intellect, the capacity for expansion and contraction, exists in the most marked degree in the first five years of life. Bloom writes: "We would expect the variations in the environment to have relatively little effect on the I.Q. after the age of 8, but one would expect such variation to have marked effect on the I.Q. before that age, with the greatest effect likely to take place between the ages of 1–5."

If you confine a small child to a tiny space, touch him very little, speak to him not at all, only tend to his physical needs, you are stunting him intellectually as surely as those Chinese mothers who bound their children's feet crippled their offspring physically. We have already seen what happens to socially isolated children in extreme environments—the irrevocable damage to their ability to verbalize or handle language. As has been written by Glenn Doman, the Pennsylvania doctor who has worked extensively with brain-damaged children and taught many to read, in *How to Teach Your Baby to Read:* "Chain a child to a bed-post and you can *make* an idiot out of him." As we have seen, idiots and semimutes are often made, not born.

As I have already stressed, children appear to grow and bloom most happily in situations of maximum stimulation. This can be true even in cases where a child does have a low and rather inelastic intelligence, as in cases of mental retardation (where IQs range from below 40 to 80 points). Maria Montessori had a revelatory experience with mentally subnormal children when she was appointed assistant doctor at the University of Rome's psychiatric clinic as a young woman in her twenties at the turn of this century. It was the unhappy Italian psychiatric practice of the day to put mentally retarded children into the asylums along with adult mental patients. One of the stark wards she visited, more like a prison than a ward, was filled with filthy, neglected, backward children. The ward matron made no attempt to hide her revulsion for them. To justify her disgust, she described how they would scrabble about on the floor after they had eaten, searching for crumbs.

Maria Montessori watched the children thrash around under their food tables looking for bits of bread and realized that they were really searching for stimuli, not food, since they had no objects at all in their ward to manipulate or feel. This was the first time she began to attach importance to the ability of objects to stimulate the intelligence of all children, normal or backward. She became convinced that these unfortunate children had potential and could be taught. Eventually she did, in fact, teach them some basic rudiments of reading and writing. What struck her forcibly was the fact of the wasted potential in all young children. She was anxious to work with normal children after this, and soon got her wish at the San Lorenzo Children's House, achieving spectacular results.

Herbert Gunzburg, a former Austrian psychiatrist who has worked in hospitals for the mentally retarded in Birmingham, England, since emigrating there in 1938, has the startling conviction that the majority of retarded children and adults can reach a measure of self-sufficiency, can bus, shop, telephone, get from place to place by themselves. He has devised a "social-sight" vocabulary for the mentally retarded, whereby they are taught key, practical words to read at sight—words like *danger, exit, entrance, keep out, no smoking.* They are taught the words with flash cards and their lessons consist of endless, laborious (for the teacher, no doubt) repetition of the same 50 to 150 crucial words, the amount depending on the capacity of the child. Along with these lessons in important "outside world" words, they are given lessons in taking a bus or a train, going shopping for simple items such as beans, bread, and butter, learning how to open a can and heat up a snack. Gunzburg's methods are being adopted by most of the more enlightened state-run day centers for backward children throughout Britain.

I was astonished to discover some teenaged mongoloid girls at the John F. Kennedy Day Center for Subnormal Children in Stratford, London, leaving their base to go out by themselves to shop for tea. The director of the center told me that from the age of three, her children were chatted to, shown colors and numbers, endlessly answered, danced with, hugged, taught to swim, and, in their early adolescence, initiated into the excitement of Gunzburg's self-help scheme. IQs were unquestionably being raised by this buzzingly active background. A number of the children at the Kennedy Center were transferring to what the British call educationally subnormal schools, institutions for the slow but not ineducable. A delightful cockiness and ebullience emanated from many of the children, I found. When I asked one five-year-old, mildly brain-damaged child if I could have a second cup of coffee from his tray of empty plastic cups, he said, "No, you've already had one."

As Maria Montessori once exclaimed, "If you can do so much to raise the intelligence of backward children—what about the normal ones?" The period from one to five years is truly a golden one, as she pointed out. When child experts discuss these years, there is an Edgar Allan Poe "nevermore" ring about their admonitions. "Nevermore" will the child absorb as much, "nevermore" will he digest as much knowledge, store as much information, osmose so many nuances of language.

Educators are continually trying to galvanize the state into recognizing the crucial importance of the first five years—with only limited success so far in Britain, though with slightly more effectiveness in the United States, especially through Project Head Start, for which the federal government provides 80 per cent of the cost, an average of around $100 per month per child; this is far from bounteous, however, and the program would have foundered long ago were it not for the dynamism of its volunteers, many of them parents.

In Britain, the state is slightly more complacent about its role in stimulating the young mind because, as I mentioned before, the primary age for first-graders is five, instead of six. However, this seems very inadequate to such thinkers as Van der Eyken and fellow believers in the desperate need for earlier education. One of these is Dr. W. D. Wall, Dean of the Insitute of Education, London University, who stated his position passionately

and succinctly in an address to the Annual Conference of Pre-
School Playgroups Association in Brighton in 1970. He gave the
following reminder to his listeners, mostly mothers and con-
verts to his point of view:

> The age of reason, we used to think, dawned somewhere around
> 12; before that it didn't much matter what happened. We are now
> acknowledging that what happens before eight, and still more
> before the age of four, is crucial to the whole of subsequent intellec-
> tual growth. . . . The enormous progress which we have made in the
> last hundred years toward equality of opportunity and equality of
> human value in our society will only succeed in its full sense if all
> children prior to coming to school have had a sufficiently rich possi-
> bility of developing fully. I have quoted this figure many times
> before but I would like to repeat it: The years up to 4 account for
> something like half the intellectual variability in human beings.
> That is to say that anything which you do with and for children
> before they go to school is likely to have two or three times the
> impact on their future growth, for good or for ill, as will anything
> that you do between 4 and 8, and still more so than anything which
> you do between 8 and 16.

He went on to say that we can no longer afford to let our
preschool children grow "like Topsy."

Dr. Wall must have known when he addressed this congress
of British mothers in Brighton that the mothers themselves
were dissatisfied with having their children grow in such a way.
One of the most heartening developments in the past ten years
in England has been the realization by mothers that their children need much more early stimulation than they—or the le-
thargic state system—would be able to give. Middle-class housewives, traditionally more ambitious for their children's school

success than their working-class counterparts, have been organizing preschool playgroups by the thousands in Britain (sixty-five hundred by 1972). The picture is not all of middle-class enterprise and working-class apathy, however. Hidden behind reserve and a certain suspicion in the working-class mother's mind that she might look and feel foolish in a kindergarten situation is usually a desperate wish for a better deal for her child. Assured now that there is no air of patronage about the organizers and the aims of the playgroups, the volunteer mothers are of all classes.

The structure of the average British playgroup is quite simple: three adults oversee about eighteen to twenty children (one salaried playgroup supervisor, one salaried assistant, and one voluntary mother-helper); the children meet for three hours in the morning in churches or town halls with health and safety regulation clearance. One of the most difficult aspects of the playgroups for their organizers is having to disassemble all equipment and store it away at the end of each three-hour morning session, as the church halls are usually needed for other activities in the evenings (several playgroup organizers assured me that they could make a fortune as stagehands after this training). Mothers pay about fifty cents (about twenty-five pence in English money) a morning for their child to attend, and each one of the groups of mothers helps out for one morning under a system of rotation. Where the Pre-school Playgroups (PPA) is concerned, the expression "mother participation" is more than just sociological jargon. The PPA could not function without them, running on an economic shoestring as it does. The playgroups get little help from the government: 80 per cent of them receive no assistance of any kind, and the others get rather low-keyed help, such as rent-reduced premises or a portion of a supervisor's salary, which is about $14 a week, far from princely.

Parent-sponsored preschool playgroups sprang up in America, England, and Canada about ten years ago in response to official neglect about how to educate the under-fives (the feeling among mothers seemed to be that even a semiprofessional and amateurish playgroup was better than nothing). As I have said, in England the PPA has become increasingly unstratified in a class sense, though its origins were originally middleclass. I have seen PPA groups functioning in some of the worst slum and demolition areas of London under supervisors with cut-glass Oxford accents and mother-helpers with almost unintelligibly thick Cockney accents. One of the reasons for the homogeneity of the English PPA is that there has been no program for the culturally deprived child of preschool age such as Project Head Start (although the primary schools in poverty areas may receive extra government grants under the Educational Priority Area Scheme). The PPA has government sanction but minimal financial aid, although the movement now has official recognition. Since April 1, 1971, the organization has come under the umbrella of the government's social services.

With self-help forced upon them, middle-class mothers in the United States and Canada have banded together in an organization called Parent Cooperative Preschools International (PCPI) with a journal published in Bethesda, Maryland, and an executive office in Quebec. Like its sister organization in Britain, the PCPI is a rambling, loosely connected body, held together less by legislation than by good will and the occasional annual meeting. House magazines form the central, unifying voice: the PCPI *Journal* for the Canadian-American preschools group, a magazine called *Contact* for the PPA (the journal editors keep in close written contact). The PCPI schools vary; some have morning sessions only, others both afternoon and morning.

Because Project Head Start concentrates on giving a preschool experience to the underprivileged child, the PCPI is necessarily a more middle-class affair than its sister organization in Britain, picking up where the government leaves off in helping the under-fives who do not qualify as "poor." Except for the existence of the PCPI and expensive private nursery schools, the middle-class child has been left to its own or its parents' devices.

It has been supposed that the more comfortably off parent will give his child the necessary intellectual nourishment in his preschool years and that nothing need be done on a governmental level. Educators appear to believe that the middle-class mother will see to it that her child gets to a private and professionally run nursery school, and this may be the case, although statistics to prove it are elusive. In any case, a middle-class mother will tend to read more to her child, to converse with him more, and this in itself may provide him with sufficient preschool stimulation for his mental needs. But it is known that in the majority of cases, the disadvantaged child in the urban ghettos will not be given this kind of attention, especially in the realm of language.

The creation of Head Start in 1965 to provide such stimulus for deprived children was one of President Lyndon Johnson's most inspired pieces of legislation. But however worthy Head Start has been, it has also left a great many children of low-income families in the cities out in the cold; according to a 1970 report from Mayor Lindsay's Task Force on Early Childhood Development, of 825,000 children under six in New York City, only 57,000 were in some sort of preschool program.

Presumably this huge number of neglected preschool children also includes members of the middle class, the children of reasonably well off professional parents. I tend to agree with Jerome Bruner that this group of parents is also in need of help with their very young children.

"I think it's a terrible mistake for everyone to think that the only people who need help are the poor mothers," he told me during an interview. "It isn't true. Mothers of all classes are interested in getting help for their children. Your middle-class mother can be just as perplexed about what she should do in the way of giving her child the right books, toys, and stimulation."

Obviously, the very nature of the voluntary, parent-run, preschool playgroups precludes the possibility of a strict educational kindergarten structure as found in the private Montessori and Froebel* schools. However, most of these structured kindergartens are overbooked, as well as prohibitively expensive for the majority of parents. And many mothers and fathers find structured kindergartens too rigid, in any case.

While the playgroups are definitely more casual in their approach than a Montessori nursery school, the playgroups do owe a great deal to both Froebel and Montessori. They have absorbed Froebel's idea of the child-oriented room in which a child may roam freely and explore, and Montessori's belief that a child learns by feeling and seeing more than a parrot memorizing. The existing Froebel and Montessori schools in both Britain and North America are so overextended that they welcome the growth of the playgroups, which help syphon off the heavy demand for places in their schools. When I telephoned Mrs. Phyllis Wallbank, head of the Gatehouse Montessori School in

---

*Friedrich Froebel, a German educator (1782–1852) who predated Maria Montessori, was the first to crusade for child-oriented classrooms.

Islington in northern London and one of the few remaining pupils of the Italian educator, to ask her for an appointment for a magazine interview, she was reluctant at first. She was frightened that more publicity would swell her already overburdened waiting list (at nearly $500 the kindergarten year, this is rather impressive going). However, I did get to see her, going along with several U.S. embassy cultural affairs people (the Gatehouse School is for nursery school educators an equivalent of Mecca for Muslims and receives a phalanx of visitors every day). Mrs. Wallbank speaks of Maria Montessori lovingly but with a clear eye. She recalls how she had to find a long tablecloth for Montessori's lecturing table on the many occasions the Italian educator spoke in London when she was nearing the age of eighty. "She knew her face was beautiful," says Mrs. Wallbank. "She wasn't so sure about her legs."

Mrs. Wallbank conceded that a great many of Montessori's principles, especially her philosophy of "learning by seeing and touching," are being adapted by amateurs, as in the international playgroup setup, but she did not seem perturbed at this gentle plagiarism. In fact, when I asked her what she thought about the explosion of playgroups all over England and the United States and the freewheeling use of a somewhat diluted Montessori method, she replied unhesitatingly: "A bit of a good diet is better than none at all."

Her phrase "a bit of a good diet" sums up the playgroup movement fairly well, though "bit" is a little grudging; I would place the level higher than that. Still, the playgroup education formula, or lack of one, is certainly loose. The organizers and mothers and volunteers operate on the object-stimulation theory and rely heavily on the use of materials, both animate and inanimate, which are thought to arouse intellectual curiosity:

sand, water, modeling clay, slides, climbing frames, plants, and small pets such as hamsters. And of course the playgroups are infinitely more mentally stimulating than is one lonely, distracted mother in a cramped apartment. What parent could reasonably provide sand and water and clay in her living room, even if she were wild enough to wish to do so? And there is substantial evidence to back up the belief that object-stimulation does enhance a young child's intelligence: sand and water do reveal movement and measure, crayons and paintboxes help distinguish color, clay modeling helps hand coordination, bead counting unveils early mathematical mysteries. And though there is no systematized attempt to teach reading, the existence of a drawer marked with the letters CHALK, a book corner, and the reading of stories do introduce the child to certain words and to the world of books and stories and familiarize him with classical tales and nursery rhymes.

One of the supporters of the belief that objects themselves help to stimulate the young mind is Dr. David Krech, a University of California psychologist, who has written that "a great intellectual nutrient for a young, developing mind is freedom to roam around in a large object-filled space." In one experiment, Dr. Krech discovered that young rats in stimulating, enriched surroundings developed thicker brain cortexes than rats in deprived environments, though he does not force the child-rat analogy too far. One recalls the frequent comments of first-grade teachers that the children who come to them from a nursery school will stand out over those who have stayed at home with Mother: they are more alert, more sociable, and, well, brighter. Whether it is because they have had the opportunity to explore stimulating materials, to draw and model, or simply to have questions answered by attentive adults, the nursery

school children have a distinct advantage over non-nursery
school children.

There is no doubt that a dedicated, devoted mother with a
peaceful spirit and time on her hands could do just as much for
the growth of her young child's mind as any nursery school or
kindergarten (and in fact in the preschool years when most of
a child's crucial language patterns are learned, she *has* been his
sole teacher). However, as Urie Bronfenbrenner, Cornell University's professor of psychology, has written in *The Two Worlds
of Childhood: U.S. and the U.S.S.R.*, contrasting the Russian and
the American child, the pattern of life in Western society does
not permit people to become overly interested in their children
(the Russian's response to his offspring is more spontaneous and
loving, he feels). In the United States, he says, "the amount of
time spent at work and going to work, and the social obligations
imposed by many occupations and professions, effectively ex-
clude time for one's children."

Dr. Bronfenbrenner's view is extreme. Russian mothers also
spend a great deal of time trotting off to factories and usually see
their children only at brief intervals before bed and on the
weekends. A Russian mother also has her life eased by the existence of a devoted *babushka*, a grandmother willing to serve as
baby-sitter. Such grandmothers are far rarer in America, where
the family unit is less extended than in Russia.

The framework of the modern nuclear family—a lonely
mother cut off from relatives, stuck in small, cramped quarters
all day long if she cannot find a part-time job which gets her out
—does not lend itself to golden mother-child dialogues (too
often the opposite occurs—the mother feels she will scream if
she hears another word from the child). And for many mothers,
especially the poorer ones, their life-style has not prepared them

for hours of child enrichment; too often their modest and realistic goal is to cope with the barest needs of everyday existence.

And so the full responsibility for developing young minds would seem to rebound upon early childhood education centers, be they playgroup or kindergarten.

Now that we know that the very young mind is like a highly sensitized print, ready to have stamped upon it more than it ever will again, how can we afford to neglect it? We cannot risk this waste of human potential.

5

Language Deprivation:
Effect on Speech and Behavior

The old adage about the poor getting poorer and the rich richer should be disappearing in a modern society where the state shows some evidence of caring for the welfare of its citizens. Unfortunately, this is not so. In fact, the division continues to widen, and the middle-class child of caring professional parents, say, is likely to inherit a much more satisfying chunk of the earth than his peer from a lower socioeconomic group. The most valuable asset a middle-class child acquires from his parents is his grasp of a more complex form of language. A number of studies have indicated that the middle-class parent has a tendency to talk to his or her child from the earliest years, to answer questions methodically and precisely, to explain why a demand is being made, and to clarify why it should be followed.

And what is so remarkable about this middle-class garrulity? Who needs it? you might ask. The answer is that the young child does. There is an indisputable link between the development of higher thought processes and reasoning ability and the growth of language, as we have seen: one nourishes the other in a complex cyclical motion.

What exactly is a "richer" grasp of language? James Drever, an American language expert who wrote about children's vocabularies in the early part of the century, put it this way: "Environment affects the nouns, interest affects the verbs, and mental grip is shown by pronouns, adverbs, prepositions and conjugations." Of course the process is not this pat, but Mr. Drever is not too wide of the mark. I overheard a child saying fancifully: "What would happen if I dug through the earth with a spade very quickly? Would I reach China sooner or later? If I were to find gold there, could I keep it, or maybe bank it so that I could buy you a mink?" I copied the sentence down from this particularly bright seven-year-old girlfriend of my son's and then analyzed it. In that one flight, the child had used two conditionals *(would, were)*, a spatial word *(through)*, an adverb *(quickly)*, and a conjunctive *(if)*.

An economically deprived child may have a firm grasp of nouns and verbs but he will fall down badly with the more subtle and necessary components of language, those refinements of syntax so often left out of the linguistic armory of the underprivileged child: prepositions like *under, over,* and *through,* connectives such as *although,* pronouns such as *which* and *who.* As A. F. Watts writes in his book *The Language and Mental Development of Children:* "Those teachers who work in slum districts know only too well that a few nouns eked out by a few gestures can be made to explain a great deal and to get children to make the effort to speak with greater fluency is not a simple task." Watts suggests that this linguistic poverty can make for deep feelings of inferiority and loss of self-esteem. One sees this particularly in the case of poor adolescent children who come to think of school not as an oasis away from the squalor and confusion of home, but as a hostile camp. They tend to leave school as a result.

The sad fact is that a working-class child often enters school at five or six "linguistically starved," in the words of Sir Alec Clegg, the enlightened chief education officer of West Riding, Yorkshire. The working-class child's chances of academic success are almost predetermined—and not in a happy direction. Since in many state schools in Britain and public schools in the United States, the weakest students are given the poorest teachers, their condition will not be improved there, either. Sir Alex has often stressed that school for a slum child merely mirrors the squalor and meanness of his own home. There are hopeful signs of change in the dismal picture, however. In Britain, teachers are being encouraged to work in educational priority areas (a high-flown term for slum areas) and are given an extra $200 a teaching year, not exactly a princely sum, but some inducement, nonetheless. The new "open plan" schools, whose history I shall trace later, have made grade schools a happier place for disadvantaged children, too, both in Britain and America.

Basil Bernstein has expounded the thesis that the working classes and middle classes speak two different languages, and that poverty's greatest crippler is in the realm of language. Bernstein's studies of the language patterns of poor children in the East End of London in the early 1960s and his published findings have had an enormous impact on American scholars. It was a happy coincidence that the Head Start program began at about the same time that Bernstein published his powerful thesis. Never before had American teachers had such a rich opportunity to study the language patterns of their own poor preschool children. What they discovered, amazingly, was that the slum child of Hackney in London's East End was as deprived as, say, the black child in a ghetto of Washington, D.C., and in a similar way; the poverty which revealed itself on the tongue was in each case very much alike. Everything that Bernstein was saying about linguistic deprivation and its effects on London children seemed applicable to disadvantaged American children (it is no accident, for example, that Bernstein is one of the most widely quoted scholars in the *American Journal of Negro Education*).

The twentieth century has been rich in its studies of the child. Freud showed us the crucial importance of the first five years emotionally; Piaget revealed that the child has a different concept of volume and number from the adult; Bloom pointed out that half of a child's intellectual development is completed by the age of four; and then Bernstein set forth the stunning hypothesis that a child's speech patterns dramatically affect his thinking and behavior and that economic poverty can mean irreversible intellectual impoverishment. Bernstein's effect on international thinking concerning the child has been incalculable. Harvard's Jerome Bruner believes that Bernstein's *Social Class and Linguistic Development*, published nearly a decade ago, was a kind of watershed for the revolution in thinking about the need to educate children earlier. Typically, Bernstein is far from being a household word in England, for countries tend to be rather casual about their own pathfinding native sons (do the Swiss know Piaget inside out? I doubt it.)

Bernstein discovered in his studies of the speech patterns of working-class and middle-class children that the middle-class child spoke a more elaborate and qualitative speech than his working-class peer, a more complex speech that enabled him to "verbalize his feelings." Bernstein found that in the case of the middle-class child, the word *mediated* between the expression of feeling and what might have become a hostile act ("I don't want to play with that, Mummy, because . . ." instead of a frustrated pummeling, to give an example of my own).

The working-class child's form of language, Bernstein found, was short, grammatically simple, often unfinished, with poor syntactical form, filled with repetitive conjunctions such as *so, then, because,* lacking in subordinate clauses, limited in adverbs, adjectives, and impersonal pronouns, and replete with rhetorical phrases signaling self-approval for a personal statement already made ("wouldn't it?", "isn't it?", "you see"). Bernstein calls this working-class linguistic pattern a *public* language as opposed to the *formal* language of the middle-class child (who is far more fortunate in being able to respond to the *public* language as well—as far as usage goes, he is bilingual in a sense.)

Bernstein's startling hypothesis, which carries great and understandable voltage for both American and British child experts disturbed about juvenile crime rates in the ghettos, and violence generally, is that these truncated speech patterns do not allow for deep feelings of guilt. As working-class children cannot *internalize* or verbalize their more tender feelings, these feelings tend to become blunted or atrophied, he believes. As he writes: "A *public* language is a linguistic form that discourages the verbalisation of tender feelings—and consequently the opportunities for learning inherent in the verbal expression of such feelings. . . . it will tend to minimise the experience of guilt . . . so permitting a range of anti-social behaviour." The recent

London adolescent subculture, the "skinheads," with their shaven heads and lethal laced boots (for kicking), are a good example of the transcribing of guilt-free inarticulateness into violence. Their war cries "Want bovver?" (bother) and "Want aggro?" (aggravation), which are not so much questions as threats, are classically truncated speech patterns. The ghetto signals for violent action, "Burn, baby, burn!" and "Get whitey" approximate the phrases of the aggressive "skinheads" in verbal thinness; they are all sharp, emotive, and guilt free.

Bernstein has stressed that the conversations of the working classes are limited to the immediate event and do not include any discussion of relationships between concepts, of any re-creation of the past or much reflection on the future. Hilda Taba, a San Francisco State College educator, found that her studies of the diary material of lower-class children in city slums tended to confirm Bernstein's conviction of the meagerness of conversational exchange in poor homes. In one group of twenty-five eighth-graders, aged about twelve or thirteen, only one child said that his family used the dinner hour to discuss the day's happenings. Most parents used that hour to mete out punishment for misdemeanors committed the day before or to allocate chores for the following day. The children come to detest adult company, and this feeling translates itself into hostility toward schoolteachers. In class they tend to tune out the minute the teacher begins to speak, associating grown-up conversation with threats and reprisals. Miss Taba goes on to say that the term "culturally deprived child" denotes only a group of children who were formerly called "slow learners," "under-privileged," or "underachievers." All these terms, as well as "disadvantaged," "lower class," "working class," are deeply unsatisfactory; no one can pretend to like them. Nevertheless they have a specific reference, denoting in the United States the 18 per cent of the U.S. population characterized by severe poverty, unskilled labor, and unemployment. In Britain, the term "the submerged tenth," more poetic, and also more vague, refers to this same sad iceberg beneath the surface of Western life.

More elaborate, qualitative speech from a parent, as well as teaching a child language, also tends to elicit a more civilized response from him. Bernstein writes: "When a middle-class mother says to her child, 'I'd rather you made less noise, darling,' the child will tend to obey." The words *rather* and *less* have softened the command, and yet the implicit warning is there that if he goes on being a nuisance, he may meet up with something more harsh, such as a slap. The working-class child will tend to have "Shut up!" and a cuffing dealt him simultaneously; he gets no linguistic cues which might induce him gradually to cool his actions. As a result, a freer use of violence characterizes the behavior of a poor child. Miss Taba cites the case of an eleven-year-old boy who thought teachers were funny: "They're afraid of a leetle beet of fighting," he said disparagingly. What the boy was referring to was all-out gang warfare, complete with broken bottles and flick knives.

Interestingly enough, the child analysts of the so-called Freudian school, with Anna Freud as their doyenne, have always been interested in the effects of inadequate speech on a child's actions. A member of the staff of the Hampstead Child-Therapy Clinic in London told me that the clinic now makes a point of taking "deprived" children into their nursery school at a slightly earlier age than they had previously—at two and a half years instead of three—because of their realization of the importance of speech in early years. She felt that the psychoanalytical viewpoint, and one which echoed the conviction held by herself and other members of the Hampstead Clinic, had been best expressed by Dr. Anny Katan, who writes:

> If the child could verbalize his feelings, he would learn to delay action, but the delaying function is lacking. . . . When the child has later acquired the art of verbalizing, he will still cling to the earlier method of acting upon his feelings instead of mastering them through verbalization. . . . If this process of acting upon feelings continues for a considerable time, the results will be fully evident. The child's ego will become fixated upon acting upon his feelings rather than attempting an adequate means of mastery. . . . The young ego shows its strength by not acting upon its feelings immediately, but by delaying such action and expressing its feelings in words instead.

What Dr. Katan is saying in Freudian terminology reminds me again of the black nursery school teacher in Boston who commented that once her children could talk, they stopped "breaking up the joint." A quick hitting out, an incapability to delay gratification—these are the characteristics of the inarticulate, disadvantaged child.

It should be made clear that when educators and sociologists attempt to analyze the speech patterns of the poor child and their effect on his behavior, they are not guided in any way by snobbishness. Bernstein has recently emphasized that he does not wish to turn working-class children into perfect little middle-class models, nor does he wish the working-class child to lose his rich, pungent accents. His plea is rather more for increased nursery school education with strong community roots and more participation by mothers. And truly it would be sad if the fertile, slangy language of the streets were lost. Anyone who has ever heard slum children vying with each other for a supremacy in insult at streetcorners, will know what quick fluency and inventiveness these verbal battles contain: the expressions used aren't Shakespearean but they are certainly colorful. In a Head Start panel discussion at Claremont, California, in 1966, Herbert Rosenberg, a speech therapist in the Pasadena city schools, made this passionate plea for encouraging the poor child to retain his "emotional" speech, as he called it: He said:

> I recall some children who would not talk. I told one boy how much I liked him and that I wanted to give him something to keep. I gave him foreign stamps and told him they were from Germany and India. He asked what states these were and then he took hold of them and said "Man! I'm going to keep them till the day I die." This is the emotional kind of speech to which I referred earlier. It is beautiful. These children say in three words what would take us ten minutes.

When I worked in the canteen of a black youth club in London's Notting Hill a few years ago, I was constantly amazed at the language of these teenagers, a combination of inarticulateness, total reliance on four-letter words to plug up the grammatical and verbal holes, and occasional dazzling bits of visual imagery in words. One fourteen-year-old, for example, who was trying to explain that he was not really a coward because he had not hit a bully back said: "Maybe I didn't hit him but I sure roughed him up good on the phone later."

Another of the teenaged wits at the club made me reexamine my nebulous role as voluntary worker behind the canteen counter when he wheeled up to me and said, "They pay you for selling these cups of coffee and chocolate to us?"

I shook my head. His eyes opened wide: "Lady, you gotta be crazy. Nobody in their right heads works for nothing."

A great many streetcorner slum dialogues are rich in wit and expressiveness and the fast talker is deeply appreciated; often the verbalizer becomes the leader. Malcolm X was a Boston streetcorner philosopher.* Still, it is a tough school and limiting, I would guess, to all but a handful of minor geniuses who are able to thrust their way through to the top regardless of early deprivation.

When a street child does get to the top, you can be almost certain there is a strong verbal mother somewhere in the background. It is a game you might call *"Cherchez la mère."* I always wondered how it was that the late George Jackson, with a childhood history of reformatories and prisons instead of schools, managed to write so eloquently, and where it was that he had picked up such a rich grasp of language. Jackson answered my question in his interview in San Quentin prison with Jessica Mitford, published in the London *Observer* on August 28, 1971, a week after he was shot dead in prison. To a question about who had stimulated his imagination as a child, he replied that it was his grandfather and mother:

My mother had a slightly different motivation than my grandfather. Her idea, you know, was to assimilate me through the general training of a black bourgeois. Consequently her whole presentation to me was read, read, read. Don't be like those niggers. We had a terrible conflict, she and I. Of course I wanted a life on the streets with guys on the block and she wanted me to sit on the couch and read. We lived in a three-story duplex and the only way out was

---

*See Hakim Jamal, *From the Dead Level: Malcolm X and Me*, (London: Andre Deutsch, 1971; New York: Random House, 1972).

through the kitchen. It was well guarded by Big Mama. I'd throw my coat out of the window and volunteer to carry out the garbage and she wouldn't see me any more for a couple of days. But while I was home, Mom made me read.

"Talk to your child!" a Head Start booklet entreats, and the movement to make mothers aware of the essentialness of mother-child dialogues before the age of five continues to gain momentum. But there is evidence that many working-class parents—with notable and increasing exceptions—do not particularly appreciate a highly verbal or bookish child. Working-class parents tend to value action, not words, and most children are touchingly eager to comply with parental expectations. A middle-class child of under six or seven is not expected to be especially useful about the house, so he is much more likely to occupy his leisure time drawing, reading, or watching television (and this usually selectively with parental guidance, which in itself makes it educational rather than just drugging). In contrast, a working-class child may soon discover that his mother would prefer him to be socially competent (be able to clean and dress himself, shop, deliver messages, buy cigarettes from the machine for her, take clothes to the cleaners, and so on) than sit in a chair and read.

However, although the child who learns to be skillful at putting the clothes in the local laundromat for his mother certainly knows how to make his way in the world, to cope with machines and money, he may find himself lagging behind in his reading at school. Hilda Taba recounts how it is that school failure and social class are closely connected.

Among the children from such conditions the usual difficulties that plague the public school in large cities are magnified. They show generally poor performance. They have a high proportion of failure, of drop-outs, of reading and learning disabilities, and innumerable life-adjustment problems. Patricia Sexton's tables [in her book *Education and Income*] show a consistently lower performance on practically every index: they have lower I.Q.'s, achievement, and grades; poorer health; and are beset with deficiencies in reading and language, the two chief tools on which success in school depends. The yield of merit scholars by professions and income levels dramatizes this discrepancy. In producing merit scholars the professors' families are at the top, and especially so the sons and daughters of librarians. This group produces 234 merit scholars per 12,672 families. At the lowest end are the laborers. They produce one merit scholar per 3,581,370.

As the American sociologist Patricia Sexton points out, privilege and deprivation are self-perpetuating. While the manual laborer's son or daughter who goes to college or the university is likely to be a gifted human being, it would be surprising if a doctor or lawyer's child did *not* go on to some form of higher education, just as a matter of course. Disraeli's concept of two nations,* poor and rich, and seemingly destined to survive side by side in perpetuity, is pointed up with distressing clarity whenever school success or failure is examined. Miss Sexton's findings are echoed in a report published by the British Universities Central Council on Admissions, which showed that the children of professional men accounted for 31 per cent of the accepted candidates for admission to universities in 1969. The

---

*In Disraeli's novel *Sybil*, the young Chartist agitator Morley says: "*Two nations* . . . who are formed by different breeding, are fed by different food, are ordered by different manners, and are not governed by the same laws . . . The rich and the poor."

remarkable aspect of this is that their fathers comprised only 8 per cent of the "economically active males aged between 45 and 59 in Great Britain." In contrast, the children of manual workers accounted for only 27 per cent of the admissions, although their fathers composed 64 per cent of the male population. Higher education is very undemocratic.

While investigating the emotional side of socially competent but academically inadequate children, Dr. Kellmer Pringle, the British child psychologist, found that those who were expected to take on a lion's share of the household duties were often deeply hostile and disturbed at school and usually extremely backward in reading. In her book *Social Learning and Its Measurement,* she cites the case of seven-year-old Paul, whose bereaved mother had made almost a little substitute husband of the young primary schoolboy. Though of average IQ, he had not even made a start at reading, and when asked about his favorite spare-time occupation, he said: "I mostly look after Mummy and our baby."

In *Four Years Old in an Urban Community,* a study of the behavior of four-year-olds of the two classes in Nottingham, England, sociologists John and Elizabeth Newson found that 81 per cent of the manual workers' children were expected to do some of the shopping, compared with 72 per cent of the middle-class children. In the matter of toilet training, they found that only 49 per cent of the middle-class children were independent in this respect, as opposed to 62 per cent of the working-class children.

But while they discovered that working-class under-fives tended to be brisk "do-it-yourselfers" compared with their more socially incompetent and dependent middle-class equivalents, in the matter of language, fantasy, and verbalizing, the middle-class child left his working-class counterpart far behind. The

Newsons attribute this entirely to mother-child interaction. If a middle-class child speaks with verbal richness ("an echo is the shadow of a sound" is one I recall), he is apt to feel a rush of motherly approval. The working-class child may be told not to speak stupid nonsense. The ability to fantasize in this verbal way helps a child to keep his interior life healthy and his ego intact, and it is tragic when this capacity is repressed. As Dr. Katan writes, this verbal fluency is conducive to emotional health because "verbalization increases for the ego the possibility of distinguishing between wishes and fantasies on the one hand, and reality on the other. Such children are able at an early age to differentiate between pretend and real."

The Newsons found that middle-class mothers actively encouraged children to be fanciful, to veer away from the literal in speech. Forty-five per cent of the professional and managerial classes said that fantasy was an essential part of their children's play life, compared to only 14 per cent of the unskilled-class mothers. They found that the extent to which reading stories was a regular part of the child's bedtime pattern was another example of class differentiation: for 48 per cent of the middle-class mothers (rising to 60 per cent in the professional and managerial class), songs and stories were normal at bedtime, but this was true for only 24 per cent of working-class households.

What a poor child misses most desperately is the process that Dr. Gertrud Wyatt described as feedback, mentioned before, the willingness or ability of the mother to act as an interpreter, to go into lengthy explanations, to correct grammatical errors. Working-class mothers like to see their children looking clean, obeying orders, and being active, not running on at the mouth, giving lip, asking "time-wasting" questions. Dr. Herbert Sprigle, Florida educator of deprived preschool children, describes how he picked up a worm and showed it to his class and asked them what it was. In unison, he writes, they said, "Bait." He asked them how they knew it was bait. Several of them replied, "Mom said so." If there was anything mysterious or engaging about the life cycle and composition of the earthworm, these children were not about to learn about it from their mothers. A worm was bait, said mom, now go away.

Gail Perry, a teacher who worked in the District of Columbia's poverty program, wrote in a teacher's magazine a year after the creation of Head Start that for the first six months after they came to her, her group of preschoolers were almost mute, totally incurious about the playthings surrounding them and never asking questions. She concluded that since no one had ever encouraged them to ask questions, they had stopped asking them.

I was reminded of Miss Perry's comments about poverty children's not asking questions or knowing how to play, or even how to hold a pencil or a crayon, when a Jamaican cleaning woman brought her five-year-old daughter with her to work at my house for the morning. Little Denise was bright-eyed, pert, and beautifully attired in a white smocked dress and up-to-the-minute laced suede sandals that must have cost her mother a week's salary. She sat and stared at me and smiled but never spoke and made no attempt to play with my son's toys strewn throughout the house. We went out to the patio garden and she stumbled over a plastic toy bucket. I asked her if she wanted to play with it. She asked: "What is it?" She had no concept of it as a receptacle for water, no idea that playing with water could be fun. Presumably, though her poor mother lived with a bucket of water in her hand for much of the time, Denise had never asked her what it was for or what it did. Or if she had asked, her mother hadn't the time or the inclination to reply. Though a good-tempered and devoted mother, the only words the woman spoke to Denise were orders ("Wash your hands," "Comb your hair," "Be still").

Bringing up children in slum conditions is never easy for a mother; the child-rearing role is made doubly exacting for the disadvantaged mother by the all too frequent absence of a husband or a stable male companion. The effect of having no man around is deleterious to the growing child, especially a prepubertal or pubertal boy. The void created is often injurious to the child, resulting in a shifting, "to-hell-with-it" attitude, a despair that creeps through adolescence and prolongs itself into early manhood. As the German analyst Alexander Mitscherlich writes in *Society Without the Father:*

> It is difficult for the child to find his identity because, instead of seeing and getting to know his father in his working world, too much is left to his fantasy. The same situation is repeated during the pubertal crisis of identity. He cannot easily find his identity in roles performed by his father . . . but has somehow to pick his way and make up his mind between a vast number of possible occupations of which he can have no real knowledge, and no first-hand knowledge based on childhood experiences. All this must give him a sense of isolation. . . .

If the crisis of identity is acute because a boy's image of his father is shadowy, how much more disturbing to be left with no father at all, which is so often the case with children in the ghettos.

When there is not even a male figurehead in the home, the mother tends to become autocratic and matriarchal, forced to adopt the exhausting dual role of disciplinarian *and* housekeeper. The effect on black mothers of this lonely role was carefully documented by Norma Radin and Constance K. Kamii, two teachers in Ypsilanti, Michigan, a city of 23,200 people thirty miles west of Detroit, in a preschool research project. They interviewed 44 low-income black mothers with young children, over half of whom were husbandless, and compared their attitudes and approaches to child-rearing with those of 50 middle-class white mothers who all had husbands. They found some stark class differences in attitudes toward bringing up children. The black mother tended to be repressive and puritanical, punishing her child severely for evidence of sexuality or for bad language. While wishing to shield her child from the world's problems, she had little interest in the child's own voiced troubles. The overall picture of the low-income black mother that emerged from their study was of an isolated, joyless, overprotective woman, terrified of outside problems such as debt and brushes with the law or landlords, very anxious to keep her children out of harm's way but not very concerned with their "inner thoughts." Verbal communication with her child seemed to be on the most basic level, largely confined to directives and imperatives of the "Wipe your feet," "Close the door," "Turn that down" variety. The middle-class mother was more concerned with her child's thoughts and tended to respect him as an individual in his own right.

The two researchers found that the all-consuming idea of the black mother, financially insecure and overburdened with responsibility, was to keep order and control in the home. There was no time for such fripperies as an exchange of ideas. The teachers concluded that the desire to impose control made the mother deeply authoritarian. When a child has discipline constantly imposed from without, he loses the ability to create his own inner discipline. As a result, he arrives at school ready to let rip physically but with a severely crippled language grasp. This combination becomes a trial for the nursery school or grade school teacher who has to cope with him in class. She finds her reasonable requests for order dissipate into the air. Poverty children are so accustomed to external force and short, sharp commands that they are inured to them. Their authoritarian upbringing has created a kind of inner chaos that makes quiet, unaggressive behavior almost impossible for them to achieve, especially at first.

A vivid description of the deprived child's school behavior when released from the authoritarian controls of home is given by Gail Perry in describing her unruly but ultimately endearing under-fives in the Washington poverty program:

> Some of the children showed insecurity, distrust and anger in a more physical manner—again not necessarily atypical to a middle class preschool group but to greater extremes than I had ever seen. In the boys, the fact that they exaggerated their "fighting" and loud boisterous behavior may in part have been an effort to preserve a male image that was so often lacking at home. . . . One little girl, who was alert to everything that went on and capable in many ways, exploded with high-pitched screams whenever frustrated. Her shaking rages lasted five to ten minutes and occurred three or four times a morning. She was quick to pull another child's hair, bite, and hit, and one day attempted to stuff one of the smaller boys into the wastebasket. . . . These preschoolers needed a great deal of assurance, love and understanding, and patience from their teachers. . . . These children all seem to need to challenge and test authority. . . . Now I was the cruel authority these youngers were testing and challenging.

While the black slum child's environment may be particularly unconducive to the acquisition of a rich cognitive grasp of language, it should be emphasized that language deprivation is not a matter of race but of background. A child's lack of adequate language learning comes from an absence of meaningful dialogue with an adult in his crucial preschool years, and this is prevalent in both white and black lower-income groups. The mother becomes the powerful, commanding, matriarch, short on words, long on quick orders, in most poor homes, whether they be in London's economically deprived boroughs such as Hackney or Stepney (where the Cockney mother may be found struggling to raise her family against depressing economic odds) or in the heart of Detroit.

What might be described as the home ecology is the barren ground from which the linguistically deprived child springs. These homes are overcrowded and bereft of any sign of the printed word except perhaps for a racing sheet or a tabloid. They teem with sensory experiences. Sociologists like Frank Riessman are anxious to point out that the culturally deprived child cannot be compared to those socially isolated children who have no early stimulus, such as the abandoned or hidden children described earlier, because their lives are lived in a veritable whirlpool of noise, confusion, blaring radios, fighting adults, screaming police sirens, and street disturbances. While I would agree with Riessman that these children do not lack for sensory stimuli and exciting (upsetting?) experiences, this unconnected barrage of stimuli does not strike me as particularly enriching and I suspect that it leaves the lower-income child as linguistically impoverished as any socially isolated child. The resulting behavioral patterns are remarkably similar. In fact, the condition of the severely culturally deprived child has often been compared to that of a deaf or institutionalized child; the same backwardness, inattentiveness, lack of responsiveness, and weakened sense of self are present.

One thing is certain: this kind of life experience does nothing to enrich a child's capacity to conceptualize or to help him to understand the content of his own experience. While he may pick up plenty of words in the process of growing up in these surroundings, they are simple labels to him and do not extend themselves into generalizations or conceptions. Most poverty children know what a ball is and dutifully answer "ball" when asked to name one. But the idea of roundness, or a multiplicity of games that can be played with it, of its looking like a smaller version of some round planetary object such as the sun or the moon, that a fist can be "balled"—all these themes on the variation of the ball do not occur to a deprived child. In the same way, teachers who take deprived children to the zoo will find that they dutifully label all the animals, but that the *idea* of all wild animals, of the African countries from which they derived, of the concept of keeping them in humane captivity, of the differing habits they might have, escape them. The mental outlook of deprived children is characterized by such *concreteness*.

So, far from being stimulated by their busy environments, poor children appear to be blunted by them, operating intellectually on the most limited level where the sight or knowledge of one animal or object does nothing to set up a chain reaction of ideas concerning them. It might well be that the working-class child is suffering from an overabundance of meaningless stimuli in the home before entering school. He has probably cultivated a self-protective ability to tune out in order to escape the barrage of sensory experiences to which he has been subjected; the smells, the voices, the drunken brawls, the top-volume television. Certainly the child from the lower income family often arrives at school behaving like a deaf-mute, only exploding into violence occasionally to show he has a healthy larynx. Along with the cultivated isolation, poverty children display a startling unconcern with outside violence, a blasé acceptance of it (they will rush to a window if a police van shrieks into the vicinity, eager to find out "who's getting it"; violence is a familiar sideshow, not particularly remarkable).

The slum child often has what the psychologists call a low self-image, his ego presumably having been battered down by disinterested, authoritarian adults. At the Boston North Point Project for disadvantaged preschoolers, teachers tried to make four-year-olds aware of their identity by standing them in front of a mirror and asking them what they saw. Many of the children stated frighteningly that they saw the teacher, not themselves.

Poor children use words to attract attention to themselves or to make demands, not to elicit information. Educators working with them emphasize that the child may be engagingly quick to say "Yes, I know that one" when asked a question (before the question is finished) or "Look at this" or "Gimme that!" The poor child is less interested in what he is saying than in the reaction he gets from what he says. Another characteristic of the deprived child's language is what the two University of Illinois educators Carl Bereiter and Siegfried Englemann call the "giant word" syndrome. For example, when the arithmetic statement "Two plus one equals three" is quoted, the child will repeat it as "Two pluh wunic'k three." The deprived child cannot see words as meaningful entities and so strings them all together as a result of this incapacity. Such children also tend to be unable to reverse the elements of a statement. Bereiter and Englemann found in their tests with slum children that they could not reverse words, even in the simplest form. When the children were asked to put "green and red" in another way, they continued to say "green and red," seemingly unable to switch the two colors over to "red and green." The idea of word reversibility is alien to a culturally deprived child, his grasp of language inflexible.

The most distressing outcome of this inflexibility in handling language is that it does not improve with time; it gets progressively worse. In his studies of 167 first- and fifth-grade black and white pupils from twelve New York City public schools, psychologist Martin Deutsch found that the six-year-old lower-class child was more verbal than the equivalently poor ten-year-old. Deutsch calls this the "cumulative deficit" phenomenon. A culturally deprived child's language appears to develop in a downward spiralling motion, shrinking rather than expanding with chronological growth. Deutsch concluded that at the first-grade level, the disadvantaged child's experiences had given him enough stimulation to provide him with at least a limited grasp of vocabulary and language usage. By the fifth grade, however, he found that even this inadequate command had deteriorated. This descent from bad to worse is an almost certain future insurance for dropping out from school. To give a factual example of this phenomenon, the Texas Education Agency, in charting the careers of educationally disadvantaged Spanish-speaking children in Texas, found that between 40 to 60 per cent of the approximately 100,000 non-English-speaking first-graders entering each year dropped out permanently by the end of the elementary grades.

If language skills are not learned early in the child's life, they do not necessarily improve in a school situation, even with bright children. Bernstein found in some testings that even the brightest working-class high school students, who shone in mathematics, fell down hopelessly on verbal tests in contrast to private school students of the same age—that a kind of branding on the tongue had occurred during the early years which we now see as being irreversible.

Many people are repelled by the idea that a child can excel academically because of an advantaged background. I am reminded particularly of a teacher friend of mine at a public grade school near Broadway in upper Manhattan, who teaches fourth-grade children from deprived homes (her school is in the catchment area for a large number of welfare-hotel families). She has read a great deal of the sociological literature concerning the disadvantaged child to help her in her own understanding of their difficulties. She said that at times she felt the studies made by Deutsch in New York and Bereiter and Englemann in Illinois, among others, were detached and chilly: "They hover over those poor kids with beady, scientific eyes, happily taping their verbal disorders. Ugh, it makes me sick," she declared passionately. Like so many other liberals, she is distressed by the constant reference to "middle-class" and "working-class" models, especially since the "middle-class" child seems to come off so much better.

Still, although some sociologists and psychologists have ripped into their research on slum children with a gusto and briskness that borders on the inhumane, society may some day have reason to be grateful for their assiduousness. Some concrete results and helpful changes have already occurred in the 1970s in the wake of this orgy of U.S. studies on the disadvantaged child, first sparked off by Bernstein. Better teaching methods which help both the privileged and the underprivileged child are being instituted in the first and second grades ("enriched environment classes," "the unstructured day," and so on), the often brilliant "Sesame Street" continues to try to bridge the preschool educational gap for the neglected under-fives, and the validity of certain testing tools, the conventional IQ test in particular, have been placed in serious doubt as a consequence of these U.S. studies on class differences and over-all early linguistic neglect.

It just may be that the disadvantaged child will get a better deal in the future and that his crippling language handicaps be dealt with more effectively and sensitively. If so, those poor "poor" children submitted to gruelling experimental tests in language laboratories will have performed a great service.

6

IQ Tests

We have seen that working-class children and middle-class children speak two different languages. In view of this dramatic difference, a great many teaching methods and diagnostic tools have come under heavy fire as being too heavily oriented toward middle-class children. Are they?

In a curious way, since the revolutionary findings of Bernstein and his followers, *middle class* has almost become a dirty word. Producers of children's television programs will speedily mount the ramparts if a critic says their programs are too middle class. Perhaps the swing against the term, suggestive as it is of the complacent, the smug, of bourgeois values and cozy economic standing, is a little extreme. Still, I think the backlash against middle-class reading methods and other communications media for children is valid. Why should poverty children, who have none of the linguistic tools inherent in a middle-class child's repertoire, be judged by these alien standards?

One of the diagnostic tools to come under heaviest fire as a result of the researches of the 1960s is the IQ test. Is it "culture fair," as Bernstein himself has asked? Geneticists, the believers in the dominance of inherited intelligence, have recently made a big splash in both America and Britain, arguing in behalf of the emotionally charged point that whites are more endowed with intelligence than blacks as proven in the higher IQ scores of the former. The two leading protagonists of the genetic supremacy argument, Professor H. J. Eysenck in Britain and Professor Arthur R. Jensen in California,* have brandished IQ test scores like fused grenades, making the explosive air around the subject of inherited racial superiority even more heated than it is, something no multiracial nation needs. While no one would accuse the two social scientists of fixing the scores (black children in both countries do tend to score lower than the white population), they have neglected to emphasize the most important point where IQ tests are concerned—their essential unfairness.

There is a healthy concern among educators themselves about whether the tests are not too geared to middle-class experience and language. A white eight-year-old child with educated

---

*For their arguments in favor of genetic rather than environmental influence on intelligence, read Eysenck's *Race, Intelligence and Education* (London: Temple Smith, 1971) and Jensen's "How Much Can We Boost IQ and Scholastic Achievement?" *(Harvard Educational Review,* Vol. 39, 1969).

professional parents might breeze through the Stanford-Binet or Wechsler intelligence tests (the two most frequently used), scoring over 100 with ease; his black counterpart with a dramatically different background of verbal neglect and slum environment might have trouble in scraping by over the 90 point mark. But does this mean that the white child is brighter? No, it does not. It may mean simply that the language of the IQ test is foreign gobbledygook to the black child. There is strong proof that the tests need reshaping if they are to be considered valid. At the moment, they are flawed and prejudicial.

First of all, it is unfortunate that the IQ test has been tossed into the racial arena. It was never designed to be there by the inspired scientists and scholars who originally conceived of the idea of "measuring" intelligence. In the mid-nineteenth century, French child study experts thought that intelligence was reflected in a person's facial characteristics and head shape (just as the Colonel Blimpish remarks that early colonial administrators were supposed to have made about the natives' slow-wittedness having "something to do with the shape of their heads"). They traveled up a number of scientific blind alleys measuring the head bumps of mentally deficient children trying to gauge the degree of their feeblemindedness. In fact, the history of IQ tests traces to this early desire to categorize the mentally defective and had nothing to do with measuring degrees of intelligence in the normal child.

In 1838 the French scientist J. E. D. Esquirol began to get warm when he said that perhaps the physiognomy of a mentally defective child was less important than his ability to verbalize. It was the beginning of the idea that language was a good measuring point of intelligence. After sixty years of groping by others, Alfred Binet finally took this idea into fuller flowering and conceived his largely verbal method of appraising intelligence in 1911, a test designed to place a child's mental capabilities somewhere in line with his chronological age.

In World War I, military personnel in the United States, happy with this new diagnostic toy (especially the revised and modernized version of Binet's test perfected at Stanford University), had a field day and delighted in giving blanket tests to new recruits; officers were sifted away from doughboys by the quality of their scores. Schoolteachers were joyful about the tests, too, giving group tests with abandon and placing the scores on children's school reports, pinning them down forever like butterflies. It was very comforting for teachers; it helped them to know where they thought their pupils stood. This practice continued through World War II.

I recall how a group of us at our Massachusetts high school (which I attended after my family was evacuated from Manchuria) discovered that a certain number at the back of our reports was our IQ score. The preening on the part of those who had achieved over 130 (to repeat, 80 is where normalcy begins, 100 is average, over 120 is college standard, over 150 is the "gifted" category) was fairly stomach-turning. However, one friend, who previously had been sunk in feelings of inferiority about his intellect, was galvanized by the astonishing statistic (135) on the back of his card to try for officer status in World War II and later for Harvard. He is now a professor of mathematics at a college, a long way from school failure. Still, high IQ scores and personal happiness, like love and marriage, do not necessarily go together, though scores often do predict occupational success. However, no claim has ever been made for them as emotional barometers or gauges of potential stability.

The knowledge of a high score can definitely bolster sagging self-esteem, as in the case of my math teacher friend. In the same way, a child with a lower IQ may be saved from unnecessary badgering by a parent after testing if the parent then knows that the child is not being lazy or obstreperous but is working to his ceiling (in these cases, the parent is informed of the result, rather than the child, for obvious reasons).

"There is no one in my profession," an educational psychologist told me, "who regards the IQ test as the ultimate criterion. An IQ score is just one tool in a whole battery of diagnostic tests on why a child is falling down in his school work. And no IQ is fixed. I have seen IQ scores soar by as much as twenty points in several years' time after the conditions which have been depressing a child's intelligence—an unhappy family or school situation—have been improved."

Two factors in the IQ picture that have been glossed over place the tests in serious doubt as an ultimate criterion. One is the fact that taking the test itself is an emotional experience, and a child may be unnerved by the surroundings in which he takes it, the pressure to be speedy, and the strangeness of the tester. Sometimes, too, a tester can make a *faux pas* out of simple friendliness and a desire to put the child being examined at ease. Frank Riessman tells the story of a young black boy named James who achieved a very low score on one occasion and a much higher one on the second. The black pyschologist giving him the test discovered that what had made James so sullen and unresponsive to her first lot of questions was the fact that she had immediately called him Jamie. The boy detested this instant intimacy, he later confessed. "My name is James 'cept to my very good friends maybe," he told her. When she reverted quickly to calling him James, his score rose in response to her testing.

Another grave flaw in the tests is that they are largely verbal, and the language used, especially in the vocabulary sections, has very little relevance to a great many children from different cultural backgrounds, for example to American Indian children in the U.S. West and to Asian children in Britain. In other words, how can you test the intelligence of a child by confronting him with a question that deals with an object of which he has no experience? Amazing as it may sound, for example, two of the key words in the Wechsler Intelligence Scale for Children (WISC) are *fur* and *diamond*; are these likely to be a poor child's best friends? The vocabulary subtest of the *Metropolitan Reading Test* contains such items as *moose, spectacles, toboggan, blueberry,* and *bear.* When would a ghetto child have last seen a moose, or gone for a mid-winter's snow ride on a toboggan?

One of the most heartening developments made in early childhood education between 1967 and 1972, with the new emphasis on studying the disadvantaged child, is the awareness of the validity of a child's personal experience as part of his learning process. More and more, children are being asked to talk and write about what happens in their lives, in their project apartments, concrete playgrounds, slum streets, or urban renewal areas, and less about what John and Jane are likely to be doing with their farmer dad on his antiseptic farm in, say, the Midwest. When I visited a new open plan primary school in Clapton in London's East End this year, I saw five-year-olds making up their own vocabularies with detachable letters: words like *telly, Mom, chocolates, Dad, football.* They were being encouraged under the Breakthrough to Literacy program* to make up words that were most familiar to them, since word recognition and,

---

*A recent reading program launched in 1968 under the Nuffield and Schools Council Programme in Linguistics and English Teaching.

subsequently, reading, became easier when it related to the child's immediate personal experience.

The sad fact is that IQ tests, both the Stanford-Binet and the Wechsler, have not caught up with this tremendous advance in understanding the mind of the child, although they are the two tests most used in primary schools (the Wechsler test is thought to be marginally more fair as it places less heavy emphasis on verbal skills and has a larger section dealing with "performance," that is, the manipulation of picture puzzles and mazes, and so on). But on the verbal side, both tests, including the Wechsler, relate only to a middle-class child's experience as they are presently constructed. As has been pointed out by Robert Havighurst, University of Chicago educator, certain nouns in traditional IQ tests given culturally deprived children would mean little or nothing to them: words such as *fireplace, chandelier, wallpaper, salad fork, dining room.* As Havighurst says, words that might be more familiar to deprived children, such as *pump, coal, stove, lamp, rain,* rarely appear on intelligence tests.

Allison Davis* a colleague of Havighurst's, replaced the remarkably middle-class words found on IQ tests, redolent glossy women's magazines in their drawing room gentility, with more down-to-earth samples. For example: instead of "Cub is to bear as gosling is to 1 ( ) fox, 2 ( ) grouse, 3 ( ) goose, 4 ( ) rabbit, 5 ( ) duck," he substituted "Puppy goes with dog like kitten goes with 1 ( ) fox, 2 ( ) goose, 3 ( ) cat, 4 ( ) rabbit, 5 ( ) duck."

Even when a child answers a question correctly according to his own experience, he may be graded as having answered it incorrectly. I. E. Sigel, professor of psychology at New York's

---

*For a description of Davis's tests on disadvantaged children, see his book *Social Class Influences upon Learning* (Cambridge, Mass.: Harvard University Press, 1948).

University of Buffalo, in an article called "How Intelligence Tests Limit Understanding of Intelligence," criticized in particular one test given to Mexican children. He cited the case where these children paired pictures of cups with tables instead of with saucers in intelligence tests. They were marked wrong, though it was perfectly obvious that in their own homes, cups did go directly on tables, and saucers were unknown.

In the same way that these Mexican children had no experience of a saucer, a deprived child from the city slums would be unlikely to know the answers to the questions relating to the following words from the WISC vocabulary test, along with the unexpectedly Onassian *fur* and *diamond* already cited: *sword, cushion, belfry, stanza.* Well, he may have heard of *cushion*, yes; but *belfry? stanza? sword?* In many ways, the verbal content of the WISC test has the remote feel of that "Postillion, postillion, our stagecoach has been struck by lightning" phrase found in the French "everyday" conversation manuals of my youth. As Bernard Coard, a West Indian educator working in London, has written in *How the West Indian Child Is Made Educationally Subnormal in the English School System:* "The vocabulary and style of these I.Q. tests is white middle-class. Many of the questions are capable of being answered by a white middle-class boy, who, because of being middle-class, has the right background of experiences with which to answer the questions, regardless of his real intelligence."

The existing IQ tests are also defective in that they fail to measure a child's potential for creative work. A close look at the Wechsler test, which as previously noted is fairer to culturally deprived children in its testing of performance as well as verbal skills, still fails to show any proper test of creative ability. In the WISC section on performance, five of the tests do not involve verbal skills; these are picture completion, picture arrangement, block design, object ascendancy, and coding (the latter requires that the child fit the right symbol to the right letter). Not one of these tests can give any indication of creativity.

The most hopeful sign on the IQ front is that educators themselves know the tests are fallible and are constantly analyzing them and attempting to improve them. Few intelligent scientists regard them as conclusive, definite criteria (this is why they are such weak ammunition in any argument concerning hereditary versus environmental effect on intelligence pointing to inherent racial superiority). The workings of man's mind are still as mysterious as any moon rock, and the business of measuring intelligence a comparatively young study. One scientist who is not satisfied with the IQ test as a final measurement is Dr. M. D. Austin of Edinburgh University, who believes that the unemotional person is more inclined to do well in IQ tests since his rational approach to life fits him for answering questions coolly and speedily. Austin tested groups of students and found that the emotional, wild dreamers ("divergers," as he calls them) did well on open-ended tests and the more pulled-together, repressed, and tidy-minded students ("convergers," in his terminology) excelled in the standard IQ tests.

Other experiments with IQ tests tend to back up Dr. Austin's theory that they do not favor the creative child. Havighurst speaks of an experiment in the American Southwest conducted by a university art teacher, who made systematic comparisons of the drawings of Hopi Indian children with American white children and found that the Hopi drawings were far superior. Yet these same children were found to be far below their white peers in verbal intelligence tests. The art teacher concluded that the Hopi children painted as a way of life; it was their cultural expression. The white children talked.

Poor IQ scores are no longer being accepted just as that—poor

IQ scores. More and more, psychologists are asking, If they're low, *why* are they low? Bearing in mind that these tests fail to reveal the temperament of the subject, testers have been experimenting with the personality, color, and makeup of the examiner himself. They have done so because they realize that, though the subject being examined may be unable to show *how* he's being affected by the examiner, a very strong effect may be taking place all the same. In 1971 the British psychologist Peter Watson made a study of West Indian students at a high school in East Ham in East London and found that the young teenagers scored ten points higher when they thought they were being given an ordinary test, not an IQ test (IQ tests inspire feelings of inferiority in black children, underlining what the sociologists call their "lowered self-esteem," for they are relative strangers in a white school culture). Scores climbed by as much as twenty points when Watson's West Indian assistant gave the tests. Such swings in scoring, pointing to an emotional background that examiners have been ignoring up to now, have also seriously weakened the Jensen-Eysenck argument that blacks are automatically endowed with lower intelligences by their genetic inheritance.

Because the unfairness of the traditional tests has become apparent, new intelligence tests are being devised in Britain and America which are tailored more accurately to variations in children's experience and culture. Eugene Grigsby, III, a Californian urban studies expert, devised these questions for black teenagers:

1. A soul brother is—A Mr. Charlie B Barry Goldwater C Cassius Clay D Ringo Starr
2. Preachers are easily recognized by their—A Manners B Clothes C Deeds D Words E Cadillacs

3. The opposite of square is A Round B Up C Down D Hip
   E Way-out
4. How many people can live in two 9 x 12 rooms if they take
   turns sleeping? A 12 B 16 C 21 D 18 E One big one
5. A White Negro A Doesn't exist B Is literary jargon only
   C Has many enemies D Is found only in the movies E Is
   a political term

London psychologist Dr. Judith Haynes has devised new tests
for West Indian, Pakistani, and Indian children geared to assessing their learning capacities more fairly than the traditional IQ
tests (she works in Hounslow in Southwest London, an area
with a large immigrant population). In her book *Educational
Assessment of Immigrant Pupils*, she describes giving experimental
tests to 125 Indian children. These tests helped the children pick
up knowledge as they went along, rather than forcing them to
rely on acquired cultural experience. In one test, Verbal Learning I, the examiner places 31 objects in front of the child (for
example, dice, tube, string, plug, strainer, reel, ribbon, pliers,
file, screw, peg, spool). The child is then encouraged to touch the
articles he recognizes when the examiner says the names and is
given eight timed trials in which to learn the names of six of
these objects. Clearly a child can reveal his degree of learning
capacity (and consequently be measured) with a test such as this,
which is less dependent on what he already knows than on what
he can take in during the test. Dr. Haynes also emphasized that
the attitude of the examiner should be relaxed, sympathetic, and
free of racial bias. She also pleads for a less rigid reliance even
on these more fair tests. "The danger of relying too much on
tests cannot be too strongly emphasized," she states. "No matter
how wide a battery of tests we use, we cannot depend solely on
the tests themselves in taking decisions about a particular child

any more than we can expect to decrease the proportion of culturally disadvantaged or verbally underdeveloped children simply by diagnosing their condition."

Dr. Haynes and her colleagues ask for a less reverential attitude to traditional modes of testing intelligence. Are they right? Is the IQ test thoroughly outmoded?

In certain circumstances, it is not, as these psychologists would probably agree. If a parent knows his child is reasonably bright and yet he or she is doing poorly at school, that would be the time to give him a traditional test, providing his own background assured that the content of the test was reasonably familiar to him. IQ tests are valid predictors of how a child can perform as long as the emotional climate of school and home does not depress his innate intelligence (and, in these cases, the discrepancy between high score and poor performance would show that some changes urgently needed to be made).

But no score should be judged in isolation. A real live child is always much more than a plus or a minus on an indexed score card.

7

Television: The Child's Third Parent

In the past twenty years, America and Britain have bred a generation of child television viewers, an ever-increasing horde of young spectators. This is not to say that the child of the 1930s or 1940s who preceded him did not have his occasional dose of visual excitement. But it was occasional rather than constant. He was given fleeting visual thrills. He had his weekly film on Saturday afternoon, those gleeful jamborees where he sat in the dark for an entire half-day watching Disney cartoons and Abbott and Costello and indulged in an orgy of bubble gum chewing, popcorn munching, and chocolate gorging.

I myself have only to hear the theme from one particular

Laurel and Hardy film that is occasionally resuscitated for children's TV to receive a Proustian barrage of memories of Saturday afternoons in the dark in a small suburban Massachusetts movie house—the remembrance of rustling candy papers, the fruity smell of small boys' tennis shoes, the overall electrical feeling of mass expectation and thrall.

And the thrill received from flickering images on a screen has not palled. Perhaps this is the real miracle. Though modern children are subjected to literally thousands of hours of television during their preschool and school years, a glint of pleasure can still be detected in the eyes of most children when they are seated in front of their favorite television program. But most children's viewing is disproportionately larger than the time they spend doing other things, as is proven by any number of staggering statistics on children's viewing.

It has been estimated that 97 per cent of American homes have at least one television set: even those families living below the "poverty line" ($5,000 a year or less per family) will have the all-important piece of household furniture—the box of a million fantasies and dreams interspersed with a million yawns—in some corner of the living room or even the bedroom. By the time an American child has graduated from high school, it has been calculated that he will have seen 15,000 hours of TV. A Nielsen rating claims an audience of six to seven million preschoolers (half the U.S. population of three-, four-, and five-year-olds). As the preschool child has an endless amount of time on his hands, if he is not at nursery school or kindergarten (and the majority of disadvantaged children do stay at home in their preschool years, as we have seen), he is apt to be watching television for seven or eight hours a day. Buckminster Fuller, the great iconoclastic architect, has called television "the child's third parent."

One fact of urban life in particular that has accentuated parental dependence on television is the fact of living high in a project block; it is a form of imprisonment for the young child, a restricted ecology that cannot fail to blunt a child's spiritual and intellectual growth. High-rise blocks are not built to encourage a mother to shoo her under-fives out to play. A report by William Stewart for the British National Society for the Prevention of Cruelty to Children published in September 1970 called high-rise living for families "restrictive, undesirable and productive of a good deal of human suffering." People have known for some time that high-rise living had serious drawbacks, that it did nothing to improve a woman's mental state. The fact that most mothers living up high in housing projects are also poor has not added to the pleasure of their existence. To worry about how to pay the market bills *and* about Johnny's falling out of the window from the fifteenth floor is a bad combination for serenity.

High-rise apartments do not encourage community spirit; young mothers are isolated, and fears about their children's falling out of windows or down elevator shafts or off balconies become obsessional; mental health deteriorates. And of course a tense mother can inspire a corresponding tension in her child. According to some specialists in child development, a child living high in a tower block can develop a dismaying set of nervous symptoms all his own, revealing itself in behavior that is nothing like his mother's, even though it springs from the same living conditions.

For a child to escape into the relative freedom of a nursery school or a day care center is difficult as there are not enough nursery school places to meet the demand for them, leaving far too many children at home with a distracted, hard-pressed mother. Mrs. Marion Easton, Director of the Hudson Guild Child-Care Center in downtown New York City, told me when I met her in 1971 that she always had a huge waiting list for preschoolers. At that time, she had a waiting list of forty children and did not know when she was going to fit them in. As far as she knew, most of her New York colleagues directing day-care centers were in the same position. She had often been stunned by the children when they first came to her, she told me, shocked by their aura of withdrawal and apathy, by their muteness. Many of the preschoolers she took into her center had never been out of their project blocks at all until they came to her. No incubated chick had ever been so confined. The idea of playing was alien to these young passive all-day television viewers. Gradually they begin to thaw, according to Mrs. Easton, surrounded by playgrounds, paint pots, blackboards, cages of gerbils, extensive housekeeping corners, sinks for water play— and most important of all—chatty, affectionate teachers.

The description of the project block child who first enters the bewilderingly social world of a day-care center was eerily similar to that given to me by a London psychiatric social worker who works with families living in Millwood, the high-rise complex on the Isle of Dogs in the Thames. "We see children who are bad-tempered, won't play on their own, who sleep and eat badly," she told me. "Because they have led a passive existence with their mother—cooped up with her perpetually and told to be still all the time—they develop quite a bit of inner rage. This makes the child surly and aggressive with his mother. But then when he goes to school, the very opposite occurs. He becomes the victim. As he has not learned to stand up for himself or to be part of the hit-back culture, he is singled out for bullying. So he is apt to be aggressive at home, passive at school, two conflicting attitudes, neither of them particularly healthy."

What has been remarkable is the way high-rise blocks have continued to shoot up in Britain, Europe, and America in the face of a great deal of evidence that they are unsuitable for young families. Nineteen years ago, American sociologist Anthony Wallace made a survey of low-rent, multistory housing projects for a Philadelphia housing authority, focusing his attention on the Jacob Riis Houses on the lower East Side of Manhattan, a project with 1,768 dwelling units built in 1948. While he conceded that Jacob Riis had its comforts compared to the slums it had replaced—it was warm and vermin free and had efficient utilities—he spoke of the mother-child clashes and painful attempts at controlling or supervising children properly from sky level:

> Several mothers remarked on the difficulty of maintaining communication with and control over their children, when once these children were old enough to ride elevators and play on the playground. . . . She (a mother) cannot control him effectually by yelling out of an upper-storey window. The outcome is that the older child cannot effectively be controlled at all if he is outside the apartment and the mother isn't. . . . This leads, I suspect (and rather paradoxically), to a rather precocious independence of small children, which parallels that to be seen on slum streets . . . The alternative to this radical independence is an equally radical dependence, achieved by keeping the child in the apartment . . . The whole conception of discipline in the family is affected by this . . . the control consists in preliminary admonitions backed up by severe punishment, if trouble is reported.

Nearly twenty years after Wallace wrote this, his diagnosis appears to have been ignored. More and more high-rise homes have been built, no doubt perpetuating this unwholesome form of disciplinary action on the part of frantic parents feeling anxious and cut off from life below.

It is more than possible that the fact of overcrowding, whether in high apartments or low slum ones, is intellectually stunting for the preschool child as well. In what he calls an "armchair analysis," University of Illinois psychologist J. McVicker Hunt suggests that crowding is a severe handicap for the child during his second year. "As the infant begins to throw things and as he begins to develop his own means of locomotion, he is likely to find himself getting in the way of adults already made ill-tempered by their own discomforts and by the fact that they are getting in each other's way." One sure way to get a child to sit still and to ensure that he won't get underfoot is to place him before the television set. It is not really surprising that poverty conditions often create zombie viewers, children who move hardly a muscle for hours while plowing through dense Westerns and family comedies that are probably incomprehensible to a preschooler.

The program "Sesame Street" was such a revolutionary innovation in the field of children's communications in November 1969 when it began because it was the first series designed entirely for those neglected small minds in slums and tower blocks in the ghettos. "Sesame Street" was also a pioneering effort in a number of other ways. It was the first program to be created out of the sociological findings of the 1960s, building on the thinking and hypotheses of those distinguished scholars, sometimes known irreverently as the "Three Bs," Bernstein, Bruner and Bloom. "Sesame Street" has been called "sociology's child," and with some justification. The guiding principle and thought of "Sesame Street" was Bloom's dictum that the child develops half of its intelligence by the time he is four years old and that therefore something drastic had to be done in the field of communications to help this age group. The research of "Sesame Street" into other fields of child development was prodigious (I heard Bernstein and Bruner mentioned at least ten times during my interview with the program's executive director, Mrs. Joan Ganz Cooney, in the first week the show was launched). David D. Connell, vice-president and executive producer of the program, has boasted that if all the "Sesame Street" research were weighed, it would come to 247 pounds, at $15,300 per pound.

The "Sesame Street" producers have never erred on the side of modesty, and perhaps it was just as well that they indulged in self-congratulation during those first weeks in November 1969, for they were able to convince an apathetic public that they had indeed unwrapped a special present for the nation's children. Up to that point, it was doubtful that many Americans had realized that a large segment of the nation—its preschoolers, numbering some twelve million—was being intellectually neglected. After all, wasn't the children's fare on television wholesome enough? There were those nice men, Mister Rogers and Captain Kangaroo, with their low-keyed, homespun, face-to-camera monologues and "Romper Room," where you could see a kindergarten in action. And there were Tom and Jerry beating the daylights out of each other on Saturday mornings. And couldn't the Three Stooges be seen kicking each other in the slats every other uproarious minute at about the same time? Wasn't that enough?

Well, no, it wasn't, said the "Sesame Street" producers. In an August-September 1969 issue of *American Education*, Edward L. Palmer, research director of the Children's Television Workshop, the organization responsible for the existence of "Sesame Street" spoke of his about-to-be-delivered baby as "an unprecedented and potentially significant experiment in educational television." He wrote excitedly of how it would be beamed to 163 public television stations across the country, of how it was to be constructed as a series of 130 hour-long color telecasts "designed to prepare young children for formal schooling" to run at first for twenty-six weeks, and how it was to have a sharp "instructional impact."

It was to be the most expensive children's series ever televised. The money to make it—$8 million—came from a variety of private and public sources: the Carnegie Corporation, the Ford Foundation, the U.S. Office of Education, the Office of Economic Opportunity (the agency which administers Head Start) and other federal agencies. The federal backing was later to become food for controversy, like so many other facets of "Sesame Street" when the initial enchantment engendered by the series wore off for some teachers and educators.

It was no accident that "Sesame Street" was partially financed by the same federal agencies that also backed Head Start. From the first, the aims of the "Sesame Street" producers were similar to those of the Head Start project; in fact, "Sesame Street" was designed as a kind of Head Start at home.

"We're after the poor kids," Joan Ganz Cooney told me emphatically when I interviewed her, "mainly because we know the lower-class child can be improved by viewing. We can't fool around with the middle-class child and his values. A middle-class child will have the language he learns on television reinforced by his parent. The poor child gets no such feedback. Yet we are convinced that the poor child knows much more than he's able to articulate. There's nothing wrong with his reasoning process. It's just that he lacks information. We're trying to supply a great deal of information to the disadvantaged child so that he won't go to school with a deficit. If the middle-class child has a deficit of information, we know that he can make it up in school. The poor child just gets discouraged in a school situation if he arrives with this deficit."

She went on to explain that "Sesame Street" aimed at enriching a poor child's vocabulary, the area in which she thought his deficit was the most apparent. It was clear from the way Mrs. Cooney spoke that she had read a considerable amount of the literature on the culturally deprived child; in particular, there were echoes of Martin Deutsch and his phrase to describe a frequent syndrome in the poor child's life, that of the "cumulative deficit."

"We're not so interested in teaching the poor child concrete words," she continued. "He'll probably know them. We want to concentrate on the prepositions—words like *over, through, in, out* —words that will make stories more meaningful to a poor child. Take the phrase that I read in one children's story recently: 'Meanwhile back at the farm . . . .' What would this phrase, thrown out so casually, mean to him? What would *meanwhile* mean? Or even *back*? Or *farm*? A story like that could block him from the start. He just wouldn't move on. We want to help slum children to move on."

The show was first conceived in 1968, more than a year before it was launched officially. The thinking of the program's planners went something like this. They decided that children liked adult television better than their own, especially the commercials, because they were quick-moving, full of jingles, easy to remember, kaleidoscopic. So they incorporated Madison Avenue techniques into the teaching of the ABCs, basic numbers (counting up to ten), clarification of prepositions and pronouns, and the recognition of certain basic forms and shapes such as circles, squares, and rectangles. Everything was to be contemporary and recognizable to an inner-city child. The setting of "Sesame Street" would be "essence of inner city,' an anonymous, fairly slummy cul-de-sac where people sat on doorsteps only a banana skin's throw away from the nearest garbage can. Two of the presenters would be black—and, as it turned out, rather beautiful—the so-called married couple, Matt Robinson, the high school science teacher, and his wife, Loretta Long, an occasional blues singer, a calm and loving pair. These two attractive people, much in evidence in all the shows, were to get away from the all-white feel of so many past children's programs.

The program would attempt to humanize its young audiences as much as possible by revealing the unspoken but apparently strong feeling of racial harmony on Sesame Street, where blacks and whites would flow in and out of each other's fairly ramshackle kitchens borrowing eggs, not trouble.

And what, exactly, were these preschoolers supposed to be learning? Gerry Ann Bogatz and Samuel Ball, two members of the staff of the Educational Testing Service, Princeton, New Jersey, the organization that directed a nationwide evaluation of the launching of "Sesame Street," writing in an educational journal, gave some idea of the great "Sesame Street" research build-up that preceded the program's initiation:

> The evaluation of *Sesame Street* was a job that began in the summer of 1968 . . . The participation of Educational Testing Service in the *Sesame Street* venture dates back to a series of curriculum conferences set up by the show's producer, the Children's Television Workshop. The meetings were called to establish the specific behavioral goals of the show. What selected set of instructional objectives

could a television show reasonably be expected to teach millions of children in 130 hours? By the end of the summer of 1968—more than a year before the show was to go on the air—a highly specific, behaviorally stated set of goals had been provisionally selected.

Anyone who believes that the "Sesame Street" teaching aims were a lightweight set of objectives surrounding a rudimentary grasp of the ABCs and a knowledge of how to count up to ten would be in for a shock if they read the actual written, stated goals of the program, set out in a confidential paper. I was lucky enough to get hold of this confidential paper, the second one sent out by the program's producers for the 1970–1971 experimental season. This official statement was put before the Schools Committee of the Independent Television Authority in June 1971. At this time, the "Sesame Street" producers were meeting with resistance from British companies who felt the series was too American and that the commercial techniques had been overdone. Spearheading British resistance to "Sesame Street" was the British Broadcasting Corporation's director of children's programs, Miss Monica Sims, who pronounced the series "passive and didactic" and deplored its "commercial, hard-selling" techniques.

The confidential "Instructional Goals" sheet was to be a powerful weapon to win over the British commercial companies, as the BBC had rejected the series. It was a hard-hitting, no-nonsense, we-know-about-the-need-for-children-to-pick-up-cognitive-skills document designed to overcome any fears that the series was somehow a half-cooked and poorly thought out affair.

Prereading goals listed rather mysteriously under the heading of "Symbolic Representation" were to be an ability to recite the alphabet, to match up letters, to recognize and label them, and to differentiate consonants from vowel sounds. Under "Words," the child was to learn to "match his words," a process whereby he would be able to select an identical word from a set of printed words and to know that words had boundaries and could not run into one another.

The "Sesame Street" "Instructional Goals" paper is thick with abstruse terminology to describe fairly simple processes. For example, from a section called "Temporal/Sequence/Spatial-Sequence Correspondence," we learn that this means simply a child's ability to read words from left to right. "Decoding," we discover, refers to the ability of a child given the word *ran* subsequently to recognize *man* and *can* with a little switching around of the alphabet. The number of reading words that the "Sesame Street" student was to have at his command seemed relatively unambitious compared to the other skills he was to learn: this was a list of twenty words comprised of such unrelated terms as *bus, love, telephone*, and *exit*.

The "Number Goals" listed for the small viewer included "matching," "recognition" (given a verbal label, the child can select the right number to fit it), "labeling," and "recitation" (this last heavy word merely meant that it was hoped that the child could recite the numbers from one to twenty).

In another section, the "Instructional Goals" paper states its now well-publicized hope that the child will learn to recognize geometric shapes such as circles, squares, triangles, and rectangles. Anyone studying the favorable reactions to the teaching aims of "Sesame Street" will read of the five-year-old who comes into his mother's room shouting about his own pillow: "It's a rectangle, Mom." In my researches on "Sesame Street," I came across a great number of articles quoting this little boy's happy outburst; it cropped up so often, in fact, that I began to wonder if he was not apocryphal—or else the brainchild of an inspired publicist.

In Part II of the "Instructional Goals," one runs across more words that show that its researchers had read their Piaget—in fact, must have totally immersed themselves in him. Beneath the overall title of "Cognitive Organization," we read that the child will be tutored in "Perceptual Discrimination and Orientation," and "Visual Discrimination": these high-flown terms involve "matching" (where the child can match a given object or picture to an object similar in form or size), "recognition of embedded figures" (given a form, the child finds its counterpart embedded in another picture), and "part-whole relationships" (the child learns to structure parts into a meaningful whole).

In another strongly Piagetesque section called "Classification," the designers of the show demonstrate the way in which they have attempted to reinforce a child's sense of how objects relate to one another. ("Which of these things belongs with those?" and "What properties has it?" Example: "If the object is a ball, is it both *round* and *red?* What else does it resemble?")

While the lofty and pedantically presented aims sometimes invite incredulity, it is easy to see that the "Sesame Street" producers had read their literature on poverty children. They seemed to know well that the disadvantaged child is at his most deprived in the realm of conceptual knowledge and therefore the aims, while ambitious to the point of foolhardiness, have a laudable side in their avowed goal of teaching concepts. The thinkers behind the program also appear to realize that the deprived child has an impoverished sense of self. There is a section in the "Instructional Goals" paper called "The Child and his World."

The method used by these testers in their research, begun in 1968 and carried through until the end of 1971, is a fascinating commentary on the way psychologists and sociologists have come to view a child's social class as an all-important factor in his capacity to learn. The ETS testers make no bones at all about the fact that they knew the "Sesame Street" viewers could be influenced by class considerations (shades of Bernstein again). In describing their two years of testing of 1,300 three- to five-year-olds throughout the country, they wrote:

> Another set of measuring instruments that was developed was intended to assess the background variables whose presence might affect the amount of learning achieved by a child viewing *Sesame Street*. Examples of such variables included the vocabulary level of the child, whether stories were read to him by his parents or siblings, and the mother's educational aspirations for the child. . . . the test locations selected were Boston; Phoenix; Durham, N.C. (inner-city black and white); suburban Philadelphia (middle class); and northern California (rural).

In their avowed aim of closing the gap between the disadvantaged and the advantaged child, the "Sesame Street" producers brought class into the arena of children's communications, a major revolution in itself. Whether they succeeded in closing the gap or not is perhaps a secondary consideration before this tremendous breakthrough in program-planning thinking. Long after Big Bird the Muppet fades from screen memory, "Sesame Street" may be remembered for taking this big step. It made communications history.

But did it help neglected minds?

The "Sesame Street" producers were sanguine, even cock-

sure, about the aptness of their educational goals and pedantic
in the way that they went about setting them out. It would be
negative and sweeping to say that they failed to achieve these
goals. But their grand design for the preschooler contained serious imperfections. Fortunately for the sake of future children's
television programmers, these flaws have been carefully
analyzed and observed.

What the optimistic "Sesame Street" producers could not
have anticipated in those first days of their debut in November
1969 was the criticism that was to greet them from intelligent
viewers, especially after the initial acclaim. And what acclaim!
Newsweek, a few days after the start of the show, described it as
"one of the best-researched programs in television history" and
then praised it for its imaginative efforts to reach "the forgotten
million."

But in a few months, some excessively sour comments about
the program began to find their way into newspaper and magazine columns—critical commentary from university professors,
grade school teachers, parents, and scholars from all over the
country. During the next two years, these lashings were to grow
into a full-blown controversy, though to be fair, the program
continued throughout to elicit praise as well, particularly from
such weekly news magazines as *Time* and *Newsweek* (in November 1970, for example *Time*'s cover story subtitled it "TV's Gift
to Children"). But criticism was savage and consistent, and in
time was to come from Britain as well. It is interesting to chart
the chronological history of the controversy that raged over the
program during 1970 and 1971.

The first powerful salvo against "Sesame Street" turned out
to be the most savage of any to come. With its use of violent
language and vitriolic comment, it might have come from the

pen of some eighteenth-century essayist. The author obviously relished showering invective on the object of his loathing. The latter-day Jonathan Swift in this case turned out to be a Boston University professor of education, Frank Garfunkel. He ignited the letter page of the *Boston Globe* on January 1, 1970, with his blanket condemnation of the show. He termed it "intellectual genocide for preschoolers" and excoriated it for nurturing irrelevance and dehumanizing the learning process. In one particularly biting paragraph, he accused the producers of treating learning as an act of titillation. Most condemning of all, he said that they had presented the program as a palliative for a certain group, a "pill-taking" process for the poor. He claimed that this patently ignored the complexities of the individual child and obscured the fact that direct personal interaction between child and adult was what caused the elusive process of learning to take place.

On a practical, less emotive level, he pointed out that parroting numbers and letters without regard to their ultimate use was an empty exercise in itself. What Professor Garfunkel achieved by this last comment was to touch on the rather old-fashioned quality of the program—not in its techniques, of course, but in its teaching. I agree with Dr. Garfunkel wholeheartedly. Rote learning of numbers and alphabetical letters went out with ruler slaps on the hand and flip-up desk tops, and runs counter to all that is new and experimental in elementary school education, as is exemplified by the "open plan" type of learning for example.

Professor Garfunkel's final criticism about the futility and unimaginativeness of rote learning was soon echoed in the *Saturday Review* by Robert Lewis Shayon. His comments were far more muted and equable in tone than the Boston educator's but they also mirrored doubts concerning the program's content. He wrote that the acquisition of cognitive skills such as those involved in learning letters and numbers hardly answered the question of society's ills. He emphasized that this kind of learning was mechanistic in feel and did nothing for the emotional needs of the child, which, in a technological society, were dangerously neglected.

By March of 1970, six months after the program had been launched, the voices of disgruntled teachers were beginning to be heard. Spearheading the attack in a teachers' magazine, *Childhood Education,* was one of its editors, Mrs. Minnie Perrin Berson. In an article entitled "Ali Baba! What Have You Done?", she urged parents and teachers to take a sharp look at the program, which, as she put it, parents had helped to pay for anyway, through federal funds and local public television membership. In a hard-hitting, if rather school-mistressy manner, she invited them to examine the aesthetic standards of the show. Opening with a scathing reference to Mrs. Cooney's claims that children revealed a 90 per cent attention level for "Sesame Street" compared with a 65 per cent level for the prevailing educational TV fare, she queried Mrs. Cooney's methods of obtaining this research: was it by measuring the eye-blinking quotient of children seated before the tube? "Aimez-vous eye-blink research?" she asked archly.

It became clear further on in the article that she also did not care for what she conceived of as the "vulgar" tone of the program as a whole, "the flickers and perks of animated cartoons, live actors, burping puppets, film clips, and any other hocus pocus that can be turbined into sixty busy minutes." She suggested feelingly that this kind of pratfalling humor did nothing to stimulate finer sentiments in children. Mrs. Berson was not even very impressed by the handsome black couple who lent a domestic note to the program; she thought they played a sort of unrealistic "nicey house" to a child audience that could not possibly recognize them as real.

As for the high-flown claims of its producers, Mrs. Berson did not see that "Sesame Street" was in any way an improvement on some of the past children's programs that tended to explore children's fantasy and feelings gently and unspectacularly. She cited "Captain Kangaroo" and "Mister Rogers" as two fine exponents of a gentle, low-keyed approach to the viewing child.

Mrs. Berson's impassioned denunciation of "Sesame Street" sparked a barrage of heated mail from kindergarten teachers, teachers' colleges, parents, and early childhood education experts. One kindergarten teacher, Bernice C. Nossoff, of Whittier, California, wrote that when she was asked what she thought of the program by parents and colleagues, her honest negative answer had caused shock and dismay: "I was treated," she wrote, "as if I had desecrated the flag or defiled the institution of motherhood!"

Miss Nossoff then went on to try to evaluate the program in terms of her own teaching experience. Most inappropriate, she thought, was the emphasis on symbols for this particular age group. Driving home a symbol of constant repetition merely compounded the error, she felt. She had discovered that, in her teaching experience, children in their early years learned best when the visual input was stable and consistent and not presented in what she described as a "winkety blinkety" way.

Young children learn from personal experience, she stated, and their "little bodies had better be experiencing, or the learning does not take place." In this assertion, the kindergarten teacher touched on a crucial nerve of the "Sesame Street" controversy: didn't the program induce children to be too passive? Later on in the year, the British Broadcasting Corporation's head of children's programs, Monica Sims, condemned the program largely on the grounds of its encouragement to passivity. To be seated for a solid sixty minutes while kaleidoscopic images bounced off the retina and repetitive jingles attacked the mind and ear seemed almost brain-washing in its approach, in Miss Sims's estimation, a view closely allied to the kindergarten teacher's from California nearly four thousand miles away.

But not all teachers were finding the show too passive and kaleidoscopic at this time. Mrs. Berson's invitation to reply to her "Ali Baba" attack drew praise as well as criticism for the program from teachers. One teacher, Mio Polifroni, took it upon herself to circulate a questionnaire about "Sesame Street" to 107 southern California middle-class families with children in private, cooperative, and college laboratory preschools. Parents praised the personal relationships portrayed, the climate of friendliness conveyed in the black-white encounters. That "Sesame Street" undoubtedly helped prepare children for school was an almost unanimous response from these parents.

But plenty of brickbats flew the program's way, too. Some parents were repelled by the crude slapstick, others felt the monsters, instead of being endearing, were frightening, guaranteed to cause nightmares. Others questioned the validity of learning numbers and letters. A great many said that they wished it could be more low-keyed and less noisy.

Mrs. Cooney's attitude toward the controversy expressed in the *Childhood Education* columns combined hauteur and irritation. She wrote:

Dear Mr. Cohen:

Thank you for your letter of March 17 enclosing the copy of *Childhood Education* carrying Dr. Berson's article.

Both Dr. Palmer and I have been too busy to get a reply to you by your deadline and frankly, I find the tone of Dr. Berson's article so emotional that it defies a reasoned reply.

She represents a middle-class viewpoint which really ignores the needs of the disadvantaged children with whom we are most concerned.

> Thank you for writing.
> Sincerely,
> JOAN GANZ COONEY, President,
> Children's Television Workshop

It is amusing to see that old deprecatory bugaboo *middle class* turning up again in Mrs. Cooney's letter, guaranteed to crush. At that time, Mrs. Cooney could not have anticipated that the word would be leveled at her own program. But this in fact did happen, and some members of the black community, especially in New York City, condemned it for embodying too many middle-class values and teaching methods.

One of the most penetrating analyses of just how effective "Sesame Street" was in its attempt to stimulate language learning appeared in the *Teachers College Record* (Columbia University) in September 1970.

The article, "Fog over Sesame Street," was written by Samuel Kliger, a New York consultant on early childhood education. He introduced his trenchant, well-informed critique with a faint kiss blown toward "Sesame Street." He conceded that it was a masterful bit of entertainment—a "beamish" program, as he put it. "What child won't squeal with delight to see a baby deer, a squirrel drinking milk from a baby's bottle . . . to puzzle over the knuckle-headed behavior of Buddy and Jim."* But educationally speaking, "Sesame Street" "did well feebly," he wrote, quoting Theodore Roosevelt's famous phrase.

A significant criticism leveled at the program by this educator was that it tended to barrage the child with too many sensations all at once. The rat-tat-tat presentation of quick images to strengthen the verbal message was a questionable method to teach language or to enable a child to conceptualize. An input of information and words had to be absorbed unhurriedly, he believed. As an example, he cited the program's illustration of Piaget's conservation experiment with children (described earlier) and criticized the programmers for using an opaque container of milk which had not permitted the observing child to see how full the container was. Then the programmers had given the child a quick answer as to which container really held the most liquid, not allowing him to teach a child to conceptualize, in his opinion.

A child learns by a process of interaction and feedback from the environment, Kliger declared, and not so much by "show and tell." Preschoolers repeating letters by rote as they did in "Sesame Street" and calling out words without real understanding, reminded him of Pavlov's slavering dog responding to the bell heralding food. "What is truly dreadful about rote knowledge," he added, "is not only that it precludes discovery, as Professor Bruner always stresses, but one never knows whether the student repeating the rote fact is revealing knowledge or concealing ignorance."

He concluded his essay by stating that the partial failure of

---

*The show's two hopeless white-coated unhandy men.

"Sesame Street" mirrored the failure of all educators who had not conceived of new strategies, both in the media and in the classroom, to deal with what he described vividly as the "slum-damaged" child.

Professor Kliger's pleas for less conventional teaching methods for the underprivileged child were repeated in one of the most influential and powerful attacks on the program made during the entire duration of the controversy which raged around it. This attack was made by Dr. Herbert Sprigle, director of the Learning to Learn School in Jacksonville, Florida, a preschool program for disadvantaged children, in an article entitled "Can Poverty Children Live on Sesame Street?" appearing in the March 1971 issue of the educational magazine *Young Children*. Dr. Sprigle described himself as appalled by the construction of the program, a visual presentation of facts that enabled children to glean information in a "passive, effortless fashion." In his direct experience of poverty children, he had found that what they needed most was the interest of an adult and an opportunity to "see, touch and manipulate objects." They needed tactile, *not* passive education, he asserted.

Dr. Sprigle felt that the program merely contributed to the concrete-mindedness of a poverty child by its incessant reference to objects rather than the concepts behind the objects. He cited the example of one of his pupils, whom he called Victor, who was exposed four or five times to one "Sesame Street" episode in particular where a man picks up a ringing telephone, says "Hello, Harry," and then proceeds to deliver a string of words beginning with the letter *H*. At the end of the fifth episode, Dr. Sprigle asked Victor if he knew any words beginning with *H*. Victor said, "Oh, yes, sure—*man.*" When Sprigle corrected him, Victor said, "Oh, *telephone.*" It was obvious that

Victor was focusing on the two concrete objects, the man and the telephone, and that this elaborate visual preamble to the teaching of the letter *H* had misfired with him—or worse still, totally confused him.

Dr. Sprigle's article was taken more seriously by his colleagues in the teaching field and by other critics of "Sesame Street" because he had tested the program's effectiveness on real poverty children and was therefore speaking from experience and not sounding off abstractly as had so many other critics. What Dr. Sprigle had done was to select twenty-four pairs of disadvantaged children and then divide them into two groups, one an experimental group which he called the E group, the other a control group which he dubbed the C group. Both groups were from Head Start kindergartens in his area. The experimental or E group used the "Sesame Street" curriculum, following up the day's program with activities suggested by the material distributed by the Children's Television Workshop for teachers (material which, incidentally, many teachers professed to find very expensive*). The control group attended another school program for the same length of time and were exposed to numbers, letters, shapes, and language. The C group was also exposed to a great many learning experiences such as field trips to the zoo and to fairs, and emphasis was given to their social and emotional development. The E group, it appeared, remained restricted to the less peripatetic "Sesame Street" teaching format.

---

*To quote from *Nation's Schools*, March 1971: "Surprisingly few teachers had any major criticism of the show's content and most adverse remarks were related to the price of the supplementary materials—*Sesame Street* records and book—which many teachers feel are too expensive ($19.95)."

At the end of a given period of time, equal in length for both groups, the Florida educator gave them the Metropolitan Readiness Test, a test for five and six year olds who are about to enter first grade geared to assessing their familiarity with word meaning, listening, matching, alphabet, numbers, and copying. On all six measures, Dr. Sprigle found that the control group scored significantly higher than the "Sesame Street" students. He found the TV graduates disappointing on all scores: "Their oral vocabulary, ability to understand phrases and sentences, to pay attention, to reason, to recognize letters of the alphabet, their number knowledge and visual-perceptual skills are poorly developed," he wrote.

What he discovered was what many child experts thought should have been evident from the start—that "Sesame Street" would not stand up as the sole preschool learning experience, that it was valuable as a supplement only, and then usually when the child viewing could discuss points in the program with a parent or teacher.

Generally, Sprigle's experiment had shown him that poverty children would have a tough time living on Sesame Street. He was not sure they should even try.

At this time, skepticism was accorded most testings of the show's effect on children. While Sprigle supporters applauded his findings because they disapproved of the program's content, the "Sesame Street" producers could point to the Educational Testing Service's findings and claim that these results proved its excellence and effectiveness. Samuel Ball and Gerry Ann Bogatz published their evaluation of the impact of "Sesame Street" on middle-class and working-class children in October 1970, nearly a year after the program began. They concluded from their findings that the child who watched the program the most was the one who gained intellectually the most. Gary M. Ingersoll, an Indiana University educational psychologist, queried this hypothesis, saying that those who watched it the most were those who had started with higher intelligence scores on the pretest, in any case. What Ball and Bogatz had proven, he stated, was that "smart children watch more and learn more." This was not news, he pointed out: Wilbur Schramm and his colleagues had discovered this a decade ago when they made a study of children's viewing habits in Canada, Colorado, and California.

Meanwhile, criticism of the program rumbled on over the heads of the testers. In one biting attack, a New York journalist, Linda Francke, reported that members of the black community disapproved of the program on the grounds of its encouragement of white middle-class values. In an article in *New York Magazine* following hot upon the Sprigle essay (which she quoted at length), she reported that one black high school teacher had dismissed it by saying: "You can know all the ABC's in the world and still hate people and still misunderstand people. *Sesame Street* is the same thing you get in a typical All-American white elementary school."

Miss Francke spoke to a number of day-care center heads and discovered that what they most objected to in the programs was the lack of reality on the Street: a place where everyone is beautiful to everyone else, where there are no drunks and dope addicts, and puppets recite verses in a never-never land. In this, they echoed the comments of Urie Bronfenbrenner, professor of psychology at Cornell University, who said: "The children [on the show] are charming. Among the adults there are no cross words, no conflicts, no difficulties, nor, for that matter, any obligations or visible attachments. The old, the ugly or the unwanted is simply made to disappear through a manhole."

In what I would consider an excess of oversensitivity, several black day-care directors said they were offended by Oscar the Grouch, the muppet with the lopsided face of melancholy outrage who lives in a clean trash can. They felt that he symbolized acceptance of a lower status in life—an "I-live-in-a-slum-and-I-like-it-and-keep-it-clean" kind of Uncle Tom-like passivity. Remembering the earnest, well-intentioned liberals I had met on the Sesame Street production team, I could imagine how misunderstood they must have felt. Oscar an approved symbol of black apathy? God forbid.

But Miss Francke's interviews with day-care center directors did suggest a disillusionment with the program which was reflected in my own interviews with Manhattan social workers and day-care center personnel. Mrs. Marian Easton, director of the Hudson Guild Child-Care Center, told me when I saw her in the autumn of 1971 that she did not put much emphasis on the program for the education of her preschoolers, half of them project children with working mothers recruited under the Head Start program.

"I feel it's too passive," Mrs. Easton told me. "We like to see constant interaction between teachers and children during the day and lots of active play. We don't mind using 'Sesame Street' at the end of the day, though, when children can afford to be passive."

By now the most frequently voiced criticism was that the program was too passive. And what, by contrast, was an active program? One television producer once defined an active program as one resembling a particularly well-written and lucid recipe—so engaging that the person reading it is galvanized into getting up, going into the kitchen, and trying it out. And, as many had noted, the "Sesame Street" children, either on the set or off it watching, never seemed to get up and go off and do anything.

John Holt, author of several popular books on children's education, summed this up succinctly in a May 1971 issue of *Atlantic Monthly:* "Learning on *Sesame Street,* as in school, means learning the Right Answers, and as in school, Right Answers come from grown-ups. We rarely see children figuring things out. . . ."

But the unkindest cut of all was the rejection of "Sesame Street" by the British Broadcasting Corporation in the late autumn of 1970. The corporation's decision was based on much more than simple dislike.

The most important reason was *length:* the CTW thought that for the program to be effective it had to be shown each day for five days a week for the requisite sixty minutes. This would have meant that five hours a week of the BBC's precious children's hour time (only eleven hours a week were allotted to children's programs at that time) would have been spent in showing an American program geared to American children's tastes.

When I went to see Monica Sims at the BBC's Television Center in Northwest London in July 1971 to further discuss her decision, it was apparent that she knew she was in good scholarly company, for she quoted several of the American critics of the program.

It was clear that Miss Sims's idea of an underprivileged child was at strong variance with Mrs. Cooney's.

"My idea of an underprivileged child is the young person who has to rely on television almost exclusively for his stimulation, the child who is the victim of adult neglect, whether he be rich or poor," she told me. "But it's no good for a deprived child to be put in a TV ghetto—that's why we don't make special programs for immigrants. We have found that children themselves hate to be categorized."

If Monica Sims had an overruling conviction about what children's television should be about, the key words would be *active involvement*. She felt she had most succeeded if one of her programs induced a child to go away from the set and do something suggested in the show. What had shocked Miss Sims about "Sesame Street," though she conceded it was excellent entertainment, was that its creators wanted to *fix* the child before the set.

"When Mrs. Cooney was asked if she wanted to keep the children glued to the set, she said yes, because once they got up they might not come back." Miss Sims shook her head in disbelief. "You see, I'd be happiest if they left, if we'd stimulated them enough to go do their own creative thing."

One assumes here that Mrs. Cooney, having read her sociological literature on poverty children, had felt challenged by the slum child's noted lack of concentration and therefore considered her program a triumph if it engaged his unremitting attention for a solid hour five days a week. She must have felt misunderstood on a universal scale that her efforts to counteract an educationally undermining feature of disadvantaged children had been interpreted as authoritarian.

Nevertheless, Mrs. Cooney might well have experienced a sense of satisfaction from the profound effect her program has had on the British television industry itself, particularly on the commercial companies. To say that "Sesame Street" rocked the British children's media-makers would not be exaggerating. It forced the various companies to reexamine the content of their own programs and ponder more fully exactly who it was that was watching out there. Up until that time, British research on its infant audiences was more emotional than analytical.

"Sesame Street" set many producers in Britain wondering if this sentimental, shadowy approach to its audiences was really good enough. Lewis Rudd, head of Thames Television's children's programs, the company which produces about 50 per cent of all the children's programs on the commercial channels, was openly grateful to "Sesame Street," "We're very thankful to 'Sesame Street' for giving us the nudge we needed. While I don't think we have the same problem as they do in the States—I mean the vast numbers of educationally deprived children under the age of five—I think the program has opened our eyes to a whole new area: made us think more about this age group than we ever have before. I would define all children who don't go to school before the age of five and who can't go to nursery school as deprived—in this sense, of course, we have an enormous audience who qualify."

A year after Rudd expressed this opinion, his company launched its program for preschoolers, "Rainbow," a twenty-minute show aired every weekday for ten weeks. Its avowed aims were "to entertain and to educate . . . that 80 per cent of children under the age of five who had not the opportunity of attending nursery school and gaining from the stimulation of contact and activities outside the confines of his own immediate family and environmental situation." "Rainbow" aimed to extend children's vocabularies, help with a knowledge of the alphabet, and sharpen word and quantitative concepts. Does this sound familiar? It even had a muppet who helped out, a yellow, froglike creature with a zipper for a mouth who could have be spawned right from the "Sesame Street" pond itself. Derivative was certainly the word for it. But, then again, why not?

After all the uproar surrounding the introduction of "Sesame Street" to Britain, the program did finally get time on British regional channels, and was seen on Saturday mornings by children in London, Scotland, and Wales in the autumn of 1971. Its reception was curiously anticlimatic, causing slight comment among the critics and surprisingly little excitement among viewers, parents *or* children. One of the reasons might have been that Saturday mornings are weekend shopping mornings for British mothers, and preschoolers invariably accompany them on their rounds. The adult comments hardly seemed relevant to the central arguments raging around it in more aware circles (Was it too passive? too middle class? and so on) and centered instead on its Americanisms. Do our children really want to speak of "garbage" instead of "trash," of "cans" instead of "bins," of "elevators" instead of "lifts"? went the critical commentary rather chauvinistically and trivially. Still, the Children's Television Workshop with Mrs. Cooney at its head, didn't allow the sniping to deter them from making more educational-cum-entertaining television for the under-ten's. "The Electric Company," a series very similar to "Sesame Street" in its aims to educate the disadvantaged child (but the seven to ten age group this time) followed closely afterwards, using, in its producer's own words "electronic wizardry" to help teach reading skills. The "Sesame Street" techniques of flashing images and words over and over again in a repetitive way was retained in spite of the by now familiar criticism that this was a slightly brainwashing way of teaching. Explaining how they were teaching the word "energy" to young viewers, for example, a CTW press sheet reads: "A voice in an echo chamber comes over the speaker as the whole word 'energy' appears and sounds it out, first syllable-by-syllable, and then the whole word at once. At the same time, the printed word expands in rhythm with the voice, then returns to its original state." Does this sort of image-on-the-brain-and-eyeball approach really teach a child to read?

No one knows. Certainly children are reading less well now than ever before, both in England and America, so television cannot be said to be child's most effective primer, even though the medium appears to be a superb information-giver.

But "Sesame Street" and "The Electric Company" are at least trying to make their young viewers more literate and the CTW should get full marks for earnest endeavor. American educator, John Gardner, quoted in a November 1970 issue of *Educational Leadership*, is much fairer to Mrs. Cooney and her colleagues than most scholars. He writes: "Technological breakthroughs like *Sesame Street* are the only hope for a radical upgrading of educational quality on a massive scale. Anyone who doesn't recognize these breakthroughs as the first limping troops, the vanguard, of a mighty host is just out of touch."

Most important of all, the humming international interest and violent reactions that "Sesame Street" produced revealed a gratifying new awakening of interest in the very young child's mind and in the media that was being created for him. This suggested that the early childhood educators and propagandists for better learning sooner (and especially language learning) had finally aroused a dormant public.

8

What Does Television Teach?

During the entire "Sesame Street" controversy, no matter how bitter it occasionally became, no one ever denied that the children watching *did* learn something. Arguments raged over whether it was useful or not to have a child learning the alphabet, which a great many considered an old-fashioned method for learning to read. But primary school teachers who welcomed the "Sesame Street" graduates into their first grades did concede that the children arrived knowing the alphabet and how to count to ten. Whether "Sesame Street" had been the right sort of teacher was at the center of the controversy, not whether it had succeeded in teaching at all.

That a child does pick up a great deal of information from the television set is undeniable. In fact, it is thought that the younger child absorbs more from the tube than the older one as he is more impressionable and possesses that receptive quality of intellect that Montessori called "the absorbent mind." Many people lament this fact, seeing the preschool child like some captive animal in his living room cage, picking up lumps of mental fodder that he can neither swallow, digest, nor use properly in any way. This pessimistic view was expressed in 1971 by the concerned experts attending the White House Conference on Children, who professed themselves shocked to find that the "child of America is growing up in captivity . . . where . . . his prison is his culture. His prison is his environment. His prison is his communication."

A child is captive before his TV set, and there is evidence to support the belief that children in urban ghettos (those "poor kids" that Mrs. Cooney was after, presumably) are more captive than others. Research carried out in 1969 by Dr. Bradley S. Greenberg and his colleagues at Michigan State University revealed that the urban poor spent twice as much time before their television sets as the rest of the population. The attitude of the poor he interviewed was that they positively trusted and liked the medium, preferring it to all others.

I think it would be fair to say that for the poor child, both the preschooler and the teenager, television is the major leisure activity. The findings of the U.S. National Commission on the Causes and Prevention of Violence of September 1969, headed by Milton S. Eisenhower, tended to confirm this view. The commission found that the poor black population respected the messages of the box, believing that it "showed it like it was" (in view of all the intensely unreal white, middle-class comedy situations—for example, "I Love Lucy" and the "Dick Van Dyke Show"—this perception has a sad irony about it). Poor teenagers, according to the commission, relied on television as a "primary source of socialization . . . and . . . in the absence of family, peer and school relationships allowed it to become the most compatible substitute for real life experiences."

The reliance of the middle-class child on the medium is far less all-embracing, though TV viewing, even for the more fortunate, is the predominant leisure activity.

But rich or poor, exclusive or prime leisure activity, what does a child learn from television? This question is buried in doubt and confusion. The opinions of the "we-don't-really-know-its-effects" group can be read in profusion, particularly in the U.S. *TV Guide*, which is filled with good writing on the subject but is consistently inconclusive; as the magazine is linked with the industry, it would not, after all, be very intelligent to commit hara-kiri by announcing that TV had a devastating effect on young minds. In a compilation of articles from the *TV Guide* of 1969 called *TV and Your Child: In Search of an Answer*, editor Merrill Panitt writes self-righteously: "It is time that someone—and we believe it is *TV Guide*'s responsibility—set down exactly what is known and what is not known about how television affects children." Predictably, the magazine goes after the answer and does not find it. And of course they are being honest. There does not really seem to be one.

One view that has general support from child experts in both America and Britain is that young children between the ages of three and eight are particularly susceptible to observational learning. Milton Eisenhower's commission was concerned that this extreme observational sensitivity to the medium did not necessarily have beneficial results, because children at this age could not distinguish between reality and fantasy and believed that what they saw on television was a reflection of the real world. Young children are not cynical about television (health-giving cynicism comes later in their teens, fortunately); they love it and trust it. For reasons no one quite understands, there is a decline in viewing among children after the age of ten. Between eleven and twelve, this is especially true of the brighter child. Wilbur Schramm calls this the "yawning age." Could the boredom arise from the fact that the bright child does finally distinguish between reality and fantasy? Whatever the reason, the older child may abandon his early love. The young child is unerringly faithful. James Halloran, director of the Center for Mass Communications Research at the University of Leicester, has confirmed that the work carried out at his center backs up the Eisenhower commission's diagnosis that young children have a tendency to confuse reality and fantasy on their TV screens.

The confusion of reality and fantasy must certainly cause a child anxiety. If a young flesh-and-blood boy can come close to being smothered or crushed to death by some horrific plant from outer space—and I saw this incident in "Lost in Space" with my seven-year-old—wouldn't the child viewer believe that he, too, could be consumed by a similar sci-fi monster, maybe in his backyard when mother was busy? The nightmare potential for the young mind that cannot dissociate reality and fantasy should never be minimized.

A happier effect of television on the young child is its capacity to increase his store of information and to expand his vocabulary. In these two capacities, television is an effective educator. Probably no one who has observed a child's interest and increase of information during a televized global event would feel like quarreling with this viewpoint. I jotted down some of the words that my son, then nearly seven, began to use during that memorable week in late July 1969, after Neil Armstrong had taken his "giant step" on the moon: his new stock of words included *docking, gravity, blast-off, orbit,* and *lunar.*

The moon landing, of course, was the supreme example of the image and the word coming together on the screen. And even if children did confuse reality and fantasy on this occasion, it did not seem to matter—adults could hardly credit their eyes, either, particularly in that stunning moment when the ghostly white-booted foot first came out of the capsule searching for the moon's surface.

The pollution problem is another world development that has riveted the attention of the young. Watching the BBC news magazine program "Nationwide," a show that captures child audiences and adults alike by its convenient six o'clock timing and simple, direct approach, my son managed to accumulate a wealth of words about man's wanton destruction of his planet. I listed a few when he was eight years old and aroused to the point of nervous anxiety about pollution (a child's reaction to television is highly emotional)—*untreated sewage, industrial waste, population explosion, oil slicks, environment, carbon monoxide, pesticides, ecology.* It has been found that some of the most effective television teaching has occurred in the realm of science. As a deliverer of fact, the medium can be superb. As an instiller of feeling or emotion, its role is less well defined.

Unquestionably, today's children know a great deal about science and have impressive vocabularies to back up information gleaned from the tube. But this hopeful picture of a generally more broad-based knowledge of the world surrounding them breaks down in the matter of just how *continuous* or relevant this knowledge may be to the total store of information in their minds. In many ways, young children resemble those self-improving adults who immerse themselves in *How to Improve Your Vocabulary* manuals and end up by blinding their friends with polysyllabic words that jut up from their sentences like pylons in a flat rural landscape—incongruous, misplaced, signaling and signifying nothing that has gone on before in the sentence.

One of the most interesting studies on television as a vocabularly expander was conducted in 1960 by Dorothy Reese Montgomery, a fifth-grade teacher at a school in Carbondale, Illinois. Having been struck by the wide fund of information her nine and ten year olds seemed to have about the world, she set about trying to discover if these enriched vocabularies had done anything to clarify actual events for them, or whether in fact the children harbored misconceptions about these world happenings. She compiled a list of twenty-nine questions concerning social studies, health, and science, and gave seventeen of her students an oral test on them. Each child was asked to name the source for his answers. Not surprisingly, the majority of the answers given were stated to have come from television. For example, in the section on social studies, Miss Montgomery asked the children why pioneers had gone to live in California long ago. Five out of eight of the children answered "for gold," citing various television shows as their source of information ("The Californians" and "Wagon Train" topped the bill as the information-giver in this instance).

When the children were asked how the Wild West (or Far West) differed from their own home in midwestern Illinois, six said it was hotter and six said it was not as modern. One boy replied, rather ominously, "More gunfights." Eleven of these

thirteen answers were said to have come from television programs. The children had automatically assumed that cowboys
came from the past and therefore that the West was somehow
less modern than their own environment. This sort of time-
confusion—and therefore confusion of reality—prevailed. The
answer that the West was hotter also revealed a distortion of
fact. From having seen cowboys like James Drury in "The Vir-
ginian" or others like him loping around in blinding sun with
dust-covered boots, the children had concluded that the West
was always blazingly hot, nothing that a San Franciscan on a
foggy January day would be able to confirm.

To the question "Who makes our laws?" the children had an
amazing collection of answers; three said the president, one
judges, one the Senate, three the governor, one the state, two the
people, and six policemen. It is sadly significant that the largest
number of children selected policemen as the prime makers of
the law. The misconception here is perfectly understandable,
since the chief enforcers of the law on crime-busting programs
is usually the state trooper screeching up a highway to ap-
prehend the criminal, or else the police snapping on the hand-
cuffs at the end. It is obvious that the children had confused law
enforcement with law making.

In her investigation of how her pupils interpreted certain
words encountered on television (*prairie, award, commercial,
lawyer*), she found that she got 110 correct answers out of a
possible 170, most of them influenced by television. The children's conception of a lawyer, for instance, was always that of
a person defending someone accused of a crime. Here again,
their interpretation was very nearly right. But while you cannot fault a child for saying that a lawyer defends an accused
person, it is obvious that the complexity of the legal profession

has escaped him—that of the lawyer as financial advisor or as tool for warring parties in divorce or libel suits, among other things.

Information from television is too often a half-understood affair, as in this case. This is why thinking educators have stressed that information alone out of context is sometimes worse than useless, and that to be valuable, information per se must be aired in child-adult discussions. Miss Montgomery was alarmed to find, for example, that while her children had extensive vocabularies, they often missed the meanings of the words, and also "knew definitions of words that they could not read for themselves."

What she concluded from this short but intriguing study of her ten-year-olds was that the children had learned a great deal from television but that the information had been picked up in an isolated way "with no feeling of the continuity of these happenings."

In other words, just as we saw that language learning was most valuable in the very young child's case when it was part of a feedback process with an interested parent or adult, television information, too, is best utilized with the help of a grown person lending verbal guidance. Dr. John Condry, professor of human development and psychology at New York's Cornell University, puts it succinctly:

> Children develop intellectually by collecting information from practically every experience they have with the world around them, and then integrating this information into their own conceptual systems. . . . This, in turn, requires that the child be exposed to an increasing variety of increasingly complex experiences, and, at the same time, have the availability of feedback to correct error.

Dr. Condry then goes on to say that the major source of feedback should of course be the parent. But we can see that parents have abdicated much of their guidance role with the advent of television, and a pernicious situation has arisen; television, the information-giver, has also become the major baby-sitter and thus much information goes into the child's mind uncorrected.

I was struck forcibly by the incompleteness of television as a teacher recently when a nine-year-old boy came to stay for the weekend. He had been watching a British TV comedy program, "The Comedians," a sometimes innocuous, at other times unexpectedly blue Friday night entertainment. A music hall comedian on the program told an elaborate joke about a country grocer who, upon finding his shop egg boxes perpetually empty, goes into a nearby henhouse and says: "O.K., chicks, come on, now tell me—who's on the pill?" The boy watching with me guffawed. Amazed that he had apparently understood the reference, I asked him to explain it to me. He said: "Well, you know. The contraceptive pill. It makes eggs disappear from a woman's stomach." It transpired that he had heard a lecture on sex education at his enlightened private school in London. When he heard the egg box joke, he put this TV gag and his own knowledge together. It was an impressive mental juggling act for a nine year old, I thought. But clearly he had got hold of a huge factual error. He had understood the contraception pill to be a magical something that made existing eggs disappear like so many magician's rabbits. Neither his mother nor his teacher had bothered to clarify the actual medical truth for him: namely, that the pill was hormonal and prevented ovulation. The child had collected, sifted, and collated his information all very deftly and on his own—and come up with a half-truth.

Parents and teachers have been extremely lax in guiding their young charges in the use of television. If most Western children have become a race of passive viewers, apparently hypnotized by the "boob tube," then the adults responsible for these children can blame only themselves. In an exhaustive, fifteen-year study of Illinois pupils, Dr. Paul Witty, Northwestern University professor of education, found that "only a small percentage of the pupils indicated in 1965 that their parents counseled them regularly in the selection of TV programs." He discovered that his sampling of young people watched television an average of twenty hours a week. This meant that twenty hours of their waking week in their homes was spent in unattended TV viewing.

This fact serves to emphasize the sense of alienation that exists between parents and children, the indifference between and separation of the generations that has characterized the modern, nuclear family since the end of the World War II. In America, this phenomenon is at its most extreme, undoubtedly because there is more television to see. In other countries, as previously noted, television often does not start until the late afternoon. This may account for the sharp differences in children's viewing statistics in various countries: fourteen hours a week for the British child, for example, seven hours a week for children in Germany. The American child is the world's heaviest viewer, but children in other industrialized countries are not lagging far behind.

That parents are selfishly grateful for the electronic childminder in their homes is evidenced in a great many studies of children's viewing habits. Two American child development experts, Robert D. Hess and Harriet Coldman, backed up Dr. Witty's findings in a survey they made in 1962 of parents' views concerning the effects of their children's televiewing. They reported:

(1) In the majority of families the young child watches almost as much as he wishes, and, for the most part, views programs of his own choice.

(2) In the majority of families, mothers make little effort to supervise either program selection by the child or the total amount he watches.

(3) In most families, the father has little voice in determining the television behavior of his child.

Teachers' attitudes toward television are often ambivalent. When my daughter was ten years old and attending a private school in London, the teachers took a how-dare-you-waste-your-time-before-the-set tone that fell on the deafest of small ears. To an essay with the loaded title "Should Children Stay Up Late Watching Television?" my daughter wrote this miracle of pious hypocrisy which netted her a B+:

I think you should stay up if it is a good program on television like Nature or a good play. If you have a friend appearing on television and your mother says you can watch it, do! If you watch to all hours you will become mentally lazy. If you watch a very late horror film you must be prepared to have nightmares and feel awful in the morning.

When teachers are not adopting this how-dare-you-watch-so-much attitude, they tend to exhort each other to make better use of television programs, both the educational ones shown at school and those they know the children watch at home. American and British educational journals are filled with vaguely scolding articles leveled by teachers at other teachers for being so indifferent to the potential of television teaching. How much guidance they do in fact give or not give would be hard to ascertain. In overcrowded schools, catchment areas for children living in working-class, industrial towns, perhaps all a teacher can do is try and keep his head above water, and so he should not be blamed for not making better use of the media he has at hand. In one blackboard jungle school I visited in the Midlands, the teachers admitted using the television set as a breather during the Schools Programs, educational half-hour shows shown in grade schools and high schools. In turn, many of the children confessed to utilizing this time to do their homework. The quality of the reception was so bad, the light so inadequate (sunlight was beating on the somewhat ancient, glaucous eye of the set), that I could only sympathize with the children for using their time to better advantage.

I visited quite a few high schools in various parts of England when I was writing scripts for a series of six high school educational television programs for Granada Television, the commercial company that operates from Manchester. At one point, I was sent out to look at a "typical" school audience at a comprehensive secondary school (a mixed high school with children of varying degrees of ability streamed into different classes). This high school was located in a semi-industrial town in Berkshire, about twenty-five miles from London. The series of documentaries we were working on, called "The Facts Are These," was to be beamed at fifteen-year-olds and would be concerned with social health subjects of direct relevance to his age group (three of the topics, for instance, were "Drugs," "Cigarette Smoking," and "Venereal Disease").

The greatest problem faced by the Schools Programs producers is the complexity of the audience at the other end. With British schools "streaming" their pupils into four ability groups ranging in degrees from bright to dull, it is a challenge to try to create a program that will make some sort of impact on all of them. My producer, Pauline Shaw, thought the best way to acquaint me with my audience was to send me along to observe a school that was composed predominantly of "low-ability" students. Script-writers in the past had had a tendency to write above the students' head, it appeared.

If I had had any thoughts of writing above heads, the profile of the school I was to visit given by the official of the Independent Broadcasting Authorities' Education Department, helped to dispel them. With a clarity verging on callousness, he described the school as "a mixed bag of white and black immigrants—Italians, Poles, some West Indians—and English children of low ability, working-class sons and daughters in the lowest stream (fourth) with IQs generally of below 100."

Observing about twenty-five boys in the first group, I felt a creeping despair: the rundown given me by the official appeared to be chillingly accurate. The boys, about fourteen years of age, were watching an educational film on the British National Health Service called "Healing the People" under the surveillance of a young tousled gym teacher who had just come off the football pitch. We saw endless stills of Florence Nightingale tending wounded soldiers in the Crimea, and the boys' inattentiveness reached fever pitch. The frantic football teacher asked the boys for their opinions of the program when it had ended. There was a sort of uproar which might have been booing. Finally, one remark could be distinguished from the rest: "It was ruddy boring." When the weary young teacher asked, "*Why* did you find it boring?" the boys snapped with extraordinary vehemence, "It's boring because it's boring, that's what!" This closed the discussion.

We had much better luck with the second group of twenty-five boys and girls, this time led by an efficient young history teacher who obviously commanded respect. We were shown a program from a Granada series, "The Messengers." The series relied on film clips from well-known films to try to show how movies had philosophical and moral messages to deliver as well as entertainment. In this program, called "The Unlucky Ones," the producers tried to show children how cinema directors looked at the physically and mentally disabled. To picture the plight of the physically disabled, the producers had taken a sequence from the film *Reach for the Sky*, the true story of RAF hero Douglas Bader, who lost both legs before World War II in an airplane training accident. When Bader had his accident and the film showed the twisted wreckage, one fourteen-year-old boy commented: "Serves him right for trying to show off." The teacher winced. The film seemed to be failing in its efforts to humanize.

However, the classroom went silent at the clip of a Judy Garland film, *A Child Is Waiting*, designed to show children some scenes concerning the mentally deficient. When the teacher questioned them afterward about their feelings concerning the handicapped, they gave serious, impressive answers. One black student, a tall, overgrown boy in worn jeans, explained that some people tended to laugh at madhouse scenes or at the antics of the demented because, as he put it, "we've never experienced it." The teacher did not let up, though such answers were slow in coming, and by the end of fifteen minutes or so, the children were interrupting each other and the air was electric. The teacher then stopped guiding the discussion and let the children take over. One girl spoke of her own paralyzed younger brother and said that what was needed most in caring for him was patience.

In the space of one morning, I could hardly have been treated to a more dramatic example of the good and bad use of television in the classroom: in one case, the pathetic, jumbled, unguided use; in the other, a masterful, stimulating, imaginative handling of an emotive subject.

One of the most difficult facets of educational television is to know just how teachers are handling the programs. The British Schools Television Services sends out cards to teachers and asks for their own reactions as those of their pupils to individual programs. In many cases, the teachers do not bother to write back. We knew that one of our programs had made a great hit because we received an avalanche of teachers' postcards concerning it. In fact, we realized that our series had struck a chord because all six documentaries elicited hundreds of cards. Apparently, the teachers were grateful for the airing of problems of more immediate relevance to their pupils than, say, a leisurely stroll around the Scottish highlands or a discussion of wheat-growing in East Anglia.

In any case, to judge from the overpowering reaction, the most effective documentary in the series had been the one on VD, called "The Other Side of Love." It was the first time such a loaded subject had been filmed for adolescents in a Schools Program, though Schools Programs have been in existence in Britain since 1955 and the problem was no newcomer to this age group. Our theme had been that sexual permissiveness was the largest single cause of the epidemic, an idea that might have been new to the young viewers. We were lucky in our presenter, a frank, eloquent venerealogist from London's Middlesex Hospital who presented the facts without a trace of embarrassment or patronage. It confirmed us in our opinion that a "talking head" could engross children if the subject was gripping enough and the "head" himself possessed an attractive, direct manner.

By and large, the teachers agreed in this commendation, with the exception of one high school principal from Manchester who found the program morally unsuitable for either his girls (or his staff!) to watch; but this rather Wesleyan figure was alone in his condemnation. Talking about the program, one teacher from a high school in the Midlands who had shown it to twenty of his girl students wrote in a heartening report, a report which also revealed his own excellent capacity to guide:

1)   The class was very absorbed. Reception was clear and pace of program excellent for understanding. Very unsensational balanced approach of film was rewarded by complete lack of embarrassed giggling.

2)   Follow-up was very rewarding. Some vocabulary ("promiscuous" "groin," "confidential") need elaborating for these girls to make sure points essential to understanding were grasped.

In contrast, another teacher from a high school near Manchester who had shown the program to a classroom of 90 fifteen-year-old girls, wrote this dispirited and dispiriting little note:

1)   Girls awe-struck.
2)   Because the problem was presented as very much one which falls within the teenage range, the group experienced emotional reticence in discussion. Showed little wish to go beyond the program.

The imagination reels—to have a roomful of receptive, powerfully affected girls and to be unable to elicit any form of discussion from them on the subject afterwards! It does show that the medium must have effective, adult reinforcement as well as the message.

Perhaps in the future, television programmers and teachers could try to achieve more direct contact. The liaison between the two in both America and Britain has been astonishingly frail. Mrs. Cooney could point to having used the Educational Testing Service to gauge young children's reactions to "Sesame Street," but the ETS is a high-powered research unit unconnected in any direct way with primary school teachers. And we see that too often when a producer is asked to respond to teachers' criticisms, he or she is apt to reply with curtness and irritation.

In my own experience, I found that educators tended to be too overawed by television personnel, stunned by their technological know-how, and almost star-struck by the technicians ("My goodness, what lights do you need for color?" "What's that cable for?" "Do airplane noises ruin your sound tapes?" and so on.)

But contact of this kind is valuable, in spite of unease on both sides, because teachers, more than anyone else, are in a position to know what children are reading. Perhaps one of the most hopeful effects that television has on children is to induce them to read what they have seen dramatized on the set. There is definitely a rich cross-pollination effect between book reading and television viewing. Librarians are quick to place in stocks of books currently adapted and showing on the television screen as they know there will be a run on them. The children's librarian at the Marylebone Library off Baker Street in central London told me that she was unable to supply the demand for copies of Anna Sewell's *Black Beauty* when the BBC adapted it for the children's teatime slot on Sunday afternoons some years ago. This happened again, she said, when the BBC adapted Frances

Hodgson Burnett's *The Secret Garden* and later James Fenimore Cooper's *Last of the Mohicans.*

The same phenomenon— a rush on books being shown on TV—occurs in America. Edith Efron, writing in the *TV Guide,* quotes Mrs. Helen Prange, director of children's services in a Stamford, Connecticut, public library as saying: "When characters like Daniel Boone and Davy Crockett are on the air, there's a lot of reading on frontier life." Other U.S. children's librarians across the country reported a big return to classics adapted for TV over the past years—books such as *Treasure Island, The Legend of Sleepy Hollow* and *Little Women.*

When television first began to appear in average homes in 1949 (before that it was a rare middle-class toy, found only in the living rooms of the affluent), there was much doom talk about how it would create a generation of wholly visual, passive people. Reading would be a lost art and children would grow up wanting to be entertained rather than knowing how to make their own entertainment. Nearly twenty-five years later, we can see that those gloomy prognostications were far from accurate. The children's book trade has never been healthier, and television and children's reading converge and cross-fertilize; this cyclical motion has revivified the children's book industry and also enriched television significantly; the children's book industry was at its lowest ebb during World War II, when most people were without television.

But this is not to say that television has not had some displacement effect, to use James Halloran's good phrase. In Dr. Witty's fifteen-year study of pupils in the Chicago area, he found that much displacement of other media had taken place from 1949 to 1965. Each year, Dr. Witty and his associates questioned and interviewed the same pupils and so were able to chart the changes in their tastes over a period of time. When Dr. Witty began his study in 1949, only 43 per cent of the pupils had TV sets in their homes; by 1959, 99 per cent had television at home. He found that an average of twenty-one hours per week was reported to have been devoted to TV by elementary school pupils in 1949–1950. In 1965, the weekly average was twenty hours. The idea that children might become immune to the set, impervious to its charms from overexposure, was certainly disproved by this study. A the end of fifteen years, the average viewing time had dropped by only one hour. The staying power of the tube should never be underestimated.

Dr. Witty discovered that though his Illinois children spent so much time before the set, they had quite a lot of time left over for other media—books, radio, and films. However, their leisure entertainments had been partially displaced by TV. For example, before TV the children said they had spent fourteen hours a week listening to the radio; after TV, this was reduced to seven hours a week—or exactly half as much. Before TV, the pupils said that they had gone to the movies once a week; in 1965, they said they had gone every two weeks. Going to the movies still seemed a great treat. That year they reported liking *Mary Poppins* better than any other film by far, followed by the James Bond film *Goldfinger* and then *My Fair Lady*.

Dr. Witty found no diminution in the amount of time the children spent reading in the course of his fifteen years of study. In fact, 25 per cent of ten- and eleven-year-olds said that TV had led them to read certain books—they cited *Little Women, Tom Sawyer, Robin Hood,* and *Heidi,* among others. His findings have been corroborated by U.S. children's librarians. Writing in the journal *Educational Leadership* in 1956, shortly after TV began to be watched on a national scale and at the point when one might assume that it would be most likely to kill the reading habit, educator Arnold L. Lazarus wrote: "Whether because of TV or in spite of it, youngsters (both elementary and secondary) are reading more than ever, according to unanimous reports of librarians (school and public)."

An even more unexpected feature of television's effect—or noneffect as the case may be—is that it has not adversely affected children's school performances; and this in spite of the predictions of those gloomy Cassandras who claimed it would create a race of mindless zombies. Success in school has been studied repeatedly in relationship to the amount of time spent watching television, and little correlation has been reported except at the extremes of brightness or dullness (a very bright child tails off dramatically in his television viewing after the age of twelve, for instance; a slow child may increase his fare as he edges into his teens and his work shows a corresponding deterioration). However, for the majority of children, heavy television viewing and schoolwork go together in unexpectedly happy harmony. As Wilbur Schramm has concluded: "On the basis of data on hand, we cannot say that heavy television viewing, at any stage of the elementary school, significantly lowers school grades."

It may well be that what we have in the modern child is a multimedia creature. One of the BBC's most imaginative children's TV producers, Patrick Dowling, whose program "Vision On" won the British Children's Entertainment Award in 1970, believes that children can absorb a great variety of images and visual stimuli. His program is entirely visual. In it, Dowling wraps quick, rapid-fire "Laugh-In" type images around one central theme each program.

"Before I saw 'Laugh-In,' he told me in a recent interview, "I assumed that if you belted images too quickly at people, particularly children, you drove them away. But then I realized that kids loved running along behind and trying to catch up. You can bore them stiff by making things too slow. I try to get at the edge of their minds. Kids are rather grasshoppery. They like absorbing impressions from a number of different images simultaneously. Ever seen a child read, listen to music, and watch TV all at the same time? He *can* do it. It's fun making a program that short-circuits the need for speech and, of course, focusing on the arts was the obvious answer. We get a lot of letters from Indian and West Indian kids, maybe because we by-pass any language difficulties they might have."

I like Patrick Dowling's description of the modern child as having a "grasshoppery" kind of mind. It is true that he has (whether this is good for his emotional development is something else, a matter I will discuss later). He can listen to the radio, watch TV with the sound-track off, and read a comic at the same time. Just to add to the multimedia feel of it all, he may be reading a comic based on a TV cartoon character. In fact, he is almost sure to be doing so, because some of the most successful comic books to date are those that spin out the further adventures of a television favorite; the comic book industry has grown fat recently by feeding off television, particularly for the under-ten group.* Joe Barbera and William Hanna, the creators of those happy suburban neanderthals the Flintstones, that feisty, fighting pair, Tom and Jerry, and that endearing gourmand, Yogi Bear, among a wealth of others, employ six hundred people to keep their cartoon industry going, an industry that straddles both the media, TV, and comic books.

---

*This is not true of the adolescent love comics which thrive independently on teen-age sentimentality.

Another brilliant cartoonist who has thrived on the existence of the multimedia child is Charles Schulz. Appreciating "Peanuts" as I do, I recall feeling a distinct sensation of satiety with Lucy, Linus, and Charlie Brown one week when I encountered them with my children on TV, at a neighborhood film show, and in my Sunday newspaper. I have never heard a child query this extensive spreading about of adored cartoon characters; they are so used to the phenomenon that they have ceased to find it either unusual or worthy of comment. Television is such a remarkable medium that it can even resuscitate long-dead characters—darlings of my youth like Laurel and Hardy. Doubtless the two deceased comedians would appreciate their comeback if they were around to witness it.

In sum, then, what do we know about TV's effect on the young child's intellectual development? He still reads copiously. He still studies. He may even have a few television-inspired hobbies. His vocabulary may be richer. His knowledge of his universe is certainly greater than that of his pre–television era predecessor. Pointing to these optimistic findings, why does anyone worry about the effects of television? Hasn't Frankenstein's monster turned out to be almost cuddly?

Well, not quite. While we can see that television does not inflict intellectual damage—and especially not when combined with adult supervision—it may have a deleterious effect on a child's emotions and behavior. While it may make children a bit brighter, is it blunting his sensibilities? This is the frightening question, the gray area of investigation into TV's effect.

9

TV and the Child's
Emotional Development

What do we know about a young child's reactions to television? Well, to state the most obvious fact, we certainly know that he loves watching it. Most preschoolers will order their days around the set, and mothers tend to go along with this daily focus of interest, especially if the child is not at nursery school, kindergarten, or a day-care center. We also know that a child's near fixation with the set is a highly charged one. Most mothers are familiar with "television tears," those fits of a child's weepiness when they cannot make it back from shopping in time for a special show. Even an affectionate, reasonably easygoing child can register an enormous amount of hostility if a mother has bungled his or her date with a particular program. And in this era of diminished use of spanking and other forms of corporal punishment (for which, thank God), mothers rely shamelessly upon their child's desire for TV viewing to impose restrictions and mete out discipline ("If you do that *once* more, Jane, it's right to bed with no more television . . . ," etc.). It is an effective if lazy way of holding maternal sway.

Few mothers would deny that they depend on the set for the maintenance of order and harmony in their homes; for proof of this, talk to any parent with young children whose set has just broken down. As the British child psychologists John and Elizabeth Newson discovered in their husband-wife team study of 700 four-year-olds in Nottingham, the pattern of much family life, especially in the evenings, was geared more to the television set than to any parental tastes. A miner's wife described her boy's bedtime schedule to the Newsons in the following way: "Well, it's half past six Mondays; seven o'clock on Tuesdays, six-thirty Wednesdays; six-thirty Thursdays and seven o'clock on Friday; and in the weekends it's six-thirty. It's all to fit the television, you see."

A modern Western child's life would be almost inconceivable without television. As one eight-year-old primary school boy wrote in an American teacher's magazine: "In prehistoric times, before there was TV. . . ."

The only period when parents can seduce children away from the set is at vacation time. Assuming that they can afford to take them away from home to a place that is rural, mountainous, or by the sea, they may see them flowering, once they are away from an all-day electronic diet. Removed from their constricted city apartment and the tube, they may begin developing new hobbies—drawing,   reading,   listening   to   music—possibly becoming more reflective, or staying out of doors for longer periods of time. My own two discovered classical music, Kipling, blackberries, butterflies, and the existence of a bizarre red-and-black artichoke-loving beetle, one summer in the south of France when we had a month of freedom from television's tyranny (and though I have played a part in creating television programs for children, I still reserve the right to hate it at times).

The inchoate, rather shadowy dislike I felt for the TV screen that time in France, absorbed as I was in watching my children developing new interests, is mirrored in what many psychiatrists I have spoken to feel about television's pull. Mrs. Mary Pears, educational psychologist at a clinic in Southwest London, told me that she distrusted television's power to impinge upon a child's mind and time. She explained that the word *impingement* was a favorite of the late Freudian child analyst, Dr. Donald Winnicott, who used it to describe what a mother should *not* do, that is, flap around a child, talking at him and distracting him at a time when he clearly needs to be quiet, to be inward. Quiet times like this are essential to a child's creative growth. Mrs. Pears feels that TV, like a distracting, garrulous, overbusy mother, impinges upon a child to his detriment.

"Poor children, when are they ever going to play again?" Mrs. Pears asked. "I'm thoroughly tired of all this overstimulation of the young child. They are not being given the space to be themselves. What bothers me is this emphasis upon learning rather than development. The foundation of learning is creative play. And television does take time away from a child's creative play. Children who are impinged upon too often may have a false sense of self. Worst of all, they can lose touch with their own springs. Children must *be* before they can *do*."

Mrs. Pears's feelings about television's powers of impingement have been echoed by many of her fellow practitioners in the field. In his article lambasting "Sesame Street," Samuel Kliger, specialist in early childhood education, speaks of the worst of children's television, the kind that produces an onrush of stimuli: "Sensations pour in on the child," he writes. "If *all* sensations were received, pattern or form perception would be impossible. There has to be selection and suppression."

To understand why so many child psychologists and psychiatrists feel an aversion to this "inpour of sensations," it is useful to review what Winnicott had to say about the necessity for child's play. He wrote:

> a child gains experience in play, continuous evidence of creativity. Play provides an organization for the initiation of emotional relationships. . . . a child in play may be trying to display at least some of the inside as well as the outside to chosen people in the environment—an attempt to communicate some of the unconscious, the repressed.

In Winnicott's view, play is essential to a child's mental health because it enables him to express a hateful or aggressive urge without fear or arousing his mother's ire and his own subsequent feelings of guilt. A child can say, "Bang, bang! You're dead," to his mother, for example, and be pretty sure she will not take him too seriously, though he might have wanted to hurt her at the moment. Playing also helps a child to develop his own imagination, to air his fantasies; it is a great antidote to repression. Television therefore can impinge on a child's development merely by robbing him of the ability or the time to fantasize for himself. It can also take away the time he needs for acting out his own anxieties and aggressions in play.

Another disturbing factor about television's effect on the emotional development of the young child is that it presents a confusion of fantasy from fact. Most children in play enter into a fantasy with gusto, but the mere fact of being in "play"—playing fathers and mothers, or kings and queens, or mountain climbers and explorers, or cowboys and Indians—enables them to dissociate fact from fiction. When a child dresses up and reenacts some fantasy role, he may suspend his disbelief while he is doing it—seriously think he is a king or a queen in that moment—but when he removes his dress-up clothes, he steps back into reality again. And when a child "kills" a playmate with an arrow or a pistol, he knows that his friend is going to come to life after an orderly interval.

In play, a child can order his world, and his fantasies can be trotted out and neatly put away again. And worrisome situations, like the "death" of the playmate friend, can by rectified. Young children have a desperate need to see wrong situations righted. That something or someone can be damaged irreparably shocks a young child deeply.

The child who is let loose with the set, who watches for hours in an unsupervised way, is going to witness a great many messy situations that are not going to be tidied up at the end. As he confuses reality and fantasy on the screen, he is not going to believe that that pleasant cowboy who has been nastily disposed of by the bearded villain in the desert gunfight is ever going to come alive again, or that all that red sticky ooze on his face and jacket is just tomato catsup. As a consequence, he may be made desperately anxious by the seemingly unjust death of a good man. The potential for the build-up of anxiety in a child who is watching constant scenes of irreparable harm and damage is incalculable.

In addition, young children have a curious propensity to keep their television thoughts to themselves. Television does seem to produce a hush in a child. This is not really surprising. He is told to sit down in front of the set and be quiet at least a hundred times a year. Curiously, he may also tend to be quiet about what he sees, as if, subliminally, the idea of *being quiet during* and *being quiet about* were linked in his mind. And we know that children do respond with intense emotionalism to what they see filmed. Tests made by Georgia University's Dr. Keith Osborn and a colleague on four- and five-year-olds watching a bloodthirsty cartoon ("Spiderman" in this case) revealed copious hand sweating among them. Only when Dr. Osborn assured them that what they had seen "didn't really happen, was just pretend," did they seem to calm down and the physical symptoms of panic subside.

Older children do not need this degree of adult reassurance, since they are much more aware of what is real and what is make-believe. They also tend to air their fears in discussion with their friends. For example, a timorous nine-year-old boy I know got rid of some of his apprehension about the scary BBC children's science fiction program, "Dr. Who," when he talked it over with a chum in the back of the car on one of my car pool days chauffeuring neighboring boys to my son's school. The conversation went something like this:

Cocky, unafraid boy: Oh, you're nutty to be afraid of the monsters in "Dr. Who." They're just men all covered in pasta. That's not real slime. It's just macaroni and spaghetti and things.

Timorous boy: Great. Who wants to be chased on a
                       dark night by a man covered with
                       spaghetti?

It is one of the beauties of the individual child, which no amount of modern technology can dissipate, that no one young person is going to be frightened by exactly the same thing as another. Long before TV became every child's best friend, other media could produce a high ratio of fear in the child viewers (TV must not always be the chief whipping-boy). Walt Disney's two films *Bambi* and *Snow White* had an immense fear-producing content for the children of my generation. That they raised hackles was certainly true, though I do not recall any two children being terrified by the same incident: some were frightened by the wicked witch's warts and wens in *Snow White*, others by her bloodcurdling plunge from the cliff, others by the scream she gave when she hurtled down, and so on. In *Bambi*, which was not meant to terrify, I am sure, but certainly succeeded in doing so, some were horrified by the gunshot sounds of the approaching predator, man, others by the forest fire, a few by the death of Bambi's mother, and then again others by the sudden appearance of the awesome stag who turned out to be his father.

Some psychiatrists argue that fear can be cathartic for a child, that it is not necessary to be overprotective, that he will run up against conflicts and shocks in his later life and therefore should not be unduly sheltered in his early years. I cannot subscribe to this argument, certainly not for the very young child. Anything that produces unease and anxiety, nightmares, or fear of the dark cannot be welcomed. Professor Hilde Himmelweit is dubious about the cathartic value of violence on television, even for the older child: "After all, he can't identify with every murderer and robber shown," she says.

Granted, a mother cannot always predict what will frighten her child or protect him endlessly from sources of fear and confusion. Still, it would help if a mother were more on tap at TV time and relied on it less as a custodian. Even if she were to avail herself of the descriptive blurb concerning a program in the weekly television guide, it would be helpful, for she could steer her child away from something patently unsuitable. She should be chary of the medium. While valuing it as a superb source of information and a vocabulary expander, she would do well to remember that it *does* increase the confusion in a child's mind, act upon his emotions, rob him of therapeutic play time, and, perhaps worst of all, deprive him of time to have a dialogue with her.

Wilbur Schramm and his colleagues suggested that television has had such an impact on the young child because it satisfied his hunger for fantasy. This may be true, and undeniably this is part of its enormous power over children. But canned fantasies going endlessly unexplained and delivered unilaterally from an electronic device to a growing human mind can have an unwholesome effect, too. As Dr. Norman Paul, specialist in family psychotherapy and member of the Department of Psychiatry at the Harvard Medical School, writes:

Television may lead a child to withdraw from the real world by confusing him—and compounding his own confusion between real life and fantasy and thus causing him trouble in coping with the real world. . . . All too evident are the patterns of unreality that come to children through television. A child who accepts the fantasies of television as real may well absorb the idea that larger animals and people are fair game for wily cartoon mice and rabbits who gleefully impose all forms of physical mayhem upon their natural adversaries; that the western shoot-up in a saloon is the way to settle disputes; that international problems are resolved by covert theft and blackmail, hair-raising chases and ultimate murder. . . . Such questions bring us back again to the role of parents in providing empathy and a reality input to counter the fantasy of programing.

One would imagine, since a child is exposed all day to a barrage of fantasies, that he would become blasé about them, that they would lose their impact. However, this does not seem to happen. The preschooler brings fresh emotions, intensity of feeling, and endless receptiveness to the set. The real tragedy up to the present is that he has brought so much to so little.

Eleanor Maccoby, American psychologist, has stated that it is perfectly reasonable to generalize about young children's viewing habits because, as a group, their reactions to the visual images on the set are highly subjective. Their capacity to identify and empathize with screen characters is enormous, in her view. As she says:

There is reason to believe that children's attitudes and beliefs can be shaped by what they see on television, and that emotions and impulses are aroused in the child viewer to match those portrayed by screen characters; it is a reasonable conjecture that a child responds in kind to the emotional states depicted on the screen.

She goes on to hypothesize that if a child responds emotionally to the characters he sees, it is also possible that the child may attempt to match the behavior of that model, though not in a strict one-to-one way.

That children have a dynamic response to the set has been known for a long time by the commercial men, the keen salesmen who know an impressionable audience when they see one. Saturday morning advertising on television in the United States represents $20 million in network revenue and reaches 12.2 million homes and 15.6 million children aged two to eleven. A network station on this weekend morning usually includes eighteen commercials in one hour's viewing time. These commercials take up about a quarter of the entire broadcast time. And young children are extremely trusting about the products that are flashed on the screen to seduce their young tastes. Even the most dovelike mothers had to trot out and buy Action Man because of the extensive advertising campaign on his behalf —mothers who detested his kit full of war gear (what were they, anyway? a fragging apparatus? a miniature defoliant? Gelignite for urban bombings?).

And as for trying to tell children that all those cereals advertised on TV have little or no nutritional value except for the milk poured over them, convincing evangelists that God may not live would be easier. Children do make decisive value judgments from television, and they can be easily persuaded that a product is good. And the subsequent nudging of parents to buy the commodity follows naturally. One U.S. market research company discovered that "70 per cent of the kids ask their parents to buy products advertised on television and that 89 per cent of the parents *do* it." As this is the era when parents spoil their children materially but neglect them emotionally, these statistics come as no surprise.

American parents have been notoriously apathetic about television's commercial assault upon their children. When the Roper survey was commissioned by the Television Information

Office, the public-relations section of the National Association of Broadcasters, in the early 1970s to assess the effects of television advertising on children and to find out what parents thought about it, the following conclusion was drawn: "74 per cent of adult Americans approve the principle of commercial sponsorship and support of children's television programs." Apparently, the urging of the Boston suburban-based watchdog group, Action for Children's Television, to "Turn Off Television Saturdays" was leaving many parents unmoved.

But parents would do well to be less complacent about the commercial fare beamed at their young. Much of it is misleading. As the crusader for better nutrition, Robert B. Choate, wrote when he charged the breakfast cereal makers with duping young children about the actual nutritional value of cereals before the U.S. Senate's consumer committee:

> Their koala bear, says Cocoa Krispies, gives you good wind: and their Sugar Smacks suggests that it can remove the hole from your paddle and get you correctly to anticipate the next bounce of the ball. Kellogg's Apple Jacks so invigorates that kids roll up hill, and General Mills' Cheerios "makes you feel groovy all morning long." General Foods' Honeycombs bribes you with an offer of fast automobiles, and Lucky Charms is described as "the frosted oat cereal with hearts, moons, stars, clovers . . . they're magically delicious."

That advertisers' florid, hyperbolic claims can lead children down strange consumer byways was confirmed by a report published during the Christmas season in 1971 by the British Advisory Center for Education (known as ACE). This report revealed that the TV advertisers' wiles had induced little girls to believe they needed deodorants and perfume. In an announcement in the London *Sunday Times,* ACE had asked children to write to "Father Christmas" and had received a thousand replies. The content of these replies led the ACE director, Brian Jackson, to believe that television advertisements were encouraging children to expect expensive Christmas presents that would do nothing to encourage their developmental skills. He found that the most preferred toy for girls was "beautiful Chrissy with wonderful hair," while boys went for Action Man dolls and Raleigh Chopper bicycles (the latter setting a parent back by about forty pounds, or a hundred dollars).

What disturbed Mr. Jackson most about the influence of television advertising on children was that it seemed to give little girls, in particular, a grotesque and precocious idea of their needs.

It is troubling to see six-year-old girls writing to Father Christmas for "sexy" boots or pop records. A lot of girls are asking for "pureplume" (perfume?) or the latest face powder, and a teenage concern with body odor seems to have been successfully planted on little girls by mass advertising.

He added that children had become "midget consumers, demanding expensive, extensive and ephemeral possessions" *

Parents might be better advised to spend less, to give them surprises rather than fulfil the child's shopping list—and to present things which are likely to help the child's developing skills and

---

*Ron Goulart's book, *The Assault on Childhood,* published in 1970, was one of the first to emphasize that young children have been converted into avid consumers and were being manipulated by the adult advertisers.

satisfactions—footballs, ice skates, paints, a record and above all, good, exciting books.

For a prepubertal child to long for a deodorant does suggest that a successful rape of the mind has been perpetrated. Television advertisements can give a child a gross distortion of what his or her needs really are. For children to long for consumer goods that do them little nutritional good (chocolates create cavities, cereals can fatten, soft drinks fatten *and* create cavities) also suggests that a medium that sets itself up to educate the young—or professes to do so as a spin-off of entertainment—is in fact callously misguiding them. The U.S. Council on Children, Media, and Merchandising reports that children watching television receive twenty advertisements per hour, ten of which usually deal with what the child should eat or drink, with soft drinks and sweets predominating. "These advertisements are doubly offensive," the council stressed, "because they lead a child away from the ABC's of nutrition and, at the rate of 5,000 advertisements per year, stress the energy rewards of nutritionally questionable sugared products."

Mr. Choate's outrage at the cereal manufacturers was similar to the council's. What infuriated him the most about their advertisements, for instance, was that they led children away from genuine nutritional knowledge, not toward it. He underlined the need for *all* branches of the television industry to feel a sense of responsibility toward the young.

The programmers would be wise to assess the soundness of the advertisements accompanying their shows, as he advised. It is foolhardy to have a well-conceived and instructional children's television program that is cut across by advertisements that may ultimately help young viewers to rot their teeth or become obese. Advertisements that help to disseminate health misinformation in any way should be screened out of children's programs.

One of the most pernicious forms of advertising seen by the young is the "have-a-quick-pill-to-pull-yourself-together" variety. It has been suggested by some experts that the epidemic of drug-taking among American teenagers can be traced back to an early youth before the set where pills were extolled all day as impeccable panaceas for life's ills.

Another potentially corrupting facet of TV advertising for children is its capacity to create a desire for the expensive and transitory (anyone who has had a costly mechanical toy or a battery-propelled engine in the house will know of their built-in obsolescence). If a child feels he has a right to an expensive toy, it is self-evident that he will also experience grave disappointment and bitterness if he does not get it. And if a friend or schoolmate does, excoriating envy follows.

Envy in a consumer society is a difficult characteristic to eradicate, especially when it begins at the nursery school age. Some sociologists believe that consumer envy is often at the root of rising juvenile and adult crime—the why-can't-I-have-a-piece-of-the-pie-too kind of thinking that logically follows an all-day TV diet of goodies brandished on the set. It is also perfectly possible that part of the black detestation of the white has come from decades of watching "whitey" spinning around in his car or speedboat, fastening the gold watch on his wrist, getting his deep-freeze unit or dishwasher. The supermarket lootings in the Detroit, Milwaukee, and other urban ghettos in the summer rioting and fires of 1968 and 1969 were an apotheosis of consumer envy mixed with racial hatred—the logical end result of having commercial luxury goods dangled hopelessly before one by a white society.

Certainly the effects of TV advertising have not been fully

investigated, and the advertisers are obviously guided more by the profit motive than by any altruism. But this will have to change. As the ACE report stated: "While it may be harmless or within the field of individual freedom to sell and buy, the effects of advertising seem striking, of dubious value, and in need of discussion."

But for the alarmed parent who does not feel like buying her child sexy boots or Lanvin perfume, there is a ray of hope in the blessed cynicism that comes with adolescence. Dr. Scott Ward of the Harvard Business School studied the reactions of 1,094 adolescents aged twelve to seventeen years and found that they were not "hapless victims of the tube." They were stern judges of the commercials, he discovered, using words like *stupidity*, *fake*, and *hypocritical* to describe them. A keen sense of values and a discernment of what was honest and what was dishonest governed their opinions. As a group, they were unequivocally hostile to cigarette advertising because they saw it as hypocritical and insulting to their intelligence. Their favorite ads were the ones which were "funny" and slightly satirical about the product being sold.

And some children need not necessarily be into their more skeptical teens before they begin to doubt the high-flown claims of the TV commercials. As Grace and Fred Hechinger wrote of their five-year-old son John in a *New York Times Magazine* article in February 1972, entitled "Why Daddy Rushes Home to Watch Batman," "he was learning fast." Airing his doubts succinctly, John told his parents, "Everything what they advertise on TV breaks a lot."

Television advertising is not the sole culprit in the game of child-mind seduction, only the most potent because it is the one that has the largest amount of time to play upon its young audience. Businesses also grow fat upon television's power to woo. The pie can be divided up in remarkable ways. The BBC, which prides itself on not being directly commercial, with no ads on its state-owned network, dips into the market place all the same. Recently, a London businessman thought of the idea of marketing toothpaste in tubes shaped like the characters in "Camberwick Green," a BBC program for the under-fives which features puppet goings-on in a country village. Sixty per cent of the profits go to the business executive and forty per cent to the BBC. In the late 1960s, Century 21 Merchandising, a subsidiary of Associated Television, the British commercial company, linked up with a candy manufacturer and sold forty million packets of sugar cigarettes each week containing Thunderbirds picture cards based on an animated puppet program, selling them at that brisk rate as long as the series ran.

"Sesame Street" was no stranger to the joys of commercial proliferation, either, in spite of its lofty educational aspirations. In one "Sesame Street" sales catalogue, coyly called *The Preschool Things Catalog*, parents are offered a "Sesame Street" Learning Kit ($19.95), a Frog Beanbag Creature Seat ($75.00), a Clown Learning Mural ($10.00), "Sesame Street" Sound Effects ($5.00), and more than fifty other items. The toys and games are inventive and even educational, as the catalog indicates, but behind it all is the unmistakable sound of a cash register ringing.

The realization that appetite comes with eating for young children ("Mummy, give me a record of the show, a doll from the show, a toothpaste tube from the show, some candy that shows me a picture card of the show," etc., etc.) has exploded into the minds of the world's businessmen like a depth charge. If a young child's mind is being neglected by TV, his mother's purse is not.

All the arguments that television has no serious impact on children's behavior tend to look a bit specious when you gauge the enormous pulling power of television advertising on young children. If the advertisers can pour money into advertising for children, then they know it has an effect, for, to put it mildly, they are loath as a group to throw money away.

The wide-eyed innocence of the television industry about its own effects ("What, us? Create more violence?") has not always been swallowed by the less gullible members of society. In a February 1969 issue of the *TV Guide*, Senator Claiborne Pell, Democratic senator from Rhode Island, made a slashing criticism of the networks' curious propensity to fence-sit and equivocate on the subject of whether or not there is a connection between violence seen on the set and actual violence:

> ... the television industry has itself answered the question affirmatively. Its financial foundation rests entirely upon the principle that television does influence the minds and actions of people. Fortunes have been spent to prove the proposition that advertising campaigns can induce people to buy products. ... If this is meaningless, if television advertising does not induce people to do things, then should we not happily dispense with advertising, end the shrill demands upon our attention and presumably reduce the cost of the products it sells? Unthinkable? Perhaps.
>
> But, if unthinkable, the industry is then left with the untenable position that its advertising time can motivate people but its programing time does not.

The statistics about how many crimes of violence an American child will witness before he reaches his early teens are harrowing. According to Nicholas Johnson, commissioner of the Federal Communications Commission (FCC), if a child is an average viewer, he will see twelve thousand human beings annihilated annually on his set. The FCC has always been a worthy gadfly to the television networks, and Mr. Johnson's predecessor, Newton Minow, was no exception. In one emotional outburst, he said: "Children will watch anything, and when a broadcaster uses crime and violence and other shoddy devices to monopolize a child's attention, it's worse than taking candy from a baby—it is taking precious time from the process of growing up."

While children's programs per se are not loaded with murders and gore (unless you count the Tom and Jerry type of cartoon where the two characters spend a lot of time flattening each other out under slabs of concrete and such), the snag is that children watch adult television as well as their own. The U.S. networks themselves estimate that they have a child audience of 26.7 million in the early evenings. Two rather self-punishing southerners, Dr. Keith Osborn of the University of Georgia's Department of Child Development, and William Hale, a Georgia educational TV station manager, watched two weeks' worth of television, week 1 in 1968 and week 2 in 1969. During week 1 they observed 95 killings and during week 2, 83 killings. Their total viewing time was 179 hours, and their kill rate 178 deaths. This led them to the only marginally comforting conclusion that the kill rate had gone down by about one-third in a year's time, though the average was still one killing per viewing hour.* They assumed that the crimes of violence had diminished

---

*In so-called gentler Britain, the scene regarding televised violence is not much better; Christopher Ward, writing in the London *Daily Mirror* of April 26, 1972, reported 3,687 instances of torture on the screen in the year 1971.

from 1968 to 1969 because of the findings of Milton Eisenhower's Commission on the Causes and Prevention of Violence published in September 1969. The commission emphasized that American viewers had been exposed to a high degree of televised violence in 1968 and concluded:

> Television portrays a world in which "good guys" and "bad guys" alike use violence to solve problems and achieve goals. Violence is rarely presented as illegal or socially unacceptable. Indeed, as often as not, it is portrayed as a legitimate means for attaining desired ends. Moreover, the painful consequences of violence are underplayed, and de-emphasized by the "sanitized" way in which much of it is presented.

Whether children copy the violence they see on television or not is something that is still being heatedly discussed among those who specialize in work with children or the study of child behavior. No definitive proof either way has yet been found, though passionate and conflicting theories abound. Those who believe in the direct connection theory point to the copycat crimes that have occurred as a result of various crime-ridden television series. In the spring of 1971, for example, a group of fourteen- and fifteen-year-old boys were arrested in Washington, D.C., for robbery. These accomplished young thieves were happy to confess that they had picked up their elaborate and skillful techniques from the TV program "It Takes a Thief."

One student of children's behavior who believes that young people definitely do imitate the aggressive behavior they see on the TV set is Albert Bandura, professor of psychology at Stanford University, who completed a study on the effects of television on preschool children in 1965. In his study, Dr. Bandura selected three groups of nursery school children from the Stanford University nursery. One group saw a real adult assault a huge plastic clown, called a Bobo doll, with every ounce of violence he could muster. The second group watched this same situation on film, and the third group did not witness the violence on the clown doll either in real life or on the screen. After this, Dr. Bandura gave the three groups of children a wide selection of toys to play with, including the Bobo doll. Many of the toys were of an aggressive nature: pistols, hammers, mallets, guns. The children in the two groups that had seen the clown doll being battered in actuality and on the screen set about bashing it with a great show of relish, hitting it all over with mallets and hammers. Those in the third group who had not seen the clown abused played quietly and unaggressively with the more peaceful toys.

While this study seems to bear out the contention that children do imitate the screened violence they see, experts in child development who take an opposite view have pointed out that the child in an experimental setting guesses that he has been given a free hand to be as aggressive as he pleases. They emphasize that the punching bag type of toy can be a delight to knock about, in any case, and children realize that what they are doing is not really harmful.

Others have pointed out that even serious film studies of human behavior which have not pandered to tastes for violence have elicited psychopathic copycat behavior. Dr. Keith Osborn and a colleague writing jointly in an October 1970 issue of *Young Children* recall an incident at a southern college where a disturbed freshman burned down the college chapel by putting a lighted cigarette in a full box of matches and placing it near some old rags, a technique he later confessed he had learned from the classic war film *Stalag 17*. One has to assume in this case that the freshman himself was emotionally disturbed and that if *Stalag 17* had not encouraged his arsonist tendencies, something else would have. The psychiatrists and sociologists who tend to the view that it is the person who is sick first and not the program or the film, and who believe that the behavioral cause-and-effect relationship is slight, often profess themselves weary of hearing television made the chief scapegoat for the fact of increased violence in society.

Professor Hilde Himmelweit, for instance, has come out strongly against those who blame television for society's ills: "It is cheap, easy and dramatic to pick on television," she feels. In spite of this belief that television is unjustly criticized, she has urged that the networks modify their screened violence, especially before 9 P.M. "There's an awful lot of knocking about before nine o'clock in the evening . . . kitchen and living room violence with which children can identify," she commented in a newspaper interview.

On the basis of her studies, she found that children were most disturbed when they witnessed violence in a real setting that they could recognize, as opposed to, say, costume drama violence. She discovered that children reacted emotionally and powerfully to careful camera close-ups, crescendos of music, and the horrified look of bystanders. They responded much more to a stabbing than a shooting, she noted.

Her overall conclusion about television's effect is that it does not initiate behavior, it merely "stamps it in." James Halloran's studies on British adolescents' tastes in television programs tend to back up Professor Himmelweit's view. He found that the slow-witted, disturbed, and aggressive boy tended to favor the more gory Westerns. Most of the British research on the subject of children's tastes in television and the effects of the medium on their behavior has tended to corroborate the view that television merely works on an already existing personality constellation, and that it does not in itself implant emotional characteristics.

Don Harper of London's Imperial College, who with his colleagues Professor Himmelweit and Dr. Joan Munro, has published an essay on the personality factors associated with children's tastes in TV, summed up what they had felt about children's reactions: "Television can't alter a child's basic personality. It might change some of his opinions and attitudes, but definitely not his character. There was evidence in our study that the kind of personality the child has influences the types of programs he chooses to watch. A child brings his personality to the set, not the other way round."

Wilbur Schramm, Hilde Himmelweit, James Halloran, et al., have found that younger and less intellectually capable children, and usually those from working-class backgrounds, tend to prefer programs of fantasy over programs of reality. Their studies confirmed the existence of a relationship between a child's own anxieties and aggressiveness and his choice of program; usually children with high anxiety and aggressiveness prefer programs carrying a high content of violence and mayhem.

This impressive collective belief in the theory that television works on a child's personality by accentuating traits that are already present rather than creating them was best expressed as early as 1960 by Joseph T. Klapper in his study *The Effects of Mass Communication.* In it, he wrote:

The results of several studies indicate that exposure to crime and violence in the media is not a crucial determinant of behavior nor

202 *A Time to Learn*

of attitudes which might be manifested in behavior. On the other hand, there are indications that such fare may serve special functions for those who are already socially maladjusted.

The danger potential of television, then, seems to be that it may fall upon fertile ground in the form of a previously disturbed child.

One of the most encouraging developments in the field of children's TV is that the networks finally seem to be listening to the academics and psychologists. This was made clear when the British Independent Television Authority issued its 1972 code on violence for its producers, warning them to soft-pedal shows of violence, especially before 9 P.M. Significantly, the code cautioned producers to remember that they were presenting their material to "vulnerable viewers," young people who were socially or emotionally insecure, and who tended to be more dependent on TV than others. The BBC followed this announcement in March 1972 with a similarly cautious code for children stating that details of fights and weapons and scenes of bloodshed should be avoided. It warned its producers not to make the "good guys" employ the same tactics as the "bad guys," and said that "violence ought not to be presented in ways which might glorify it or present it as a proper solution to inter-personal conflicts."

These codes reveal that the networks are becoming increasingly aware of their responsibility to the viewing child. The ITA code and its reference to the emotionally vulnerable child gives us echoes of Klapper and Himmelweit; the BBC warning against the parading of easy solutions through violence shows a deference for the findings of the Eisenhower Commission. In the United States, the same concern for children's welfare is being revealed with the setting up of watchdog bodies composed of experts and parents alike, such as the excellent Action for Children's Television. Another promising development in North America is the establishment of a consortium composed of thirteen American and Canadian TV agencies, educational networks, and community stations, which are producing in-school series for five- to seven-year-olds dedicated to taking the child beyond the classroom, to extending his knowledge of other environments, and to encouraging his aesthetic sense. The series is called "Ripples" and is being produced by the Northern Virginia Educational Television Association in connection with National Instructional Television (NIT). In this series of 36 fifteen-minute color programs for children in kindergarten, the producers have attempted to extend children's feelings of sympathy and appreciation of natural beauty. In commenting on "Ripples," Dr. Rose Mukerji, chief consultant for the Early Childhood Project of NIT, has emphasized that television for children must concentrate more on their emotions (as "Ripples" does) and stress "human values, human feelings, esthetic qualities, as well as knowledge . . . with . . . *affective* content as well as *cognitive.*"

Increasingly, people like Dr. Mukerji and others are beginning to realize that while television can desensitize a child's emotions, make him callous and indifferent to sights of human suffering because he sees so much of it on the screen, it can also humanize him. The "Sesame Street" producers knew this when they shot scenes of woodland animals little known to city children. The spectacle of good mothering—a mare tending her colt, a golden retriever playing with her puppies—is a salve to neglected children in high-rise apartments and slums. Children are also keenly sympathetic to the plight of handicapped children of their own age or to contemporaries rendered miserable by natural disasters or wars. The London commercial company Thames Television tapped the spontaneous humanity of thousands of children when it took the bold and experimental step of showing a day in the life of a mentally handicapped four-year-old called David through the eyes of his twelve-year-old sister —and this was exhibited during normal children's entertainment time. The company was flooded with children's letters asking if they could help David.

We must accept that television is here to stay and that it is central to the lives of our children. However, if it is to be humanizing rather than brutalizing, producers must continue to be more aware of the complex emotional makeup of their young viewers and design their programs with sensitivity and caution. It is too crucial a medium for millions of neglected children to be conceived in ignorance of children's feelings, or merely for commercial gain.

10

Children's Literature Today: Changing Patterns

A child's first book may greatly influence his young unconscious mind. He can identify with a hero or heroine—or be left blank and unmoved—but some book, special to him, coming to him at a crucial time in his emotional development, may go a long way toward shaping his view of life and his surroundings.

Considering how emotive books are—how important they can be in the development of cognitive thinking in the young child—it is rather staggering to realize that the children's book industry has, until recently, remained rather complacent and somnolent about its dynamic effects upon a child's image of himself and those about him. But this is not entirely the fault of the children's book publishers. Rather, there has been a serious breakdown in communications between the child psychiatrists and sociologists and the trade itself. Never was I more conscious of this than when I queried Professor Jerome Bruner about whether he thought the book trade had tended to follow the recent findings of early childhood development experts such as himself. A charmingly diffident man, he conceded that he honestly had not paid the matter much thought. He did not think that any of his colleagues had given the children's book trade much consideration, either. It reminded me of my original contention made at the Edinburgh Psychoanalytical Conference in 1966 that even the best of the professionals in the field of child studies tend to keep their discoveries to themselves. It does not seem too grotesque a conception that the people who make the books for the children to read and the experts who are studying the way young human beings think should get together. But they do not—or not enough.

Of all the institutions to respond to the findings of the child experts about the verbal inadequacies and poor self-image of the disadvantaged child, the children's book industry has been the most dilatory. It has been content to allow reading to be a minority occupation for the leisured middle class. It is estimated that more than six million American nonwhite children (half of those neglected twelve million we heard so much about during the debut of "Sesame Street") are learning to read at this time from books that feature a preponderance of all-white children. The you-are-invisible game that a white American society has been so adept at playing with regard to its black population has been most successfully played in the world of children's books.

Nancy Larrick, writer about children and former president of the International Reading Association, undertook a personal survey of the several thousand trade books published for children in 1962, 1963, and 1964 and found that of the 5,206 children's trade books launched by the sixty-three U.S. children's book publishers in the three-year period, 349 included one or more black children in the text—an average of 6.7 per cent. Over the three-year period, Miss Larrick discovered that only four-fifths of one per cent of the sixty-three publishers told a story about contemporary American blacks. When some of the publishers defensively stated that they did indeed have black children in their trade books, it turned out that these were more dark faces in a crowd.

Many times, there were not even any dark faces in the crowd. In August 1965, Whitney Young, Jr., then executive director of the National Urban League, pointed out that a little Golden Book published by Golden Press and entitled *A Visit to the Zoo,* showing children visiting New York's Central Park Zoo, had not pictured one nonwhite face in the entire book. And yet the story purported to be realistic, with illustrations of a representational rather than of a fanciful nature. The publisher apologized and admitted that he had missed a chance to present a fairer picture. Other publishers were less gentlemanly about their all-white books, simply pointing out that they lost trade, particularly in the South, if they featured a black child.

But perhaps the distinctly WASP nature of the children's book industry up until the present time is not altogether surprising, as insensitive and irresponsible as this tendency is. Since its flowering in the mid-nineteenth century, children's literature has had a comfortable, middle-class ring about it. It is true that Charles Dickens showed children in positions of grim poverty and destitution, but even *David Copperfield* was not intended for young readers and has only become of interest to children in this century with the help of films and plays to feed children's interest in the book.

If a poor child appears in some of the classics, it is usually in order to underline the nobility of the well-born protagonist, or to help humanize a naturally haughty upper-class child. We see this in Frances Hodgson Burnett's *The Secret Garden*, where the imperious orphan Mary finds an earthy wisdom and simplicity that she comes to appreciate in a Yorkshire farm boy, gradually allowing him to have the gift of her trust and friendship and, in the process, becoming a nicer person herself.

If a child encountered poverty in a Victorian classic, it was usually because of a fall in circumstances; the essential well-bredness was there in spite of the lessened comforts due to a social catastrophe. The three children in Edith Nesbit's *Railway Children* had known great comfort at their roomy mansion in Kensington, South London, and days were spent being beautifully served by a neat little band of servants. Servants were taken for granted in the lives of these middle-class heroes and heroines. The family, "just an ordinary suburban" one, we are told, had "pretty clothes, good fires, a lovely nursery with heaps of toys, and a Mother Goose wall-paper. They had a kind and merry nursemaid." Along with these fruits of privilege came a cook who made a superb pigeon pie and a parlormaid with bright red hair. Suburban comfort indeed!

When their father is mysteriously led away (to prison, as it turns out), the children follow their plucky mother to Yorkshire and make the best of being newly poor. There is more than a vague suggestion that their gutsiness and resiliency are built-in legacies of their original good breeding.

Jo, Beth, Amy, and Meg, of Louisa May Alcott's classic *Little Women*, also knew better days before their father went off to war and their "Marmee" had to work to keep them in genteel style. They show dash and courage in the face of this sudden reduction in circumstances and are even able to accept that they will have fewer presents for Christmas, as we learn from the opening chapter. The romance of once-prosperous Victorian girls retaining their spirit and style in spite of genteel poverty appears to be eternally gripping reading material for the young, "relevant" or not. In 1971 a research team from Sheffield University's Institute of Education found that *Little Women* was an all-time favorite with young British readers (after Enid Blyton). The Sheffield team reported this finding halfway through a four-year project designed to present a fuller picture of the total pattern of children's reading to the government-backed British Schools Council.

The natural aristocrat hero or heroine has prevailed throughout the history of children's literature. It might have been a natural outgrowth of the classical fairy tales; the prince knew or, in any case, intuited that Cinderella was a real lady, after all, and we are led to feel that he would have wanted to marry her even if the shoe had not fit. Aristocracy and breeding will out.

While the unmistakable relish with which the Victorians viewed aristocracy and servant-filled nurseries may be forgivable—children love escapism and these scenes of nineteenth-century domesticity certainly provide it—the fact that so much of the successful literature of the past seventy years has neglected whole segments of the child population is not.

The irresponsibility of the book trade in the face of what damage such all-white presentation of life was creating, is shocking. The psychiatrists and sociologists of the sixties had made it clear that a child could respond with dangerous subjectivity to the content of literature, that prejudices and permanent misunderstanding could be instilled into children of three or four years, and that the young in minority racial groups could be given feelings of intense inferiority by the paradings of white children before their eyes in endless white adventures and situations. Sol Cohen, assistant professor in the Graduate School of Education at the University of California, speaks powerfully of the harm done by all-white toys and books to a minority child's self-concept:

> When children have a negative attitude towards Negroes even before they are old enough to read, when nursery school children cannot bear to identify themselves with a doll whose color is brown, the effect of constant repetition of the inferior, undesirable characteristics ascribed to people of minority groups may well have permanent and damaging effect upon the latter's self-concept.

It should be remembered that books are rarely if ever seen in the homes of culturally disadvantaged children, whether they be whites in rural communities or blacks in the inter-city ghettos. For this reason, the child's first picture book at a Head Start play group or first primer at grade school can seem as alien as an object from outer space. The deprived child has not had his mother read to him; there has existed none of that easy mother-love-plus-reading-aloud activity which the middle-class child enjoys almost as a natural legacy of growing up. Reading aloud to a child can become a refinement of the feedback process we know is so crucial to the development of enriched speech. Usually, a child will stop his mother with the query "What does that mean?" and her answer will add to his fund of knowledge and expand his vocabulary. But this mother-child activity withers in poverty homes, if it ever existed at all. As an example, let me quote Gail Perry, the eloquent and feeling teacher who taught in the first operational phase of the District of Columbia's poverty program in 1965. She had some violently disturbed children in her class—you may recall that one of them kept trying to push his fellow schoolmates into a wastebasket—and she felt that if she visited their homes she would gain further insight into what had created such turbulence. In order to get an exact picture of their home backgrounds, she took to visiting them, rather than just telephoning the parents, which had not been successful or given her any clues into some of her pupils' behavior. She described one home visit:

> Another child lived with her 15 brothers and sisters in a two-bedroom tenement and was being brought up by an older sister who dropped out of school to care for the younger children. The mother left for work early in the morning and returned late at night. The father made $40 a week and was therefore not eligible for welfare. Crowded living conditions gave these children no privacy. There was a scarcity of books, paper and pencils; trips to the outside world were few if any; and there were no adults with the education, time, or energy to spend on anything but the business of just surviving.

In a home like this—which must be like thousands, perhaps millions of others—it can come as no surprise that the printed page, a teacher's reading voice, is going to be a virgin and alien experience. It should also be the opening of a world of magic and wonder to a child. But is it? Unfortunately not. Too often what he is reading is completely meaningless to him, with no relevance to his own family and living conditions. The effect is to alienate him, to make him "tune out." What does all that gobbledygook about a little girl and boy, a car in a garage, a pony in a field *mean?* It does not represent most homes and it reinforces those it does—which is, of course, another kind of lie.

The smugness of the children's book publishers—and those involved with them, the readers, the bookstores, teachers, librarians—in the face of so many detailed studies of how all-white books as leisure reading material and as part of teaching in the schools can whittle away at the ego and self-esteem of a young black child, has sent many educators reeling away from children's literature in despair. David K. Gast, associate professor of education at San Diego State College, who himself had instituted a four-year study of minority Americans in children's books, marveled at the complacency of the industry throughout the early sixties, speaking modestly of his own part in altering the picture.

> But really, I'm not an old-timer because the study of the portrayal of minorities in teaching materials has been periodically investigated for the past thirty-five years. Any decent review of the literature in this field would reveal the names of pioneer scholars including: Davis-Dubois, Rollins, Baker, Taba, the ACE Committee on the Study of Intergroup Relations in Teaching Materials, Tannenbaum and Marcus. Though it's a sad commentary that, despite the findings and suggestions which were made over the years to bring about a culturally fair portrayal of minority Americans, no great interest was shown on the part of a smug and complacent dominant public, the publishers, and sadly enough, educators themselves. . . .

Professor Gast goes on to suggest that it was the heated climate of the late sixties, the conflagrations of Watts and Detroit, the assassinations, the violent protests of the young, the general social upheaval which swept the entire nation, that finally dissipated the smugness of the children's book industry.

Certainly, there has been a growth of a more sensitive approach to the feelings of child readers developing in the trade over the past few years. The presence of nonwhite children in books has risen from 6.7 per cent to 9 per cent—not a dramatic rise, but a rise nevertheless.

Child study experts and sociologists have shown that children are sensitive to the existence of racial overtones in children's books. As long ago as 1942, educator Eleanor Nolen attempted to alert publishers to this crucial point. She wrote: "The place to combat race prejudice is with the child's first books and first social relationships."

Her view was corroborated in a more detailed study undertaken by Mary Ellen Goodman, a cultural anthropologist. Miss Goodman examined the racial attitudes of four-year-olds in a northeastern American seaside town to which she gave the fictional name of New Dublin in her book *Race Awareness in Young Children.* She found that black preschoolers were keenly aware of color differences and that they reacted with extreme emotion to books that tended to underscore these differences. She studied children in integrated nursery schools, presenting them with white and brown dolls and picture books and jigsaw puzzles picturing black and white children. She encouraged the children to talk freely about them.

In her book she cites the case history of Paul B., an aggressive, sturdy, and very dark skinned black boy of four, whose mother prided herself on her light-brown hue and tended to regard him as the ugly duckling of the family because he was darker than his siblings. Paul had begun to respond to his mother's peculiar racialism with a copycat variety that was uncomfortably super-imposed on his own confused and withdrawn personality. One book, *Little Black Sambo*, had profoundly influenced his thinking. Miss Goodman writes of Paul:

> Paul's race awareness is of a medium order, but his feelings are strong. He is not clear about kinds of people, though he has a notion there is a "black" kind, and another kind which he only occasionally labels "white". He sometimes calls the black kind "Black Sambo" (his mother has read the book to him). Paul probably sees himself as actually being very dark, and he clearly prefers not to do so. He always finds white figures prettier and nicer, and he rejects "black." He tells us: "I don't like that father, he's got a black head" and "I want to tell you which one I like; I like that one (white), I don't like that black one."

White children invariably placed white dolls with other white dolls and brown dolls with similarly colored dolls. This spon-taneous classification occurred with the black children as well. One of them, Joan, a 4 ½ -year-old black child, volunteered com-ments about her parents as well as the dolls. She said: "My daddy is colored. My mommy is colored." Then she offered up this baleful comment: "The people that are white, they can go up. The people that are brown, they have to go down." An uneasy and inchoate awareness among the children that whites have a better chance to succeed in life than blacks threads its way throughout Miss Goodman's study, reflecting the fact that American society, and especially American children's litera-ture, had done nothing to improve the self-image of young black preschoolers.

There is much hope for this situation now with a spate of

delicate and attractive picture books being published, such as Ezra Jack Keats's *Whistle for Willie* and *A Snowy Day,* in which a little black boy called Peter practices whistling for his pet dachshund along the graffiti-scarred walls, of, presumably, Harlem, and then investigates the wonders of a snowy day in the city.

In the early part of this century, a picture was beginning to form about the nature of the black which stuck tenaciously throughout the first four and a half decades of the 1900s and only began to fade in the 1950s. Harriet Beecher Stowe's deferential Uncle Tom was to have many twentieth-century descendants. The image of the black imprinted on the white American's mind extended into many different media—films, plays, and, most strongly of all, into children's literature. Ray Stannard Baker, a writer who analyzed American white and black differences in a book called *Following the Color Line,* published in 1908, summed up his impression of the Negro personality in this way:

> The temperament of the Negro is irrepressibly cheerful, he overflows from his small home and sings and laughs in his streets; no matter how ragged or forlorn he may be, good humor sits upon his countenance, and his squalor is not unpicturesque. A banjo, a mullet supper from time to time, an exciting revival, give him real joys.

Blacks in films were either servile or craven, or both. The trembling and shuffling and "Oh, lawdy" of these caricatures, largely menials in white homes, sent movie audiences into paroxysms of laughter. Flick on the radio and you could hear the homespun philosophy of "Amos 'n' Andy," or listen to Jack Benny groaning over yet another one of the gaffes or malapropisms of his manservant, whose growly, stripped-vocal-cords timbre was another predictable characteristic of the male of the species.

Side by side with the film and radio depictions of the Negro as a perambulating, all-in-one minstrel show with the brain of a chick pea was a fictional stereotype found in a new and flourishing book industry in girls' and boys' adventure stories.

In 1906 an enterprising U.S. publisher named Edward L. Stratemeyer founded a syndicate to supply boys and girls with exciting stories featuring intrepid heroes and heroines, aged eight to twelve (later, with Nancy Drew and Sue Barton, the age rose to a sophisticated late adolescence). They were all white and stamped with the optimism and pioneering courage of Horatio Alger, a figure Stratemeyer greatly admired. Female pseudonyms were given to authors of the girls' series (*The Bobbsey Twins* was written by a nonexistent authoress called Laura Lee Hope). Stratemeyer was tireless, outlining all the stories himself. To *The Bobbsey Twins*, a series which appealed to both girls and boys, he added rugged adventure sagas for boys, the *Rover Boys* and *Tom Swift*. By 1930, Stratemeyer led a staggering empire with sales of his two major series, *The Bobbsey Twins* and *Tom Swift*, topping over six million copies each.

The death of Stratemeyer in 1930, combined with the depression, dented the burgeoning syndicate, and some of the series were abandoned. However, Stratemeyer's daughter, Harriet S. Adams, carried on with the industry, adding a new series to the list which she designed herself—the adventures of Nancy Drew, girl detective.

In all these adventure stories, which had the young American reading public of the twenties, thirties, and forties by the throat, blacks, if they were introduced into the stories at all, were uniformly ignorant, irresponsible, comical, and, at times, downright shifty, if not criminal. If they spoke, it was to raise a laugh, to provide comic relief from the events that carried the plots along, and their utterances were larded with some of the most tongue-twisting argot and dialect known to literature.

The two sets of Bobbsey twins, one lot of four-year-olds, the others eight, had two Negro servants to tend their wants and the needs of their spacious house on beautiful Lake Metoka in antiseptic middle-class-white land (Mr. Bobbsey is a rich timber merchant)—the Bobbseys' domestic couple, Dinah and Sam, who live over the stable. Dinah is fat, chuckly, a marvelous cook, and is described as having a "kinky head." She talks as if the watermelon which she purports to love had become permanently stuck in her larynx. In *The Bobbsey Twins or Merry Days Indoors and Out*, published in 1904, Dinah says to the four-year-old twin Freddie:

> I do declar' it looks most tremen'us real. . . . It's a wonder to me yo' chillun can make sech t'ings. . . . Fire enjuns, ain't it Freddie? Recon yo' is gwine to be a fireman when yo' is a man, hey?

Her husband, Sam, speaks in similarly fractured style in the same story:

> "Now chillun, dar am de house," said the colored man. "All yo' hab got to do is to clear out de insides. . . . Tonight I'll poah some water ober dat house," said Sam. "Dat will make de snow as hard as ice."

While Dinah and Sam are pleasant enough creatures in their antebellum, southern way and fulfill their roles as "happy family retainer" stereotypes, other Negro characters crop up in the Stratemeyer series who are far less salubrious, though just as one-dimensional. A criminal maid in the Nancy Drew story *The Hidden Staircase*, published in 1930, begins to mutter fearfully to herself when arrest is imminent: "I done reckons my old ears is playin' me false," and later, "Reckons I ain't gwine take no chances."

When arrest is unavoidable, she falls apart and begins to whine to the police unattractively: "I's just an old culled woman who makes her victuals workin'."

Self-deprecating statements such as this from Negro servants abound in the Stratemeyer books. In *Tom Swift*, there was a character called Eradicate Andrew Jackson Abraham Lincoln Sampson, always referred to as Eradicate because he eradicated dirt. In *Tom Swift and His Motorcycle* (1910), Eradicate reports of himself humbly: "I trabled all over and I couldn't get no jobs."

In the Stratemeyer series, women were invariably fat and chuckly or slatternly and surly. Men mosied around their menial chores, alternating between tipping their hats to their white employers and befuddling their minds with cheap rye. Their occupations were always lowly. James Jones, history professor at Florida State University, who conducted his own personal study of seventeen Nancy Drew books published between 1930 and 1941, found that seventeen Negroes appeared in the stories. These included five maids, four porters, two cooks, several criminals, one elevator man, and a slatternly maid who "shuffled" when she walked.

In the late 1930s, with the approach of World War II which would eventually usher in the integration of black and white men in the forces, and the increased awareness in American society of racial inequities, a softer line begins to appear in some of the Stratemeyer publications. While the black patients in *Sue Barton, Visiting Nurse* all speak in dialect as do Nancy Drew's menials, they have some remnants of dignity. With an air of surprise, Sue Barton patronizingly reflects that "all the apartments [of Negroes] were clean. . . . They had a tradition of cleanliness and were proud of it. An apartment was seldom cluttered . . . no speck of dust lingered anywhere." She also adds that they have "enchanting black babies."

By 1950, even such benign patronage was not going to be good enough for a markedly angrier black population agitating for civil rights. In 1953, the Bobbseys' servant Dinah had altered her grammar from the original porridge of double negatives, and she and her husband miraculously lost their dialects. To crown the couple's rise up the social scale, they are removed from their quarters above the stable and brought to live in the Bobbsey mansion. Such integration.

It was certainly time that Dinah and Sam were allowed to be human beings. The effect of such stereotyping did not leave black children of the 1940s untouched. In 1941, Eva Knox Evans, author of *Araminta's Goat*, now a small classic, wrote that she had encountered some alarming signs of conditioning in her black kindergarten pupils. She had been reading *Araminta's Goat* aloud to her schoolchildren as she went along. However, when she showed the class the illustrations and they could see that Araminta was black, the Negro children in her group asked, "Why doesn't she speak the way Negroes speak in books?" Miss Knox then pointed out that the children themselves did not speak the way blacks were supposed to speak in most books, so why should Araminta, and the argument passed off.

With any luck, however, the 1970s should see the final laying to rest of such damaging stereotypes. The Office of Children's

Services of the New York Public Library cautioned libraries in 1971 to guard against

> books which describe blacks in derisive terms which use derogating names and epithets. . . . These terms are either insulting or patronizing rather than humorous or affectionate. Another language consideration is the use of dialect particularly when it is phonetically written, as "gwine" for "going." . . . The next factor to consider is that of illustration . . . the black child who sees pictures that ridicule his face may be deeply hurt, feel defeated, or become resentful or rebellious. . . . At one time we had few if any children's books dealing with black people in roles other than menial. Now we have books about black professionals, judges, soldiers, sailors and cowboys. . . . Those books help the black child discover his own identity.

Another body that helps to ensure that books for children are not "whiter than white" is the Council for Interracial Books for Children formed in 1965. The council was sponsored by a number of famous educators, poets, and pediatricians, among them Harold Taylor, Benjamin Spock, Langston Hughes, and Ben Shahn. The aim of the council, centered in New York City, is to encourage children's authors and illustrators to focus on non-white subjects. The council has succeeded admirably in this over the past years.

Describing how it was that the council came into being and what it has accomplished, Harold Taylor says:

> When the American school system was finally seen by its critics among the blacks and the whites to be an elitist operation by the whites to take care of its own, the text-book manufacturers, both those on the assembly line of writers and those in the editorial offices were forced to shift ground if they were to stay in business. The Council for Interracial Books was one of the first organized

groups to tackle the problems of books for children as a cultural, social and political matter rather than a commercial enterprise.

Over the years since 1965 it has had a serious influence on the publication of children's books which could speak to the children's concerns for imaginative, interesting and honest stories to read. Aside from the white chauvinism implicit in the Jane and Dick and Spot approach to children's textbooks, the stories were so often little more than spelling and word-teaching devices that they lacked the literary imagination through which the child's sensibilities could be touched. We now have a respectable library of work which not only gives the child a way of entering his own multi-racial culture, but gives his mind and his aesthetic sense a chance to grow. The Council did not do it all but it did act as the necessary leverage.

The role of the children's librarian as a refiner and a guardian has not been confined to the racial arena only. Increasingly, librarians have taken on a sifting, vigilante role where they consider topics unwholesome, insulting, or injurious to a child's intellectual development. The vigilante role, while normally important in the racial sphere, can sometimes have ludicrous and damaging consequences. I am thinking in particular of the banning of *Little Red Riding Hood* by a midwestern library during the height of the McCarthy era of the 1950s—the word *red* alone apparently was too emotive to be allowed to rest at that time. Librarians have often erred on the side of the puritanical in the past, too, keeping juvenile books sexless and free from some of the harsher, or at least more real, aspects of life that many teenagers will meet in the often difficult process of entering and coping with adolescence. It is doubtful, for instance, if Judy Blume's book *It's Not the End of the World*, the story of a twelve-year-old girl who learns to live with her parents' divorce, would have been found altogether suitable some years ago.

But in the racial sphere—with the history of Negro stereotypes as shown in the Stratemeyer series, for example—the repugnance that some librarians feel for hitherto passively accepted books, such as Hugh Lofting's *Doctor Dolittle*, is understandable. In the light of what we now know about clear racist attitudes in children's stories, it is surprising that Dr. Dolittle was not pounced on before 1968, when it was labeled "white racist" by some New York librarians and asked to be withdrawn from the state's library shelves. Certainly the somewhat moronic African Bumpo, with his large lips and kinky hair, is a rather unpleasant stereotype. My own hunch is that Dolittle went unnoticed by liberals and integrationists for so long because Lofting's illustrations of both white and black people are so grotesque as to give them an unreal, cartoonlike quality; they are not creatures of the real world such as the Bobbsey twins and Nancy Drew, and therefore not so jarring to racial sensibilities. Mrs. Isabelle Suhl, one of the most powerful voices condemning Lofting's Dr. Dolittle as racist, librarian of the Elizabeth Irwin High School in New York City, concedes that the black community itself has made no great outcry against the Lofting books. This does not, however, make him appear any less repellent and harmful to her.

In a letter to me recently, Mrs. Suhl wrote: "It is not Bumpo alone that I object to but Lofting's white supremacist attitude which permeates all his writing and characterizations and illustrations. I feel they are insulting not only to all Africans but also to all people of African descent."

There are other cruel and insensitive stereotypes that have jarred upon librarians' sensibilities and they are not always racial. In 1970 the Ipswich Public Library in Suffolk, England, banned all Billy Bunter books on the grounds that this popular and corpulent schoolboy created by Frank Richards was more tragic than comic and that the stories would lead children to make mock of obesity, a sad and not infrequent handicap in the young. There was an outcry in the press about the high-handed-ness of the Ipswich library, much talk about their action's being the thin edge of the wedge of possible further attempts at cen-sorship. However, a quick glance at one of the Billy Bunter books (among a best-selling series in the Armada paperback range) called *Billy Bunter's Postal Order* (1951) makes one wonder if the Ipswich view was not valid:

> Bunter's fat thoughts dwelt on a gorgeous feed, on a pile of enticing, attractive, sticky things, to the exact value of sixteen shillings and tenpence. Three "bob" for the taximan, who, if he expected a tip, would learn that he had another guess coming: twopence reserved for the motorfare back: sixteen and ten for tarts, buns, cakes, ginger-pop, eclairs, doughnuts, cream puffs—it was quite dazzling.

In some cases, recent psychiatric insights have outstripped old-fashioned characterizations. In 1951 it is quite possible that little was known about the link between lovelessness and com-pensatory eating. Though no one wants to be sententious or spoilsport, couldn't children live without Billy Bunter?

British librarians have certainly decided that their young readers can try to live without Enid Blyton. The history of how English children's librarians have phased out this best-selling authoress deserves a chapter on its own as the slow axing of Enid has been a fascinating and unprecedented underground action and has passed off with little publicity or fanfare, perhaps one of the major reasons for its stealthy success.

Trying to kill off Enid Blyton has been much like slaying the multiheaded hydra. She was frighteningly prolific until her death in 1968, writing nearly four hundred books in a career which spanned thirty-five years. A check on her English-language sales one year revealed a total of £75,000,000 (nearly $200 million), not counting her foreign translations (she was translated into thirty languages, including Swahili). She wrote a book a month.

But her popularity with book publishers, paperback firms, and the children of Britain and other countries did nothing to lessen librarians' detestation of her stories and the values they contained. They loathed the snobbishness of her fictional children, their impoverished vocabularies, and the padded middle-class homes from which they sprang. Finally, they detested the moral concepts she wove into her tales, with good invariably being victorious over bad. Life was not like that, the librarians said.

What most disturbed the British librarians was the way a child would devour twenty or thirty Blytons and then cease to read at all, either more Blytons or anyone else. In some curious way, the Blyton books appear to be reading growth stoppers, and this is what they find most pernicious about them. One Marylebone, London, children's librarian told me that most of her colleagues had not gone so far as to ban them, but when the copies they had wore out, they simply did not order new ones. As a consequence, British children are forced to dig into their pockets and buy the paperbacks (which they do by the millions, for this simplistic storyteller still tops the popularity charts).

The repugnance that children's librarians in Britain feel for Enid Blyton's propensity to sugar-coat life is a very contemporary reaction. Sixty years ago no one fussed overmuch about saccharine and unreal tales concerning bourgeois little girls and boys and their happy families, and stories like Kate Douglas

Wiggin's *Rebecca of Sunnybrook Farm* and *Mother Carey's Chickens* were all-time favorites with librarians and children alike. But today there is a concern that children's books, if they are dealing with everyday life, should at least attempt to mirror reality.

One of the first books to move away from stereotyping and portray a way of life that was based on reality was Louisa R. Shotwell's *Roosevelt Grady* (1964), the story of a black migrant worker's family. Roosevelt, the young hero, has a thirst for knowledge that his father's life-style cannot sustain. Miss Shotwell's book won the Best Intercultural Children's Book Award for the story and received high critical praise in magazines and newspapers. In opposition to all these accolades was Dr. Catherine Juanita Starke, of Teachers College, Columbia Univeristy, who warned against the counterstereotype—the too-good-to-be-true black—and some observed that young Roosevelt Grady was of this ilk.

Roosevelt Grady was the best known of a number of stories about the children of minority groups which began to appear in the late 1950s and 1960s. Children of minority groups other than blacks also appeared, stories which tried to communicate something of the reality of the lives of young Chinese, Mexicans, and Puerto Ricans. Mina Lewiton, in *Candita's Choice,* wrote of a little Puerto Rican girl's successful struggle to adapt to New York City. Irmengarde Eberle told of how an amiable Mexican family learns to live in Texas in *The Very Good Neighbors.* In *The House of Sixty Fathers* (1958), Meindert DeJong wrote of the thorny experiences of a Chinese boy's existence during the Japanese war in the Chinese river town of Hengyang. This book is interesting also in that it shows us an early Maurice Sendak, accurately and unsentimentally revealing the distress in the features of the boy, Tien Pao. Even then, Sendak's illustrations had a quivering, vibrant quality and Tien Pao's pet pig, Beauty-of-the-Republic, presages some equally engaging animals that we are to see coming from his brush and pen in later years, such as the sleepy Sealyham in *In the Night Kitchen.*

The effort to bring integration into the public schools was reflected in the literature, too. One of the most sensitive of these was published by Dorothy Sterling; in *Mary Jane*, we read of the entry of a young black girl into a newly desegregated and highly intolerant all-white school. At about this time, Joan Lexau wrote *Benjie*, a story of a black five-year-old living in a starkly urban setting, a book that was widely used in the New York City primary schools for early reading pleasure. Teachers had seized upon the idea that children liked reading about young people who looked and lived like them. The trend has been called "here-and-now" literature, or sometimes, more slangily, "telling it like it is." In a burst of enthusiasm about this new drift in children's literature, David Gast penned an essay joyously, if a shade clumsily, entitled "The Dawning of the Age of Aquarius for Multi-Ethnic Children's Literature" in a teachers' magazine.

A glance at some of the preschool titles in a 1971 issue of *New York Magazine* under the heading "For the Liberated Child's Library" revealed a near obsession with reality literature: *All Kinds of Mothers* by Cecily Brownstone ("Black and white mothers, working and stay-home mothers all have an important quality in common—their love for their children"); *Mommies at Work* by Eve Merriam ("Busy moms in various occupations, trades and professions. A Must!"); *Rosa-Too-Little* by Sue Felt ("A Puerto Rican girl, who desperately wants a library card, learns to write").

The telling-it-like-it-is trend burst in upon the paperback field, too. In the 1972–1973 Dell Yearling Laurel-Leaf Library list of paperbacks for elementary schools, teachers are presented with choices such as *The Empty Schoolhouse* by Natalie Savage Carlson ("Ten-year-old Lullah Royall was thrilled at the news that the parochial schools in her state were to be desegregated. . . . But unexpected hostilities and the threat of violence make her happiness short-lived") and *Dead End School* by Robert Coles (". . . this is the story of Jim, a black boy. When his sixth grade class is moved from an old rundown school to an even older one, his widowed mother leads the neighborhood parents in a protest which results in the children being bussed across town to a new, well-equipped white school").

At the same time, the New York Public Library showed its concern for the child of the minority group and his need for an increased feeling of pride in identity with a listing of young children's books under the heading of "The Black Experience in Children's Books," a list that speaks for itself: *Black Is Beautiful, Black Means . . . , Brown Is a Beautiful Color,* and others.

The struggle for more black identity has also led to the writing of a number of books which describe famous blacks in their careers: *Black Masters of American Art* by Ronald Bearden and Harry Henderson, *Blacks in Communications* by M. C. Stein, *They Dared to Lead: America's Black Athletes* by Phyllis and Zander Hollander, and *Profiles in Black Power* by James Haskins. An effort to acquaint the American black child with some of the richness of his African heritage led to such books as *Moja Means One*, a Swahili counting book by Muriel Feelings, illustrated by her husband, Tom Feelings.

The reality approach to children's literature was finding its counterparts in Britain, though with less of a stress on the black child, since blacks are a smaller minority group in Britain than in the United States. Leila Berg has led the trend toward reality books in Britain, focusing on working-class children who live in poor, industrialized communities. Miss Berg has written for a paperback series called Nippers, published by Macmillan (London), which is being used in the primary grades as a primer. In one of her stories for the series, called *Fish and Chips for Supper*, she combines the repetition of the classical nursery rhyme with some familiar urban family behavior: "Dad, dad, go to work. Mum, mum, pay the bill." In her story *Finding a Key*, the heroine is a latchkey child who has to make her own high tea as well as her working family's when she returns home from school. *A Box for Benny*, one of Leila Berg's most skillful tales, dubbed a minor classic of the urban contemporaneity genre, tells of a small boy in Manchester's Jewish quarter.

Even those authors who veer heavily toward fantasy have a tendency to weave their fantasies against a backdrop of reality. The combination of myth and modernity is nicely mixed by one contemporary British title for kindergarten children, a story by Judith Barrett called *Old MacDonald Had Some Flats*. In the cover illustration by Ron Barrett, we see an old familiar MacDonald with his battered farmer's hat—unmistakably rural, but this time he is backed up by some uninvitingly vertiginous high-rise apartment houses.

The French author Laurent de Brunhoff, the present creator of the now internationally famous elephant, Babar, (his father, Jean, was the elephant's original creator) echoes this prevailing belief that children should have a dose of contemporaneity with their fantasy.

"Little boys and girls nowadays are used to seeing many cars on the streets, planes, and television," he says. "They are used to seeing all kinds of technical life, and I think Babar should show that part of life." This is why, presumably, de Brunhoff recently sent him to the moon.

However tortoiselike the response of the children's book industry has been to the revelations made by the revolutionary child experts of the 1960s (Bloom, Bernstein, Bruner, et al.), we can see that it *has* now responded—belatedly, perhaps, but in a stunning rush. Some conservative publishers bemoan the trend toward contemporaneity, the not always too subtle stories designed to mirror urban stresses and to boost the disadvantaged child's feelings of self-esteem. Other experts in child reading habits are philosophical about it. Josette Frank, New York resident and director for children's books and mass media of the Child Study Association of America, comments wisely on the trend in her book *Your Child's Reading Today:* "If this [the emphasis on minority groups] is sometimes done too self-consciously, and with a heavy hand, it is, nevertheless, a step toward long overdue integration in our juvenile books."

The reality literature may occasionally be a little self-conscious, it is true, but it is to be welcomed. Certainly it has touched a chord in the schools, both in England and America, where teachers are more conscious of the needs of culturally deprived children and are anxious to select books that will help them. The industry itself can have no regrets for developing a social conscience, however late in the day. Business, both in hard and soft cover, is booming. In the United States, there are twenty-nine hundred new children's book titles published each year, in England the number is slightly lower at twenty-three hundred. A report of the U.S. section of the International Board on Books for Young People published in May 1972 stated that the problem of rising costs for hardback books had led to a trend in America of putting more children's book titles into paperback; an average of one hundred and fifty new paperback titles had been reprinted from hardcover editions each year over the past five years. The fact that schools now use paperbacks extensively is one of the major reasons for this boom.

But however welcome—and, it appears, lucrative—this new approach to reality may be, some educators and child experts plead for it not to be overdone. In her article "Is There a Literature for the Disadvantaged Child?" Dorothy Seaberg, professor of education at Northern Illinois University, cautions against showing the urban child too many literary replicas of himself, emphasizing that poor children, perhaps more than others, need the therapy and sheer delight of fantasy and the flight from reality. She stressed that "escape valves are necessary for coping with the hard realities of life." She speaks of her own experience and that of her colleagues in a New York University Tri-University Project carried out in the late sixties with inner-city children, with the objective of trying to inculcate "a joy of reading" in the young children and to assess just what books did in fact inspire such joy. Dr. Seaberg summed up what she and her colleagues discovered during this summer-long experiment:

1. Folk literature and fantastical fiction seem to have the greatest appeal of all types of literary genre for the urban child.
2. If realistic fiction is employed with the urban young, it must . . . be related to real life experiences of the child. It is only then that identification can take place.

Literature for children has a mythic quality about it which no amount of reality fiction could or should remove. As Kornei Chukovsky stresses in his book *From Two to Five*, fantasy is vitally necessary for a child's emotional development. If stories are too self-consciously tailored for certain groups, they have a way of missing out on freshness and spontaneity, and tend to lack the universality and sheer joyousness of some of the greatest classics. No inner-city child has seen a bullfight or heard of a banderillero, yet Munro Leaf's *Story of Ferdinand*, first published in 1936, continues to delight children from all classes. As Dorothy Cohen of the Bank Street College of Education points out, the greatest stories for children are those that have a built-in clarity about them that makes the exotic and unknown comprehensible. As she notes, clarification of difficult terms are woven into *The Story of Ferdinand* with astonishing effortlessness; the sheer joy of rich language and alliteration seems to carry the meaning along:

> First came the Banderilleros with long sharp pins with ribbons on them to stick in the bull and make him mad.
> Next came the Picadores who rode skinny horses and they had long spears to stick in the bull and make him madder.
> Then came the Matador, the proudest of all—he thought he was very handsome, and bowed to the ladies. He had a red cape and a sword and was supposed to stick the bull last of all.

The best of the new black fiction for children seems to me to be that which embodies this classical and everlasting delight in words; if this literature also helps a minority group to further understand its culture, all the better—but a good children's book should transcend ethnic concerns and appeal to all young people. Julius Lester's *The Knee-High Man* is an excellent example of this. While Lester writes in his introduction that this collection of black folk literature is written in celebration of his people's heritage (his father was a black Methodist minister and a consummate storyteller, apparently), the sheer relish he takes in word-spinning, in rolling outrageous adjectives around, gives his stories a universal quality. Take this sentence from *Mr. Rabbit and Mr. Bear,* for example:

> But the next day he [Mr. Rabbit] was sitting outside the gate, ready for another morning of that delicious, scrumptious, crispy, luscious, delectable, exquisite, ambrosial, nectareous, yummy lettuce.

This sentence is repeated three times during the story and would be the kind of string of musical words that children would wait for expectantly and probably repeat in delight, whether they understood the meaning of the words or not. It is this combination of the familiar and the vaguely outrageous that tickles children and makes listening to a story (and eventually reading it) a joyous experience.

Certain themes are of universal interest to children and have nothing to do with urban settings or racial and ethnic differences. Though children would be too young, naturally, to describe them as such, what they appear to be concerned with most are moral values, the triumph of good over bad (which is perhaps why the stories of Enid Blyton, however limited, have an appeal). Young children are reassured when gentle Ferdinand, wrenched by accident into a nasty, noisy bullring from his daisy-ridden meadow where he slumps happily under a tree, can return to his post and continue to smell flowers. Though Mr. Rabbit is a bit of a sly-boots, no child wants him to end up in a pot, and the great pleasure derived from his sorties into forbidden territories is that he can get away with eating all that "nectareous" lettuce. They love to see tough farmers being outwitted by animals. Children breathe again when they witness the victory of the hero in Roald Dahl's *Fantastic Mr. Fox,* finally free of farmer persecution with his family in a bunker underground.

Nonny Hogrogian's *One Fine Day*, the story which won the 1972 Caldecott Medal,* also featured a fox, this time a gentler one who loses his tail and has to make a series of transactions in order to recover it. The important aspect of this story for children's peace of mind and sense of order is that he *does* recover it.

The appeal of Robert McCloskey's *Make Way for Ducklings*, awarded the Caldecott Medal when it was first published in 1941 and still going strong, probably springs from the fact that Mother Duck does manage to ferry her ducklings safely across the motorway back to the Boston Common lake.

"A Curriculum for English" presented by the University of Nebraska suggests four universal themes for children's literature that are tied up with feelings of insecurity about their home and family.

> 1) a small person's journey from home to isolation away from home; 2) a small person's or a hero's journey from home to confrontation with a monster; 3) a helpless figure's rescue from a harsh home and the miraculous creation of a secure home; and 4) a conflict between a wise beast and a foolish beast. The family unit and the home are described as ultimately good, even if, as in 3) above, it may not be so originally for a small hero. That terrors lurk outside the home in many stories—wolves, tigers, the "dread of the forest"—may reflect the mystery of the technologically-oriented outside world for a child.

---

* The Caldecott Medal was named after Randolph Caldecott, a nineteenth-century English children's book illustrator: in spite of its lineage, it is a U.S. prize.

Of vital emotional concern to the child is that wrong be put right in the stories he reads and that the feelings of insecurity he feels in his own life, those connected with dependence upon his parents and home, should be mollified and softened by the themes of those stories.

It would seem that more important than holding up any mirror to a child's life or a picturing of undiluted reality is the magic of a creative children's author himself, an author who possesses that special sensitivity that enables him to tap mythic springs and to express intuitively those universal themes which appeal to young minds and emotions. If children's literature concentrated solely on reflecting urban realities, no matter how tastefully, a new kind of neglect would be born almost more reprehensible than the neglect of the minority child seen in the 1930s and 1940s—the neglect of all children's positive need for the fantasy that nurtures and makes whole their emotional development.

11

Some Modern Solutions for Teaching the Under-Tens

Of all the revolutionary ideas that have sprung up in this century, the realization that the logic of children differs from that of adults has been one of the most far-reaching. Jean Piaget's meticulous studies showing that children, up to the age of eight, tend to think more egocentrically and in more concrete terms than adults, combined with Jerome Bruner's view that a child's readiness to learn comes much sooner than we have believed, have moved educators to reexamine old established tenets of teaching. This is especially so in regard to the contention that children are receptacles for information delivered authoritatively by adults. This teaching concept is now under grave suspicion. The new view holds that children think differently from adults, therefore, they must be taught differently. British educator Sybil Marshall summed up this new assessment of the essential difference in the mental makeup of adults and children in the following poetic way: "Children are not solely adults in the making, but creatures in their own right, as tadpoles differ from mature frogs, or caterpillars from butterflies."

In England, the new thinking about the very young child has caused a visible revolution in the structure of the primary schools over the past thirty years. Developing in a slow, almost organic way, British infant schools, especially in the Midlands and in the North, have gradually evolved a new system of teaching five- to seven-year-olds that is as far from the old rote teaching of the three Rs and parrot recitals of undigested information as a black Victorian school smock would be from a little girl's swirling plaid miniskirt. The new type of school is called, loosely, the "open plan" school and has grown without any visible prime mover or philosopher behind it. Because a number of progressive American educators have embraced the new system—and in some cases adapted it (as with the sprinkling of new "open door" schools in New York City, North Dakota, Arizona, Oregon, and in some suburban communities on the Eastern Seaboard), it has sometimes been wrongly assumed that the "open plan" infant schools in England grew from a single source. However, this is not the case, as anyone who has tried to trace its development since World War II will discover.

The great surprise for the resident of Britain, like myself, is to find that so little has been written about the "open plan" school in England itself, where it has been somewhat undervalued up to the present. When I met Henry Pluckrose, principal of London's Prior Weston Primary School and present-day guru of the British "open plan" school system, he told me that this shying away from definition on the part of "open plan" advocates was deliberate: "If we define something that is still growing, then we may stop it," he explained. America's dynamic educator, Mrs. Lillian Weber of City College of New York, has helped to make the American public aware of the virtues of the "open door" school,* especially for disadvantaged children (her first adaptation of this British plan, which she prefers to call "informal education," was inaugurated for grade school children at Public School 123 in Harlem in 1968), but England has had no such eloquent advocate. Up to this point, nothing but an occasional newspaper article has been written about the system—and these are usually hostile—although, as I write this chapter, I hear that the British government is soon to publish its solemn assessment of these schools, a paper spurred by the fact of an additional government grant of $250 million for primary school education in the next two years. With so much more money to spend on infant schools, the query now is whether or not this type of education warrants the bulk of the additional funds.

It is almost as though Britain had suddenly been awakened to its own unpublicized educational brilliance by American admiration (Charles Silberman devoted a large part of one chapter of his book *Crisis in the Classroom* to praising the English infant schools, especially those geared to "open plan"). In southern

---

*In 1965 and 1966 Mrs. Weber studied the British Infant School under the sponsorship of London University, visiting fifty-six schools in deprived areas of London, Birmingham, and Bristol. She has since written a book and made a film on the subject; she is also the consultant for the Manhattan Open Door Program, an adaptation of the British system and natural outgrowth of Head Start. It is sometimes also called the "Open Corridor."

England, the more affluent part of the country, "open plan" has been a slow grower, and in London itself only a sprinkling of infant schools in the poorer areas of the East End could be said to be using pure "open plan" school methods. To be more specific, out of over six hundred primary schools in Greater London, no more than thirty could be accurately termed "open plan." In the other London primary schools, diluted, tentative attempts to incorporate some of the characteristics of this informal education have been made, such as the abolition of report cards and set subjects. But these innovations have caused sharp outcries from parents.

In the fulsome and enthusiastic coverage of English "open plan" schools in the U.S. press, little has been written about the resistance of the British parent to these revolutionary changes. I was present at a parent-teacher meeting at the Hampden Gurney Primary School in London's central Marble Arch area in 1968 when the new headmistress was being grilled by parents for making a few innovations at the school along "open plan" lines. What enraged parents most was her refusal to continue issuing term report cards ("How can we keep a record of our child's progress?" was the general lament). One of the parents' very real complaints about the phasing out of particular subjects such as history and geography ("In real life they are not separated," was the headmistress's reasonable rationale for her action) was that in secondary school the children would be subjected to rigid subject separation and stiff "O" ("ordinary") school-leaving certificate examinations at the age of fifteen. One of the saddest inconsistencies in the British educational system is this juxtaposition of flowing, free education at the bottom and cut-and-dried, old-fashioned information ingestion at the top. It would be surprising if the English child did not emerge at the end of his school career feeling slightly schizophrenic with this free beginning and restrictive ending. In any case, the British parent has the right to feel anxious and fretful at the contradictions built into the overall educational system for his child.

As diffuse as are the origins of the "open plan" school system, certain discernible events and publications heralded its coming. The first report which could be said to disseminate the thinking behind "open plan" was the Hadow Report of 1926. Throughout British educational history in this century, government bodies have shown a propensity for sending learned groups of people under a distinguished committee chairman to examine the existing educational system and ascertain how it could best be reformed. The group report is duly published by Her Majesty's Stationery Office, there occurs a brief flutter of comment and discussion in the newspapers and educational journals—then it sinks out of view. Some brilliant recommendations for educational change have thus over the years, been proffered, cogitated over, and then quietly shelved.

The Hadow Report was primarily concerned with the education of the adolescent, recommending that he be taught apart from the primary school child, in separate buildings instead of in all-age schools, and that his school-leaving age be raised from fourteen to fifteen. Ten years after the publication of the report, its central recommendation that teenagers not leave school until fifteen was adopted (the recommendation that schools for adolescents be separated from those for primary school children was not fully enacted until forty years after its publication). Though educational philosophy was not as crucial to the Hadow Report as were some of the more practical reforms suggested in it for the adolescent student, the committee did emphasize that teachers should be more concerned with providing an enriched environment in which children could learn spontaneously and at their own pace than with the instilling of facts. In essence, what the Hadow Committee hoped would occur among teachers was what the New York educator Caleb Gattegno has described as "the subordination of teaching to learning." This idea is the central one of the "open plan" school philosophy.

The teaching of Friedrich Froebel had an enormous influence on the Hadow Committee's thinking. The philosophy of this German teacher, whose freer methods of teaching primary school children shocked his European colleagues in the mid-nineteenth century, had become widely known and appreciated in England by the time of the 1920s. Though a small, experimental school in West Kensington had practiced his methods as long ago as 1880, there was little widespread recognition of his philosophy of teaching until 1921 when the Froebel Institute was established in Roehampton, London, and its members began to organize teacher training courses along his philosophical lines. Froebel predated Piaget by a half a century, yet he could have been the Swiss psychologist's spiritual father. Like Piaget, Froebel felt that knowledge acquired by the young child had to be gradually sifted and that the child had to absorb concepts at his own rate of speed. Above all, Froebel believed in the innate capacity of a child to handle a certain amount of freedom. He thought that a teacher should follow in the wake of a child's intellectual development and not try to impose his own disciplines and tempo upon him arbitrarily.

But the recommendations of the Hadow Report, along with its revolutionary philosophical suggestions for teaching reform, went largely unnoticed when first presented to the politicians and the public. Parents were far more docile and apathetic in those days about how their children were being taught, and many teachers and educators were repelled by what they thought were free-wheeling, progressive techniques. The climate was such that it was simple for a report of that kind to disappear without trace, resurfacing in another decade, it is true, but with a milder impact because of the time lapse.

As Lord "Rab" Butler, minister of education under Churchill during the war years, has written in his autobiography, *The Art of the Possible*, it took a national catastrophe like a war to force the English to look at their educational failings with a critical eye. As he writes:

> The crisis of modern war is a crucial test of national values and way of life. Amid the suffering and the sacrifice the weaknesses of society are revealed and there begins a period of self-examination, self-criticism and movement for reform. It is remarkable how in England educational planning and advance have coincided with wars. . . . the revelations of evacuation administered a severe shock to the national conscience; for they brought to light the conditions of those unfortunate children of the "submerged tenth" who would also rank among the citizens of the future. It was realized with deepening awareness that the "two nations" still existed in England a century after Disraeli had used the phrase.

Butler was sufficiently inspired by the realization that "two nations" still applied in England to drive through his momentous 1944 Education Act without Churchill's especial benediction (in fact, he did this almost while Churchill was not looking; the old war-horse's interest in schools at that point was tepid to say the least). At the basis of Butler's act was a desire to remove the "old stigmas of inferiority" that had attached themselves to the secondary schools (state-aided grammar schools still catered to the gifted children of the working-classes; independent schools educated the sons and daughters of the middle and upper classes). His idea was to upgrade the facilities of the secondary schools with increased financial aid and to see that conditions in all types of state schools—grammar, modern, and technical—would be roughly similar. In working for this broad-based equivalence, Butler forecast the present British comprehensive schools—large, well-equipped plants for the children of all classes, resembling U.S. high schools in their democratic tone. But Butler realized that it was useless to improve at the top and ignore the upcoming bulge of children, a booming crop of war babies, who would, as he said, enter the period of compulsory schooling from conditions of family deprivation. For this reason, the act provided for a major expansion of grant-aided nursery schools.

With the war overturning old, stale ideas concerning school and class, a fresh wind of change blowing through the corridors of the Education Ministry, and a new dollop of money for preschool children, it was not surprising that primary school teachers, nurtured on Froebel, should feel free to be more innovative than they ever had before the war.

The school buildings in northern England, appalling old Victorian red-brick affairs, for the most part, had a liberating rather than a constricting effect on infant-school teachers. Again, with such dispiriting piles of ancient bricks to function in, what could one do but work around, rather than with, them? The idea gradually formed that children need not be confined to these unattractive classrooms and that the best way to avoid feeling oppressed by them was to allow the children to roam freely throughout the corridors and from class to class with less division between the ages or separation of one classroom group from another. Gradually, gracefully, and without fanfare, northern innovators poured their new wine into old academic bottles, and their ideas moved south to London and the home counties.

In 1967, the "open plan" schools were given their biggest boost by the government when Lady Bridget Plowden, chairman of the committee which published the Plowden Report "Children and Their Primary Schools," recommended giving a grant of £11 million (about $26 million) for "educational priority areas" and officially endorsed the "progressive" primary school methods in operation throughout the country. Lady Plowden's recommendations were accepted by the government.

It is no mere coincidence that the endorsement of more money for schools in deprived areas and for the "open plan" schools (the "progressive" ones mentioned) should have come in the same breath. It has now come to be realized that the disadvantaged child thrives in the atmosphere of these open-ended, child-directed schools where parents are enthusiastically invited to take part in the making of materials for the classrooms and parent-teacher dialogue is encouraged. If one of the main handicaps of the working-class child has been his lack of communication with his parent, the "open plan" schools try to help by bridging the parent-child gap. When I went to visit the Harrington Hill Primary School in Clapton in Northeastern London, mothers were busily at work in the principal's office making numbers and reading cards for their five- and six-year-olds. John Bryce, the principal of this newly constructed "open plan" school, said that it was a calculated policy on his part to involve the parents in the workings of the school ("Parents have free access to the school at all times," he told me). In this primarily working-class area with a high immigrant population, the mothers had become just as involved with their children's school activities as any keen middle-class mother in the affluent suburbs would with her PTA meetings and fund-raising teas.

A popular misconception about the "open plan" schools which exists in Britain among skeptical parents is that there is no structure to the school day. The jargon of the "open plan" schools themselves has contributed toward the suspicion—phrases like the "unstructured" or "free" day. But as John Bryce explained to me, the schools have a definite structure. ("We have assembly at eleven o'clock, for instance," he said, "and have lunch at a set time, and so on.") He subscribes to the view originally voiced by the famous British child analyst, the late Dr. Susan Isaacs, who wrote in connection with one early progressive school's "free day" that all "free activity has its necessary practical limits and is set in a general framework of relatively fixed events."

The unity and dedication of the teachers also gives the "open plan" school its strong feeling of centralization. One teacher I spoke to at Harrington Hill told me that staff meetings were incessant, and, she admitted a little wearily, exhausting. She said that few lunch hours failed to turn into staff meetings, informal perhaps, but intense. In the "open plan" school, the teacher is the anchor of the classroom, the central force about which the apparent freedom revolves. John Bryce admits that this puts a great deal of pressure on the teacher in this system.

"Generally I would say that 'open plan' is marvelous for the children, rougher on the teachers," he told me. "This is a very mixed community with 95 per cent of the pupils coming from low-cost/council houses. This was originally a Jewish community. Now it is nearly 40 per cent immigrant colored. A great many of the mothers work and there are a lot of strains and stresses. We get some pretty disturbed kids. The teachers can find it a strain. It would help if we had a larger teacher-pupil ratio—say, one teacher to ten children rather than one to twenty as it is now. In spite of these drawbacks, our teachers are very dedicated. No one feels lukewarm about 'open plan'."

Parents begin to sense this teacher dedication and respond accordingly. By a happy coincidence recently, I went to a hair-dresser's near Marble Arch with the coy name of Hair We Are. The man and wife who ran it were a definite mum and dad, very excited about their children's school. They were sending their boy, aged eight, and girl, aged six, to the Prior Weston Primary School in the Barbican area of the East End, a showcase "open plan" school run by the pioneering Henry Pluckrose (his school has become a focal point for visiting American teachers). I was amazed to discover that they lived in central London and yet were more than willing to make the trip several miles to the East End through traffic-choked city streets to ensure that their children attended the school. They maintained that their formerly insecure and unconfident boy had undergone a character change since he began attending Prior Weston. Apart from reading the papers each day with intelligent interest, he would ring them up "like a little man" when any event occurred at home that he thought that they, at work, would miss. Like their children, the parents were devoted to Henry, the principal, who was on a first-name basis with the parents and children alike (in Britain, where male teachers and headmasters are referred to by the creepingly deferential term *sir*, even this is a startling break-through).

The most significant remark made by these enthusiastic work-ing-class London parents about their son's reaction to Prior Weston was that their boy wept if he could not go to school.

This relatively new enthusiasm for school seems to me to be the key to the possible future success of this British-born system now being warmly embraced by many Americans and why I feel the "open plan" or "open door" system may be—if carefully administered—one of the solutions to the "neglected mind." This education by controlled freedom has almost completely erased the deprived child's loathing of school.

This loathing has been so common among children over the years that it has even acquired a clinical name: school phobia. It was a common enough agony experienced by young students to warrant discussion at that International Conference on Adolescence in Edinburgh that I attended in journalistic solitude in 1966. Parents of my generation certainly knew the symptoms: psychosomatic stomachaches, diarrhea, sweaty palms, tears ("I'm sick, Mum—I can't go to school"). School phobia is the illness that can grip the disadvantaged child more than any other; up to now that red-brick schoolhouse has been no haven for him, but a forbidding citadel of middle-class teaching methods, an autocratic forcefeeder of bewildering and irrelevant facts, and generally about as cozy a place to spend a day in as the Egyptian mummy section of an ill-lit museum (and probably less interesting). Too often the conventional school seems to be a place that is testing the poor child from a deprived home and finding him wanting. Dropping out is a natural future development of this unfairly superimposed feeling of inferiority.

When I asked Lillian Weber in 1971 in New York City if she thought the "open plan" or "open door"* school was a more sympathetic environment for the working-class child, she answered in the affirmative. For the deprived child, the main ad-

---

*Also referred to sometimes in the press as "open corridor," not a term that its New York advocates particularly like; "open door" is preferred.

vantage of the method, newly adopted in Manhattan in several schools under her aegis, was, she felt, that he now no longer went unobserved and ignored.

"While I don't want to say that informal education is a panacea for the disadvantaged child," she told me, "I do think that it does give him a chance to keep his drives for learning going. This type of education has this ethos written into it—there is the obligation to mesh with each child, to find out where he is. It also admits of the right of each child to have the power to *aim* and expects the teacher to meet *his* thinking. It is the primary obligation of the teacher to interact personally with the child. There is the constant awareness of the need to extend each child's thinking. Formal education with its whole-class presentation did not have such an obligation to each child. Therefore, children who weren't responding were ignored. Teaching was not done in an equitable fashion. In informal education, if a kid is at the bottom of the pile, then you as a teacher have to know where he is and figure out a way to extend his thinking."

According to some experts, the sense of alienation a child can feel in a conventional school may begin at the age of seven. In *From Birth to Seven*, a survey of seventeen thousand babies born in 1958 and followed through for six years into home and school backgrounds, Dr. Ronald Davie, deputy director of the British National Children's Bureau, found this to be the case. He writes:

> The initial difficulties of some working-class children in acclimatising themselves (to school) sometimes result in alienation. Our results show that more working-class children, even by seven years of age, are showing hostility towards teachers, or, worse still, withdrawal, depression and a "writing-off" of adult standards.

One is reminded again of the survey made by the Texas Education Agency (see p. 112) which reported a 40 to 60 per cent annual dropout rate of Spanish-speaking children by the end of their elementary grades. Such widespread discouragement has more than set the stage for the theorists of "deschooling" such as Ivan Illich, the revolutionary Mexican educator who wants existing conventional schools abolished.

The "open plan" school is definitely not a deschooling process, in spite of what some parents and observers might feel when they enter a primary class of this kind (there is much talk of its "noise level" in both U.S. and British journals, a lovely euphemism for a God-awful din). Both the "open plan" schools in Britain and the "open door" in America have a definite structure.

The structure of "open plan" schools comes with the division of the classroom into learning areas. No matter how the teacher may see fit to arrange them, they usually consist of (a) a reading corner filled with books that a child may select for himself; (b) a writing table covered with felt tip pens, paper, word and alphabet cards, and sometimes a typewriter; (c) a science area, usually containing live animals (in PS 87 in New York, I saw a cage of very Gallic-looking snails, in an English "open plan" school, a glossy white rat of Russian lineage); they also have plants, rocks, thermometers, magnets, and other materials of scientific interest; (d) a math corner with tables holding cuisenaire rods, weights, counters, measuring cups, scales, and frequently a stove for cooking under adult supervision (measuring ounces of sugar and milk, and so on, to make simple dishes, has been found to be a compelling way for the child to learn living math); and finally (e) an art corner where the children can model clay, work with water colors and collage materials, and cut pictures out of old magazines and newspapers. A section for records and simple musical instruments may also be included. In the Manhattan "open door" schools, sand and water tables usually stand in the hallways, with colorful exhibitions of the children's artwork along the walls.

Lillian Weber is careful to point out that her informal "open door" schools are only adaptations of the English kind and are not direct models. She took a cautious course in implementing the new scheme at PS 84 and PS 123 in Manhattan, suggesting to grade school teachers that they use the method as a supplement to their curriculum. Within a period of four years, the teachers themselves ceased to use "open door" as an addition and it is not the basis and all-round method for the teaching of six- and seven-year-olds at these two schools, a triumph for the method and for Mrs. Weber's tact (as a teacher of over twenty-five years' standing, she knew enough not to try and breathe too heavily down other teachers' necks).

The term "open door" is preferable in many ways to the designation "open corridor" that seems to have caught on journalistically in America. The new teaching is much more than an architectural phenomenon, though the corridor aspect is highly central to its ethos; the main idea is for children to feel that there is a community of classrooms into which they can flow from the corridor. However, the method can thrive without this corridor intervisitation, as I have seen at Harrington Hill. At the basis of the teaching is the concept that a child's learning is not sequential, that it is self-directed, that a child has his own timetable which guides him, and that an atmosphere of curiosity and joy in a classroom is more important than neat desks set in a row and quiet circumspection. The feeling is that in an enriched environment, surrounded by stimulating materials and a teacher's gentle guidance, a child cannot fail to learn. The flowing of children into the corridors in the cases of both the New York and English schools sprang from necessity and lack of space, not from a feeling that a corridor is essential to the method (though it may enhance it, as Lillian Weber certainly believes).

In England, the corridors are less important with the newly built schools, confirming the notion that they were used, in the past, much more from necessity than from being central to the learning process. At Harrington Hill, the corridors, exceedingly airy and wide ones, are used only for assemblies, entries, and departures. A air of spaciousness and of wholeness, rather than division, has been lent the school at Clapton by an extensive use of glass partitions and wide, unsectioned rooms filled with long, child-sized tables for sentence-making and writing. The rooms are deeply carpeted and a great deal of action, especially reading, is done on the floor.

It would be rash of me to be categorical about Anglo-American differences of the "open plan" schools on the basis of my visits to PS 87 in Manhattan and to Prior Weston and Harrington Hill in London. I would not care to generalize about the differences on any broad-based scale. However, there were sharp and discernible contrasts in the three that I did see. At Harrington Hill and Prior Weston, there was less of a hurly-burly (that "noise level" we hear so much about) and more apparently conventional attention to sentence-making and concentration on the subject at hand. The teachers were reasonably commanding and could be heard admonishing and hushing the children when the occasion warranted. The children rose and filed into their eleven o'clock assembly without a murmur when their teacher announced it was time; the teachers saw that they did this neatly and quietly. My observations at Harrington Hill and Prior Weston tended to give some credence to the thesis of University of New Hampshire educator Marian Hapgood that English children are more soft-spoken and mannerly than their American counterparts and therefore are better adapted to the "open plan" system. However, I do not totally subscribe to her view that noise and learning are inimical; no one has ever proved them to be. It seems to me that much would depend on the quality and tenor of the noise made; while unhappy noises are disturbing, a happy buzz can be infectiously gay, even stimulating.

One of the most telling Anglo-American differences in the setting out of "open plan" lies in the autonomy of the principal. It is hard to escape the conviction that the best of the "open plan" schools in England are vehicles for dedicated, charismatic principals like Henry Pluckrose and John Bryce, the two London stars. Their leadership is unquestioned by the teachers who surround them. Though no cracking of whips is heard, the structure in both these London schools is definitely that of a nucleus of dedicated, hard-working teachers revolving around the powerful central force of the principal. The best schools, no matter what the teaching method, have always been those with star-quality, tireless heads, and "open plan" is no exception. In one conventional primary school in London, which shall be nameless, I witnessed the sad introduction of a few "open plan" methods under the weak leadership of an unsure, vacillating headmistress. The result, for several years, was chaos and massive withdrawals of pupils by irate parents. In any educational system, there seems to be no substitute for the personal magnetism of a good head.

The "open door" schools in Manhattan have been fortunate in having the powerful personality of Mrs. Lillian Weber as their driving force. However, possibly because she is an advisor to them, rather than their on-the-spot principal, there does appear to be less unity and more noise in the New York "open" classrooms than one notes in Britain. Certainly, there was an ear-drum-destroying level of it at PS 87 when I visited it in the fall of 1971. The children were swarming around in one basement room, churning from one table (the snails) to another (cuisenaire rods) with shrieks and cries of what appeared to be pleasure. Hidden as any apparent structure was beneath this chaos, I was assured by the teachers that it did in fact exist. One of the teachers outlined it for me: there were seven classes in one unit and over 300 children in all, breaking down into 101 of kindergarten age, 102 in the first grade, and 103 in the second grade; all were aged from five to seven. The children were grouped in "clusters" of twenty, although the number was not static and these clusters of children were encouraged to flow freely in and out of the corridors three mornings and two afternoons a week. Attending each cluster was one full teacher, one student teacher, and one paraprofessional (a mother or a high school graduate, not necessarily someone with a college degree). Each child received fifteen minutes of private instruction every other day and the teachers kept track of each child's progress on separate sheets, though no report cards were ever filed. Each teacher was fully prepared to have regular conferences with parents.

I asked one teacher about discipline problems, the scourge of most urban schools in deprived areas in Britain and America, and she assured me that they were at a minimum.

"Noise isn't necessarily naughty, after all," she explained. "If a temper starts to rise, we calm it down with a group song or maybe we read a story . . . but this doesn't occur very often."

She told me that absenteeism due to sickness was astonishingly low, a dramatic change from her previous experience in teaching grade school children by formal methods.

"They hate the day to end here," she said. "They all groan and say, "Is it three o'clock already?""

One of the explanations for this widespread pleasure in school —a new sensation for the ghetto child, in particular—is that the "open plan" or "open door" method strives to bolster a child's ego by appealing to his self-esteem while encouraging learning at the same time. Most of the reading and writing taught is of the language-experience variety, in which a child tells something of his own experience in one or two sentences and the teacher writes down what he has said. In this way, a child is not cracking an obscure code about an unreal-seeming pair called Janet and John; he is reading his own story, his own creation.

The appeal to the child's egocentricity shores up the self-esteem of those disadvantaged children whose overcrowded homes have had the effect of depersonalizing them. As we have seen, severely disadvantaged children from large low-income or welfare families have great trouble in verbalizing, resembling those children who have suffered from extreme social isolation in their early years. They have trouble in speaking at all when they first enter the strange new environment of a classroom, and even if they do speak, they have difficulty in referring to themselves in the first person. Language-experience teaching, where the reading and writing is of a gratifyingly autobiographical nature and where reading and writing evolve naturally from each other (in "open plan," they are not separated into two different categories as they have been in the past in conventional schools), gives the child the feeling of belonging, of having an importance and value that is all his own.

In England a similar appeal to the ego is made by the use of the "Breakthrough to Literacy" method (see p. 120), the one used extensively in British "open plan" schools. A glance at the official brochure describing the system reveals how heavily it relies upon a child's healthy self-centeredness for its success. In a paragraph explaining the use of the "Word Maker," the brochure states: "Phonics are introduced through the *Word Maker*, a smaller folder with pockets containing written symbols. This allows the child to construct words experimentally, without the finality of writing, and to acquire spelling facility, etc."

In writing of their collection of "Twenty-four Breakthrough Books," the authors state that

> Conversations with children and examples of children's writing were used as the source for each book. The subject matter and the language are those natural to children. Hence the child nurtured on the *Sentence Maker* will find himself able to carry over this experience into reading *Breakthrough* books. Some explore an everyday incident like losing a tooth, or going to school, others involve witches and giants. . . .

As evident as is the appeal to the ego in all these devices, the Breakthrough "Sentence Maker" employs it most nakedly: "The child's *My Sentence Maker*," the brochure reads,

> to which he graduates once he can recognize a certain number of words through handling the teacher's model. Items from the printed vocabulary plus his own personal words are only acquired if he *needs* them. Thus he constructs his own working vocabulary and uses it to compose sentences in his *Plastic Stand*. . . . The child very soon produces a great variety of sentences which he reads to

his teacher and friends, writing naturally about many of the things that interest him. The child is *handling* language with confidence and ingenuity . . . because it is his own, represents *his* achievements and is fun to use.

How the Victorians would have cringed! Buttering up the little monsters—encouraging them to prattle on about themselves! No such individuality was asked of a child in those days. A look at some of the horrible, moralistic tales of that era confirms this; children were cautioned to be good, be quiet, eat up, cut their nails, and attend to the business at hand. One need only reread Heinrich Hoffmann's *Struwwelpeter* to get the nineteenth-century message. Even harmless dreamers like the absentminded schoolboy in the verse, "The Story of Johnny Head-in-Air" came a nasty cropper for indulging in his own fantasies (he eventually fell in a river and lost his writing book—horrors!). As unknown to the Victorians as a jet flight was the concept that a strong, well-defined ego in a child is a positive good and a future insurance for mental health.

But healthy egos apart, are the children reading as well as they used to when they are exposed to these self-directed, unconventional means? "Open plan" is not everyone's idea of the perfect solution for the education of primary school children. Frequently, parents are unimpressed by what they feel is an over casual approach to learning. One mother I spoke to in Maine whose son was attending a small, experimental "open door" school there said that her Benny could not add two and two and he was nearly seven years old. When she confronted the teacher with this manifest lack, she was turned away by a soft answer: "Benny will come to the math corner when he feels ready," she said. According to the mother, Benny never did.

Some complaints have come from scholars as well. Mrs. Bernice Martin, lecturer in social studies and economics at Bedford College, London, condemned the "progressive methods" in schools, finding them alien to the basic nature of the working-class child. In her estimation, working-class children felt more at ease in a structured, role-bound setting, and thus the unstructured environment of the "open plan" school disabled them "by requiring a pattern of response which they can only find radically inimical and disorienting." She thought that middle-class children took comfortably to the freer methods because they were accustomed to the playing down of ascribed roles in their home backgrounds.

What Mrs. Martin seems to be saying is that as a working-class child is accustomed to authoritarianism at home, he should have a diet of continued dictatorship at school. However, as so many child study experts have emphasized, an authoritarian background, such as the many matriarchal black homes in the ghettos, only adds to a child's passive nature and lack of any real sense of identity. A school shouldn't compound this error. The most cursory glance at the dropout figures in deprived areas of the United States where authoritarian teaching methods have been used would tend to confirm the beliefs of those scholars who maintain that a working-class child is made to feel alienated by school strong-arm tactics and strict role definitions.

When the Inner London Education Authority published a report in 1971 stating that there had been a marked decline in the standard of reading among the young in Great Britain in the past ten years, the anti-open-planners were given just the critical fodder they needed. Commenting on the new government grant for the provision of more "open-plan" primary schools in the London *Sunday Times*, education writer Allan Hall was scathing about the new teaching, describing its built-in noise level as "continuous," its regime exhausting for staff and pupils alike, and its expectations for a better education unjustifiably high:

> Educationalists assume that all children, given a "meaningful learning situation" are eager to learn. But education is still hard work. Reading and writing demand enormous efforts on the part of the child. Bright children will manage somehow. They will "flow into all parts of the building and its surroundings" making intelligent discoveries and recording their findings for the teacher's approval. But what of the rest? The plodders, the shirkers, the "can't's" and the "don't want to's"? In the open plan it's much easier to dodge the issue.

Allan Hall's slashing criticism of "open plan" expectations is very reminiscent of the outcries that greeted the progressive methods of John Dewey and his disciples in the 1920s and 1930s: the antiprogressives always tend to fall back on the view that learning is hard work and that the "fun" element will negate proper learning and encourage the shirkers (whomever *they* might be—disturbed children, exhausted by their problem families?) to shirk further. There is a déjà-vu feel about Hall's comments.

And how valid are the criticisms? According to the Ronald Davie report *From Birth to Seven* (ironically given a huge color section spread in the very same *Sunday Times*, but months later), poor reading springs more from bad home conditions than progressive school techniques. As he writes:

> A seven-year-old from a one-or-two child family is on average about 12 months advanced in reading compared with one from a family of five or more. . . . The ability to read is closely linked to fluency in

speech, and since children learn new words and expressions more by talking with adults than with other children, the time a parent can give a child is extremely important.

Davie emphasizes that this special dialogue time is at a minimum where there is overcrowding and large families.

One of the surprise findings of the Davie report was that Scottish seven year olds were, on average, about eleven months ahead of the children from other parts of Great Britain. His research team could only conclude that this had something to do with the propensity of the Scottish parent to continue to read aloud to his child (Scottish television is less all-embracing, too —there are fewer sets per family, fewer channels); also Scottish teachers were apt to start their pupils reading earlier than teachers in other parts of the country (paging Jerome Bruner once again here).

If overcrowding is at the basis of poor reading, then it is easy to see why reading has deteriorated over the past decade in England and America; poor and limited housing plus a growth in population have been the twin, symbiotic scourges of both countries in the past ten or fifteen years.

"Open plan" or "open door" has not been in operation long enough in the United States to ascertain whether or not its loosely structured methods have succeeded in teaching children to read and solve arithmetical problems as efficiently as they might in the more traditional classrooms. Even the fairest official evaluations are not clear-cut. Dr. Sol Gordon, a member of the board of trustees for the Center for Urban Education, formerly on the faculty of Yeshiva University, was not sure that the first-and second-graders he observed at PS 123 were as adept at arithmetic as they should have been. However, in this official evaluation, he did praise certain qualities of "open door":

While I found this class uncongenial to me because of the fooling around (and I dare say that parents, if they dropped in, might be taken aback) in general according to such standards as verbalization and reading levels, this class was achieving much better than I would have thought possible.... The general reading ability seemed much higher than ordinarily found in second grade in ghetto schools.

One of Dr. Gordon's most significant conclusions, more on the emotional than the academic side, was that "the children seemed happy to be at school—a phenomenon not often observed in a ghetto school."

While there are many detractors of "open plan" who insist that happiness is not all, it is evident that this new pleasure in school is one of the most remarkable aspects of this system and one which cannot be ignored. Lillian Weber is the first to caution American educators against clutching wildly at "open door" as the solution for all ills. If it is to work properly and on a more broad-based, nationwide scale, there must be a more thorough network of teacher training programs geared to this teaching method. As John Bryce, the Harrington Hill principal, emphasized, the pressure on the teacher under this new system is enormous. She must be adequately prepared to cope with this kind of pressure by taking teacher's training at the college level. In the United States, these programs are still scarce, with training centers located only at New York's Bank Street College and at the University of North Dakota. However, it is possible that the existing university training programs for teachers will adapt themselves to "open plan."

Just as the occasion of World War II illuminated the plight of Britain's "submerged tenth" for its education minister and others, the recent federal poverty programs initiated in the United States have shone great beacon lights on the deprived American child. Project Head Start alerted Congress to the fact that millions of children were being starved intellectually at a time when their rate of development was at its most crucial stage. A great if long overdue unease on this score gripped U.S. lawmakers, and in the late 1960s, at least nine bills were introduced in Congress which were concerned with child development and child care.

Day care is not new in America, nor in other industrialized nations such as Russia, Germany, and the Scandinavian countries. The idea of a mother's dropping a child off at a nursery so that she can work has been in existence since women first entered industry. World War II saw the trend widen when women joined the assembly lines both in Britain and America (the nurseries were often located at the industrial centers; this was the start of industry's vested interest in making it easy for mothers to work by providing on-the-spot day-care centers). In those early days of day care, the nurseries were almost entirely custodial; the children, usually over three years of age, were fed, kept clean, aired, exercised—their physical well-being was tended assiduously. It did not occur to either the day-care supervisors or the mothers that any other form of care was necessary.

A working mother of a very young child has had to contend with a certain amount of social disapproval. She has always been made to feel that she should more properly be at home making her family comfortable. Specialists in child development have not helped make her feel less guilty, as they have reason to believe—well-documented reason—that a child is better off with his or her mother during those first three to five years. Even many day-care authorities feel that the child's first three years are better spent with his mother. Mrs. Marjorie Grossett, executive director of the New York Day-Care Council, is of this opinion, though she supervises family day-care programs that tend to the under-threes.

However, despite social and medical disapproval, mothers have continued to seek employment, and "woman manpower," that semantic contradiction in terms, has burgeoned over the past decade. The reasons are not always for financial gain alone. In literally millions of cases, women with young children who work do so from absolute necessity. Fifty per cent of the mothers in New York City who have their young in day care (eighteen thousand in all) are in one-parent situations. At the basis of the boom in working mothers is the undeniable breakdown of the conventional marital structure and the overall increase in divorce and separation.

Other influences also contribute to the trend. Undoubtedly, the appetite for material goods, which many claim that television has whetted, enters into a mother's desire to make money. Certain consumer goods now seem indispensable to her—a television set, a car, a dishwasher, a washing machine, wall-to-wall carpets, a hi-fi set, and so on. Also, the countries of the industrialized West subscribe to a strong work ethos. To work is to have a certain dignity. Money in the pocket gives a modicum of freedom. A job and money spell independence. And recently, adding to the basic seductiveness of making one's own income is the realization that this helps a woman to become a first-class rather than a second-class citizen. The irrefutable evidence that the women's liberationists have brought to light—that women are discriminated against, legally, socially, industrially, and in a host of other ways—has added to the general feminine determination to reach for freedom and autonomy through the acquisition of a paycheck (even if that paycheck may represent unequal pay for equal work with men).

It is futile to decry the movement and wish women would become more submissive and happily housebound, more willing to cosset their husbands (a great many still think this is lovely —and more power to them if this is what they want; the point is, millions no longer *do* want this). So the clock is not going to be turned back, and it would be useless to militate against day care because it helps remove a mother from the one-to-one relationship with her infant which benefits him so greatly. The crucial need is for better and better day-care centers.

Working mothers are here to stay, and the figures prove just how determined they are to stay. The working mother phenomenon has been an explosive happening in the past twenty-five years in the United States. According to a 1969 U.S. Department of Labor report, the number of working mothers "increased more than sevenfold since 1940 and more than doubled since 1950." In March 1967, the department reported that 10.6 million mothers with children under eighteen were workers, and that "almost two out of five of these mothers had children under six, totalling 4.5 million youngsters of this age." It is significant that between 1960 and 1967, the rate for mothers of children under six increased more rapidly than for any other group. During this seven-year period, 32 per cent of mothers with children under six were working. This phenomenon has been a great defeat for those child psychologists who believe that the first three to five years are best spent with the mother. It is sad to relate, but apparently mother would rather not spend her time on a twenty-four-hour basis with her child, or, if she would, financial considerations have had to take precedence over this maternal wish.

Some of the facts concerning working mothers and their children should comfort those who see the trend as inhuman, a breaking down of warm interpersonal family relationships. First, there is little evidence to prove that children of working mothers are any less educationally alert or less well adjusted than the children of stay-at-home mothers. One of the observers on the Ronald Davie team which published *From Birth to Seven* said:

> I suspect that the things women do for and with their children have been needlessly elaborated to make motherhood a full-time job. Unfortunately, in this very process, the child's struggle for autonomy and independence, for privacy and the right to worry things through for himself are subtly reduced by the omnipresent mother.

While this comment is a slap in the face for the concerned, all day-long, ever-present mother, it could be argued that the latch-key child, thinking things out for himself in his motherless apartment, can also become a lonely, alienated figure, ripe for delinquency. Still, nothing in the Davie team's findings showed that the children of working mothers did less well at school or were in any way more antisocial or disruptive than the children of housewives.

What the more hopeful sociologists (hopeful about the undeniable trend towards less traditional forms of "mothering" and more working) say is that there is nothing wrong with a multiplicity of mother substitutes as long as the child has continuity with the same blood mother at the end of the day. The real optimists even go so far as to pronounce day-care centers an improvement on the one-to-one relationship, pointing out that they can resemble a form of extended family, with the teachers, nutritionists, and paraprofessionals involved in the running of such a center approximating those endless strings of doting aunts and grandmothers who make a South Sea islander's or African child's early years such happy, tactile affairs.

In any case, when a mother is "at risk," to use the language of the social welfare agencies, a day-care center can be infinitely preferable for her child than her disturbed and disturbing company. A mother "at risk" (and about 10 per cent of the mothers whose children were in the New York centers were categorized as such)* is one who is addicted to drugs or alcohol; these addictions usually masking deep-seated psychiatric disturbances. When a mother is comatose most of the day, or potentially violent, it is easy to see why a day-care center with its play therapy, excellent nutrition, rest periods, and the attentions of concerned, affectionate adults is a desirable alternative to her daylong ministrations (or lack of them). Day-care centers in these cases help to lower a mother's emotional temperature, making it possible for her to be much more loving to her child at night. It is more than possible that the centers reduce the possibility of child battering. The day-center directors are usually alerted to problem situations in a child's background. The centers operate in a complex way with welfare officers, nutritionists, psychiatrists, and teachers all exchanging information with each other—the main object being to get a full picture of the mental and physical well-being of each child.

In one day-care center I visited in New York, I saw a little girl

---

*In a pamphlet published in May 1971 by the Day-Care Council of New York, called *Our Children—Our Times*.

sleeping in the playground, draped over a tricycle. The supervisors let her sleep on. They explained that her drunken mother and the mother's lover brawled throughout the nights and kept her awake. For this reason, they let her catch up whenever she could and never woke her unnecessarily. This sort of sympathetic understanding and individual attention to each special case can make the centers havens for the children of problem parents. However, as Milton Wilner has written in his study of day-care centers, although the best can alleviate certain social problems, they can never totally compensate for inadequate income, poor housing, low employment, absent fathers, and racial discrimination.

But day-care centers can be great palliatives for children under social stress. The sad fact is that there are simply not enough to go around (and this is true of most Western countries with mothers of young children eager to work). In 1971 it was estimated that there were only 640,000 U.S. children who could be served in licensed centers and family homes, and ten times this number was needed to be realistic. Then, how were the overflow of children being cared for while their mothers worked? The last Labor Department survey on the subject published in 1965 revealed that less than one-half of the preschool children were cared for in their homes, approximately one-third in someone else's home, and a little more than 5 per cent in group day-care centers. Some were tended by the mother while she worked and some "cared for themselves." The casual officialese of the last phrase sends a chill through the heart.

As day-care centers are striving to be more educational, to move away from the old custodial, baby-sitting role, they have also become more expensive to run. Federal agencies estimate that they cost anywhere from $1,000 to $2,300 per child per year, depending on the area in which the child lives. As they are attempting to enhance a child's intelligence as well as his physical well-being, a high adult-child ratio is also required—a heavy expense. Ideally, there should be one adult per group of five children. For a day-care center to function at its best, it should also be rooted in the community, absorbing volunteers and interested nonworking mothers into its activities.

A danger inherent in the day-care system is that it relieves a mother of so many of her burdens of child care that it can end up by supplanting her completely. Most directors are aware of this and strive for parental involvement. They realize that what Harvard social relations professor Dr. Jerome Kagan calls "an insidious erosion of the quality of parental involvement" must not be allowed to occur.

Just how conscious some of the best centers are of this sensitive emotional area is shown by the statement in a pamphlet for parents put out by the Hudson Guild Child Center in Manhattan. Under the heading "Arriving and Leaving," it reads:

> When your child is ready to stay for the full day, try to call for him as early in the late afternoon as you can. The Center is open from 8 to 6, but nine or ten hours is too long for a child to be in a group. He gets tired and uneasy when he sees other children going home and sometimes decides he doesn't want to come at all. So remember to come on time and come early. . . .
>
> When you bring your child in the morning, take him to his teacher before you say goodbye. When you pick him up at night, come into the building or playground and give him time to say goodbye to his teacher. . . .

It is obvious in the special pleading of this note that what is sometimes referred to as the continuity of mothering is hoped for here. Mrs. Marion Easton, the Hudson Guild director, told me that what she desired above all was parental involvement and "mother reinforcement." But she admitted that "mother reinforcement" was a relatively new concept and one which the center was still struggling to achieve. Most directors share a kind of modesty about their destinies. They speak of "early days." Truly, day-care is in its infancy, without meaning to make a painful pun.

The most optimistic facet of the day-care phenomenon is that there is an increased awareness at the highest levels of the need to make them centers for early childhood development and not just high-powered baby-minders. Some of the federal pro-nouncements about child care reveal the profound influence that the early childhood development experts have had upon them. In its 1969 report, the Labor Department stated that "all must make a concentrated effort to provide more and better facilities and training for additional personnel skilled in early childhood education." And in another passage, the report put in a plea for educational play, saying that it involved "the develop-ment of skillful integration of many awarenesses and the con-stant development of new insights." Such a degree of enlighten-ment about a young child's needs would not have issued from bureaucratic pens in the past. The seminal Project Head Start was the most encouraging piece of federal legislation for the low-income child ever devised. We can only pray that future presidents will develop the program further and not be re-trogressive.

It will come as no surprise to the reader that this book— a personal and, I hope, unpretentious voyage around some of the new theories of early childhood learning and a look at how they have affected children's books and television—embodies a strong plea for a belief in the "nurture" theory of child development. The great battle that rages over which has the most influence on human development, heredity (nature) or environment (nurture), seems to me to be a rather acrimonious and unproductive one. Obviously, a subtle interaction of both influences occurs in normal circumstances. However, it seems foolhardy to minimize the effects of environmental influence, especially on the growth of human intelligence, when one examines such evidence as I have tried to present in this book.

The most important aspect of the nurture theory is its built-in hope for all children and also the very real possibility that parents can have a deep and positive effect on the enriching of their children's minds. It seems to me to be perfectly obvious that a fertile environment—a sympathetic parent and a warm and interested teacher—can stretch a child's mind, increase his intelligence. How depressing it would be to believe firmly that a child's intellect was fixed at birth, set like some immovable thermostat throughout his life.

What is most hopeful to witness is the increased belief of progressive educators themselves in the nurture theory, the trend to bolster children's egos in schools, to cooperate with parents who come from economically deprived areas and who need help themselves before they can help their own children's development, the swing away from custodial care alone.

The idea of the perfectibility of the young human being is as old as time. The Latin scholar-poet Juvenal said of children:

"Require of him [man] that he shall mould their [children's] tender nature as with his thumb, even as a man fashions a face in wax." If we were to believe the advocates of a fixed genetic intelligence in a child, then there would be no fashioning, no molding, no influencing, no extending, and no shaping. Being a parent would be an arid affair, indeed.

And I refuse to believe that it is.

References

CHAPTER ONE

Bloom, Benjamin. *Stability and Change in Human Characteristics*. New York: John Wiley & Sons, 1964.

Herlihy, James L. *Midnight Cowboy*. London: Jonathan Cape, 1966.

Himmelweit, Hilde. *Television and the Child*. Oxford: Oxford University Press, 1958.

Pringle, Kellmer. *Social Learning and Its Measurements*. London: Longmans, 1966.

Schramm, Wilbur, Lyle, Jack, and Parker, Edwin. *Television in the Lives of Our Children*. Stanford, Calif.: Stanford University Press, 1961.

Stewart, William F. R. *Children in Flats: A Family Study*. London: National

Society for the Prevention of Cruelty to Children, 1970. 1 Riding House St., London, 1970.

CHAPTER TWO

Bloom, Benjamin. *Stability and Change in Human Characteristics*. New York: John Wiley & Sons, 1964.

Davis, Kingsley. "Extreme Social Isolation of a Child." *American Journal of Sociology*, vol. 45, January 1940.

Hawkins, Eric. Paper delivered to the British Medical Association at Harrogate, England, June 30, 1970.

Humphrey, George. *The Wild Boy of Aveyron*. New York: Appleton-Century-Crofts, 1932. (Translation of Itard's reports.)

Singh, J. A. L., and Zingg, Robert M. *Wolf Children and Feral Man*. New York: Harper & Bros., 1939, pp. 3–119, 283.

CHAPTER THREE

Bernstein, Basil. "Social Class and Linguistic Development." In A. H. Halsey, J. Floud, and C. A. Anderson, eds., *Education, Economy and Society*. New York: Free Press of Glencoe, 1961.

Bloom, Benjamin. *Stability and Change in Human Characteristics*. New York: John Wiley & Sons, 1964.

Bodman, F., Sykes, K., and McKinley, M. "The Social Adaptation of Institution Children." *Lancet* Vol. 1, January–March 1950.

Coles, Robert and Piers, Maria. *Wages of Neglect:* New Solutions For the Children of the Poor. Chicago: Quadrangle Books, 1969.

Deutsch, Martin. *The Disadvantaged Child*. New York: Basic Books, 1967.

Lewis, Morris M. *How Children Learn to Speak*. London: George Harrap, 1959; New York: Basic Books, 1959.

Lewis, Morris M. *Language and Personality in Deaf Children*. London: National Foundation for Educational Research in England and Wales, 1968.

Luria, A. R. *The Role of Speech in the Regulation of Normal and Abnormal Behaviour.* Edited by J. Tizard. New York: Pergamon Press, 1961.

McCarthy, Dorothea. "Affective Aspects of Language Learning." In Aline J. Kidd and Jeanne L. Rivoire, eds., *Perceptual Development in Children.* London: University of London Press, 1966.

Nisbet, John. "Family Environment and Intelligence." In A. H. Halsey, J. Floud, and C. A. Anderson, eds., *Education, Economy and Society.* New York: Free Press of Glencoe, 1961.

Piaget, Jean. *The Child's Conception of Number.* London: Routledge & Kegan Paul, 1952.

Piaget, Jean. *Language and Thought of the Child.* London: Routledge & Kegan Paul; First published 1926. Paperback edition, 1959. New York: Humanities Press, 1959. World Publishing, paperback, 1955.

Thomson, Robert. *The Psychology of Thinking.* New York: Penguin Books, 1959.

Winnicott, Donald W. *The Family and Individual Development.* London: Tavistock, 1965.

Wyatt, Gertrud. "Mother-Child Relationships and Stuttering in Children." Doctoral dissertation, Boston University. (University Microfilms, Ann Arbor, Michigan.)

CHAPTER FOUR

Bloom, Benjamin. *Stability and Change in Human Characteristics.* New York: John Wiley & Sons, 1964.

Bruner, Jerome. *The Process of Education.* New York: Vintage Books, 1963.

Chukovsky, Kornei. *From Two to Five.* Berkeley: University of California Press; Cambridge: Cambridge University Press, 1968.

Contact. Journal for the British Pre-Schools Playgroup Association. 1 The Outgang, Heslington, York, England.

Doman, Glenn. *How to Teach Your Baby to Read.* New York: Random House, 1963.

Engelmann, Siegfried, and Engelmann, Therese. *Give Your Child a Superior Mind.* New York: Simon and Schuster, 1966.

Eyken, Willem van der. *The Pre-School Years.* Harmondsworth: Penguin Books; Baltimore: Penguin Books, 1967.

Gunzberg, Herbert. *Social-Sight Vocabulary.* London: National Association of Mental Health. 39 Queen Anne St., W.1.

Krech, David. Paper read in 1969. Also published in *Adult Status of Children with Contrasting Life Experiences,* Chicago: University of Chicago Press.

Parent Cooperative Preschools International (PCPI) Journal. Editorial and Publications Office, 6303 Phyllis Lane, Bethesda, Md. Executive and Membership Office, 20551 Lakeshore Rd., Baie D'Urfe, Quebec, Canada.

Project Head Start, Community Action Program, Office of Economic Opportunity, Washington, D.C.

Wall, W. D. *PPA—Which Way Next?* London: 1970. Pre-School Playgroups Association. 87a Borough High St., S.E. 1

CHAPTER FIVE

Bereiter, Carl, and Englemann, Siegfried. *Teaching Disadvantaged Children in the Preschool.* Englewood Cliffs, N. J.: Prentice-Hall, 1966.

Bernstein, Basil. "Language and Social Class," *British Journal of Sociology,* vol. 11 (1960), pp. 271–276.

———. "Social Class and Linguistic Development: A Theory of Social Learning." In A. H. Halsey, J. Floud, and C. A. Anderson, eds., *Economy, Education and Society.* New York: Free Press of Glencoe, 1961.

Crossed with Adversity: the education of socially disadvantaged children in secondary schools. Schools Council Working Paper 27. Evans, Methuen Educational, 1970.

Drever, James. From A. F. Watts, *The Language and Mental Development of Children.* London: George Harrap, 1944.

Katan, Anny. "Some Thoughts about the Role of Verbalization in Early Childhood." *Psychoanalytic Study of the Child,* vol. 16, 1961.

Mitscherlich, Alexander. *Society Without the Father.* New York: Harcourt, Brace & World, 1969; London: Tavistock, 1969.

Newson, John, and Newson, Elizabeth. *Four Years Old in an Urban Community.* London: Penguin Books, 1968.

Perry, Gail. "We Had a Head Start on Head Start." *Young Children,* vol. 21, no. 5 (May 1966).

Pringle, Kellmer. *Social Learning and Its Measurement.* London: Longmans, 1966.

Radin, Norma, and Kamii, Constance. "The Child-Rearing Attitudes of Disadvantaged Negro Mothers and Some Educational Implications." *The Journal of Negro Education,* vol. 34, 1965. pp. 138–145.

Reissman, Frank. *The Culturally Deprived Child.* New York: Harper & Row, 1962.

Sexton, Patricia. *Education and Income.* New York: Viking Press, 1961.

Sprigle, Herbert. "Can Poverty Children Live on 'Sesame Street'?" *Young Children,* March 1971.

Stemmler, A. "An Experimental Approach to the Teaching of Oral Language and Reading." *Harvard Educational Review,* vol. 36, 1966. pp. 43–59.

Taba, Hilda. "Cultural Deprivation as a Factor in School Learning." *Merrill-Palmer Quarterly of Behavior and Development* vol. 10, no. 2 (April 1964).

Wolman, Marianne. *Head Start and Language Development: A Panel Discussion.* Claremont Reading Conference, 1966. Washington, D. C.: Project Head Start, Office of Economic Opportunity.

CHAPTER SIX

Goodenough, Florence. *Mental Testing.* London: Staples Press, 1950.

Grigsby, Eugene. "The Urban Teacher, His Pupils, and the Language Barrier." *Educational and Urban Society,* vol. 2, no. 2 (February 1970).

Havighurst, Robert. "Who Are the Socially Disadvantaged?" *Journal of Negro Education,* vol. 33 (1964 yearbook), pp. 210–217.

Haynes, Judith. *Educational Assessment of Immigrant Pupils.* London: National Foundation for Educational Research in England and Wales, 1971.

Mackay, David, Thomson, Brian, and Schaub, Pamela. *Breakthrough to Literacy.* London: Longmans, 1968.

Riessman, Frank. *The Culturally Deprived Child.* New York: Harper & Row, 1962.

Sigel, I. E. "How Intelligence Tests Limit Understanding of Intelligence." *Merrill-Palmer Quarterly of Behavior and Development*, vol. 63, no. 9, pp. 39–57.

Taba, Hilda. "Cultural Deprivation as a Factor in School Learning." *Merrill-Palmer Quarterly Behavior and Development*, vol. 10, no. 2 (April 1964).

CHAPTER SEVEN

Berson, Minnie Perrin. "Ali Baba! What Have You Done?" *Childhood Education*, vol. 46, no. 6 (March 1970).

Bogatz, Gerry Ann, and Ball, Samuel. "Some Things You've Wanted to Know About *Sesame Street."* *American Education*, April 1971.

Childhood Education, vol. 46, no. 9 (May 1970). Prints reader reactions to M. P. Berson, "Ali Baba! What Have You Done!"

Fuller, Buckminster. From John D. Haney, "Television: Has It Changed The Child? Will It Change Your Teaching?" *Instructor*, February 1971.

Gardner, John. From Bennie Mae Collins, Evangeline Morse, and Gerald Knowles, "Beyond *Sesame Street:* TV and Preschoolers." *Educational Leadership*, vol. 28, no. 2 (November 1970).

Hunt, J. McVicker. "The Psychological Basis for Using Pre-School Enrichment as an Antidote for Cultural Deprivation." In Fred M. Hechinger, ed., *Pre-School Education Today.* New York: Doubleday & Company, 1966.

Ingersoll, Gary M. *"Sesame Street* Can't Handle *All* the Traffic!" *Phi Delta Kappan*, November 1971.

"Instructional Goals for the 1970–71 Experimental Season of *Sesame Street."* Confidential paper put before the Schools Committee of the Independent Television Authority, June 30, 1971.

Kliger, Samuel. "Fog Over Sesame Street." *Teachers College Record*, vol. 72, no. 1 (September 1970), pp. 41–56.

Schramm, Wilbur. *Television in the Lives of Our Children*. Stanford, Calif.: Stanford University Press, 1961.

Shayon, Robert Lewis. "Cutting Oedipal Ties." *Saturday Review*, February 14, 1970.

Sprigle, Herbert A. "Can Poverty Children Live On *Sesame Street?*" *Young Children*, March 1971. From a paper first presented at the 1970 Conference of the National Association for the Education of Young Children, Boston, November 18–21, 1970.

Stewart, William F. R. *Children in Flats: A Family Study*. London: National Society for the Prevention of Cruelty to Children, 1970.

Wallace, Anthony F. C. *Housing and Social Structure: A Preliminary Survey with Particular Reference to Multi-Story, Low-Rent, Public Housing Projects."* Philadelphia: Philadelphia Housing Authority, 1952.

CHAPTER EIGHT

Condry, John. "Broadcasting and the Needs of Children." In Evelyn Sarson, ed., *Action for Children's Television*. New York: Avon Books, 1971. (An edited transcript of the First National Symposium on Children and Television held by the Action for Children's Television—ACT. ACT address: 33 Hancock Avenue, Newton Center, Mass. 02159.)

Darvin, Brenda, and Greenberg, Bradley S. "Communication Among the Urban Poor—Communication and Urban Poverty—A Research Summary." CUP Research Report No. 6. East Lansing: Michigan State University. 1969, p. 36.

Halloran, James. "The Social Effects of Television." In James Halloran, ed., *The Effects of Television*. London: Panther Books, 1970.

Johnson, Nicholas. "Beyond Sesame Street." *The National Elementary School Principal*, vol. 1, no. 5 (April 1971).

Montgomery, Dorothy Reese. "Television . . . Information Utilized or Ignored." *Childhood Education*, March 1960.

National Commission on the Causes and Prevention of Violence. "Statement on Violence in Television Entertainment Programs." U.S. Government Printing Office, Washington, D.C. 1969, p. 5.

Pannitt, Merrill. Foreword, *TV and Your Child: In Search of an Answer.* (A series from the 1969 issues *TV Guide* magazine). Triangle Publications, Inc., Radnor, Pa.

Schramm, Wilbur, Lyle, Jack, and Parker, Edwin B. *Television in the Lives of Our Children.* Stanford, Calif.: Stanford University Press, 1961.

Witty, Paul. "Children of the Television Era." *Elementary English,* vol. 44 (May 1967), pp. 528–535.

CHAPTER NINE

Advisory Center for Education Report. From "TV Effect on Child's Wants Questioned." London *Times,* December 20, 1971.

Bandura, Albert. "Behavioral Modifications Through Modeling Procedures." In L. Krasmer and L. P. Ullmann, eds., *Research in Behavior Modification.* New York: Holt, Rinehart and Winston, 1965.

Halloran, J., Brown, R. L., and Chaney, D. *Television and Delinquency.* Leicester, University of Leicester Press, 1970.

Himmelweit, Dr. Hilde. From London *Observer,* March 29, 1970.

Johnson, Nicholas. "Beyond Sesame Street." *National Elementary School Principal,* vol. 50, no. 5 (April 1971).

Klapper, Joseph T., *The Effects of Mass Communication,* Glencoe, Ill.: Free Press of Glencoe, 1960.

Maccoby, Eleanor. "The Effects of Television on Children." In Wilbur Schramm, ed., *The Science of Human Communication,* New York: Basic Books, 1963.

Mukerji, Rose. "Why Not Feelings and Values in Instructional Television?" *Young Children,* May 1971.

U. S. National Commission on the Causes and Prevention of Violence. "Statement on Violence in Television Entertainment Programs." U.S. Government Printing Office, Washington, D.C. 1969, p. 5.

Newson, Elizabeth, and Newson, John. *Four Years Old in an Urban Community.* London: Penguin Books, 1968.

Osborn, Keith, and Endsley, Richard C. "Children's Reactions to TV Violence: A Review of Research." *Young Children,* October 1970.

Paul, Norman L. "Invisible Factors in a Child's Reaction to Television." *Childhood Education,* vol. 47, no. 6 (March 1971).

Pell, Claiborne. From Keith Osborn and William Hale, "Television Violence." *Childhood Education,* May 1969.

Roper Report. From Martin Harris, "The TV Problem." *PTA Magazine,* May 1971.

U.S. Council on Children, Media and Merchandising. From Martin Harris, "The TV Problem." *PTA Magazine,* May 1971.

Ward, Scott. "Children, Adolescents, and Advertising." In Evelyn Sarson, ed., *Action for Children's Television.* New York: Avon Books, 1971.

Winnicott, Donald. *The Child, the Family and the Outside World.* London: Pelican, 1964.

CHAPTER TEN

The Black Experience in Children's Books. New York: Office of Children's Services, New York Public Library, 1971. (Bibliography.)

Chukovsky, Kornei. *From Two to Five.* Berkeley: University of California Press; Cambridge: Cambridge University Press, 1968.

Cohen, Sol. "Minority Stereotypes in Children's Literature: The Bobbsey Twins, 1904–1968." *Educational Forum,* vol. 34, November 1969.

Gast, David K. "The Dawning of the Age of Aquarius for Multi-Ethnic Children's Literature." *Elementary English,* vol. 47, May 1970.

Goodman, Mary Ellen. *Race Awareness in Young Children.* New York: Collier Books, 1964.

Jones, James P. "Negro Stereotypes in Children's Literature: The Case of Nancy Drew." *The Journal of Negro Education,* vol. 40, Spring 1971.

Larrick, Nancy. "The All-White World of Children's Books." *Saturday Review*, September 11, 1965.

Perry, Gail. "We Had a Head Start on Head Start." *Young Children*, May 1966.

Seaberg, Dorothy J. "Is There a Literature for the Disadvantaged Child?" *Childhood Education*, September–May 1968–1969.

University of Nebraska curriculum. From Evelyn G. Pitcher, "Values and Issues in Young Children's Literature." *Elementary English*, March 1969.

CHAPTER ELEVEN

Butler, Lord. *The Art of the Possible*. London: Hamish Hamilton, 1971.

Davie, Ronald. *From Birth to Seven*. London: Longmans, 1972.

Gordon, Sol. From *Open Door*. Report by the Program Reference Service. New York: Center for Urban Education. 105 Madison Avenue, New York, N. Y., p. 37.

Hall, Allan. "All Out in the Open." *Sunday Times*, May 14, 1972.

Kagan, Jerome. "Day Care Plans Stress Education Role." *New York Times*, January 14, 1971.

Mackay, David, Thompson, Brian, and Schaub, Pamela. *Breakthrough to Literacy*. London: Longmans, 1968.

Marshall, Sybil. *An Experiment in Education*. London: Cambridge University Press, 1963.

Martin, Bernice. "Progressive Education Versus the Working Classes." *Critical Quarterly*, March 1972.

Pamphlet from Hudson Guild Child Care Center. 459 West 26th St., New York, N.Y. Director: Mrs. Marion Easton.

Silberman, Charles E. *Crisis in the Classroom*. New York: Random House, 1970.

U.S. Department of Labor. *Facts About Day Care*. Washington, D.C.: Wage and Labor Standards Administration, Woman's Bureau, 1969.